Courage to Learn:

A Navigational Tool for California Community College Student Success

By Daniel Ortega, Ph.D.

Ordering Information:
To order this book, or for a desk copy, please contact:

Courage To Learn Press
Tel: (323) 829-4558/ (323) 241-5201
Email: dortega721@gmail.com / Fax: (323) 241-5304

Dedication

To all community college students, past, present and future…

"Let us think of education as the means of developing our greatest abilities, because in each of us there is a private hope and dream which, fulfilled, can be translated into benefit for everyone and greater strength for our nation."

—John F. Kennedy, 35th U.S. President

About the cover….

Cover Art by:

Joseph "Nuke" Montalvo

www.nuke.one
(323) 637-5817
Josephmontalvo70@gmail.com

Table of Contents

"Education is the most powerful weapon which you can use to change the world."

—Nelson Mandela, President of South Africa and Political Activist

Preface and Dedication

With Nothing But a Dream

By Daniel Ortega

I came to college with nothing but a dream.

As a former California Community College student, I too was once in your position—trying to navigate and demystify the California Community College structure and its multiple purposes. All of that can be overwhelming; when you first begin college, those factors can contribute to your fear of being a student, especially when coupled with trying to succeed academically as a student and making sure to take the right courses. Plus, I was constantly worried about getting the correct information and accessing the resources that were available to me. I can empathize with your situation since I have personally experienced it, so the purpose of this book is to provide you with all the information to help you navigate the community college system and to promote *your* success. I wasn't always a scholar or author; I was once a student just like you, wondering what my next step would be. I didn't have a clue how to study, manage my time, decide what my major was going to be, or set goals. All I knew is, just like you, that I had a dream to become a college graduate, and I was willing to commit to the possibility of making that happen. So please, consider *Courage to Learn* your navigational tool for California Community College student success, since it speaks specifically to the structure of California Community Colleges. The information and resources in the text are what I, both as a student and now a California Community College counselor and professor, deem important information that is a must for every California Community College student and which will definitely contribute to your success and help you complete your educational goals.

I also want to share with you the story behind the title. While in my doctoral studies, I was assigned a book to read by Parker Palmer entitled *The Courage To Teach: Exploring the Inner Landscape of a Teacher's Life;* it is a great book, and I do agree with Palmer: it does take much courage to teach, and we as teachers must really look deep within ourselves while teaching and even after teaching. Yet, I also believe that it takes students a lot of courage to learn. Specifically, for students enrolled in the California Community College system, there is a multitude of students coming from a myriad of backgrounds: some might be coming back as re-entry students after taking a long hiatus; others might not have performed so well academically in high school but are using the community college as their second chance; still others, in certain urban centers in California like South Central Los Angeles or Watts, where I grew up, might come from an environment where it is not socially accepted to be in college by some peers. In my opinion, overcoming that takes a lot of courage, and that should be acknowledged and recognized. I also understand the fear of even enrolling in college because of all the issues I just mentioned. A famous quote by Bob

Marley— "My fear is my only courage"—also comes to mind when speaking of California Community College students because I do believe all of you who are reading this book and are enrolled in college have channeled that fear or trepidation into courage. So to make a long story short, I reflected on the Parker Palmer's book *The Courage to Teach: Exploring the Inner Landscape of a Teacher's Life* and the Bob Marley quote, "My fear is my only courage" and came up with the title *Courage to Learn*. Lastly, I want to dedicate this textbook to all the students who are or have been enrolled in a California Community College and show every single day that they too have the *Courage to Learn.*

Foreword

Taking Charge: Identity and Change

Student Learning Outcome:
Students will self-assess a baseline for skills and attitudes involved in lifelong learning (curiosity, transfer, independence, initiative, and reflection) by writing a reflective journal entry on how they will incorporate lifelong learning skills into their goals for higher education.

"I believe that education is the fundamental method of social progress and reform. All reforms which rest simply upon the law, or the threatening of certain penalties, or upon changes in mechanical or outward arrangements, are transitory and futile...But through education society can formulate its own purposes, can organize its own means and resources and thus shape itself with definitiveness and economy, in the direction in which it wishes to move. Education thus conceived makes the most perfect union of science and art conceivable in human experience...Education, therefore, is a process of living not a preparation for future living."
—John Dewey, "My Pedagogic Creed" (1897)

"There is, it seems, more concern about whether students learn the mechanics of reading and writing rather than grow to love reading and writing; learn about democracy than practice in democracy; hear about knowledge...rather than gain experience in personally constructing knowledge...see the world narrowly, simple and ordered, rather than broad, complex and uncertain."
—Vito Perrone, "Letter to Teachers"

"We don't need advice, theories or books, because life itself is our teacher. I have been made to understand in the depth of my soul what discrimination means. My life story is a tale of exploitation. I have worked and suffered hunger... When looking back at a life such as mine and when taking in the stark reality of it, a hate for the suppressors who have brought so much suffering to a people begins to grow."
—Rigoberta Menchu, *I, Rigoberta Menchu*

Nobody *gives* you an education. If you want one, you have to *take* it. Only you can educate you—and you can't do it by memorizing things or by passively sitting in a chair in a classroom. You have to get actively involved in your own education, take charge, and find out who you are by experience and by risk-taking; then pursue your own nature intensely.

11

Typical school and work routines discourage you from self-discovery. To know yourself, you have to keep track of your random choices, figure out your patterns, and use this knowledge to control your own destiny. It's the only way that free will can grow. If you avoid this, other minds will manipulate and control you lifelong. This book is one of many tools that will help you cultivate and customize your own knowledge and education so that they will serve you best.

The Path to Self-Discovery

I am grateful enough to have had an education that was traditional yet enlightening. I went to private school. We had a lot more freedom there than my kids do in their public schools today. As a parent and educator, I believe that we are all seeds of change—for the future. But we need tending to, nurturing and cultivation, so that we can be harvested at our peak and bloom fully. I do *not* believe in inevitability, the inability to change, or labels—especially those we inherit after being born into a world that creates divisions based on race, class, gender, geographical location, language, family, culture, sexuality, physical ability, political affiliation, and so on.

You can make change happen; you can shape your own education and future by being a person who makes change happen.

Imagine the world—your life, your future—with hope and passion. And be open-minded: be willing to dream, to learn, and to change. Change, like seeds, must be nurtured, cared for, and prized. Education, like good stories (whether in books or in conversation), can create change and build community. And while most cities suffer from a severe lack of public spaces and forums for the free exchange of ideas, institutions of higher learning, if approached with the right open-minded attitude, can challenge thinking, provoke inquiry, stimulate action, and bring people together.

You can make the change happen; you can shape your own education and future by being a person who makes change happen; you create a forum for the free exchange of ideas. Be the person who speaks up in class or questions your professor. Participate in special events and extra-curricular activities—and if none that interest you exist, organize some that do. College is a public space: seize it and speak out. It's yours: *you* own it. Share your urgency, pain, passion, compassion, anger, outrage, disbelief. Share your dreams—unfiltered, unrestrained, uninhibited.

You may meet people, read about people, or see movies about people who share their stories or viewpoints which seem like they are not for you, not your life—but they are. We are not isolated (though we may often feel that way, connected only electronically, through cellphones, texts, Instagram and Facebook profiles, and mediated through social network websites), but we share common experiences. The struggles of others are ours. We may think we can ignore them—just click away or stop reading or stop listening—but we must listen, we must read, we must learn, and we must teach. It's all relevant.

One path to self-discovery that seems to have atrophied through traditional schooling lies in finding a mentor. People aren't the only mentors. Books, this one included, can serve as mentors if you learn to read intensely, with every sense alert to nuances. Books can change your life, as mentors do. Read. Read everything you can.

Ralph Ellison's *Invisible Man* recruited people into the Black Power movement. Upton Sinclair's *Oil* and other works galvanized labor activists to take action in the workplace. Richard Wright's *Uncle Tom's Cabin* promoted unionization while his *Native Son* created a new generation of socialists. Tomas Rivera's *Y No Se Lo Trago La Tierra* documented the plight of undocumented farmworkers. Rodolpho Anaya's *Bless Me, Ultima* almost single-handedly started the Chicano literary tradition. Words can make social change.

> *Words have power: to experience them can be both inspiring and enlightening; to use them to express yourself can be liberating—and even revolutionary.*

Words have power: to experience them can be both inspiring and enlightening; to use them to express yourself can be liberating—and even revolutionary. Have you ever seen an author like Wanda Coleman speaking her mind through her poetry? Have you heard slam poet Taalam Acey break it down, ranting at breakneck speed about the injustice of the prison system? Do readings by the poet Alurista make you want to go out and fight for social justice? Well, they—and countless others across the country—have kept the emotion, the fight, the anger, the insight in their words. It is a powerful experience to hear others raise their voices, and that is a conversation that you can join. Make your voice heard.

Experiential Learning and Involvement

Often, institutionalized, traditional schooling teaches little more than the process of institutionalization: obedience. Follow the rules. Obey the teacher. Don't question authority. The surrender required of students meets the primary duty of bureaucratic establishment: to protect established order. It wasn't always this way.

Classical, non-traditional schooling teaches independent thought, appreciation for great works, and an experience of the world not found within the confines of a classroom. It is *this* education that is missing in many public schools today but still exists in many private schools—and can for you and your children, too, if you take time to be willing to learn. The ancient Greeks discovered thousands of years ago that rules and ironclad procedures, when taken too

13

seriously, burn out imagination, stifle courage, and wipe the leadership clean of resourcefulness. Greek education was much more like play, with studies undertaken for their own sake, to satisfy curiosity. It assumed that sane children want to grow up, and it recognized that childhood ends much earlier than modern society typically allows.

This means that you should participate actively in your studies; if your classroom doesn't provide the experiences that you need to learn, you should go out and create them. In other words, involve yourself in your education. Take charge of it. Make the choice to have experiences that are worthwhile and from which you will learn something valuable *to you.*

Taking Charge

School may often seem to act as an obstacle to success. To go from the confinement of early childhood to the confinement of the classroom to the confinement of homework, working to amass a record entitling you to attend a "good" college, where the radical reduction of your spirit will continue, isn't likely to build character or prepare you for a good life.

This is what can happen if you passively accept the education handed to you or take the path of least resistance to where you think you want to go. In many respects, school does exactly what it was created to do: it solves, or at least mitigates, the problem of a restless, ambitious labor pool, so deadly for capitalist economies; and it confronts democracy's other deadly problem—that ordinary people might one day learn to un-divide themselves, band together in the common interest, and take control of the institutions that shape their lives.

Once you take responsibility for your own education, you'll join a growing army of men and women all across America who are waking up and creating their own destinies. You'll have the exquisite luxury of being able to adapt to conditions, to opportunities, to the particular spirits of your kids, to whatever life throws at you—and not just surviving, but thriving.

However, it doesn't have to be this way: you can take charge of your education, your future, and control and shape your own life. This book is your road map. You shape your education; don't let it shape you. Higher education—for all its faults—is still a requirement for so many jobs, and if you involve

14

yourself in the direction of your education, it can be a wonderful, enlightening experience.

What Can You Do

You can make the system work for you; you can set your own path; you can stand up for what you believe in strongly and enact change for future generations. If you are interested in education and involve yourself, you will learn the rest on your own. Start by reading this book and following what it says. While no guide alone can be 100% complete, each mentor, each guide, each class, each instructor, each book, each article, each relative, every experience—all of these can contribute a little bit to making you who you can be and setting you on the right path to take charge of your future and succeed in your goals.

Take that to heart while reading this book: if you have questions, ask them of your instructors, your counselor, your mentors; if some parts of the book don't apply to you or work for you, discard them and keep the parts that do work and do apply. Traditional schooling operates out of the assumption that ordinary people are biologically, psychologically, or politically inferior; real education assumes that individuals are independent spirits. Once you take responsibility for your own education, you'll

> *Each mentor, each guide, each class, each instructor, each book, each article, each relative, every experience—all of these can contribute a little bit to making you who you can be and setting you on the right path to take charge of your future and succeed in your goals.*

join a growing army of men and women all across America who are waking up and creating their own destinies. You'll have the exquisite luxury of being able to adapt to conditions, to opportunities, to the particular spirits of your kids, to whatever life throws at you—and not just surviving, but thriving.

Yes, you can change your life, your future, and the world. Let yourself change. Let yourself learn.

Metacognition: Learning How to Learn

One additional thing you can do to be a successful student is to learn how to learn; this can help you determine how to maximize your study time for effectiveness and choose classes and professors that suit you. This process, or sense of awareness, is a reflective, introspective ability that you should develop over time: it involves learning over time about the ways in which you learn best.

And, as many instructors and bosses will be different in their approaches, metacognition can help you thrive in environments that are different from your ideal circumstances.

Learning Styles:
Visual, Auditory, Kinesthetic, Verbal, Interpersonal, Intrapersonal,
Linguistic, Logical-Mathematical, Musical

In his book, *Frames of Mind: The Theory of Multiple Intelligences* (1983), theorist Howard Gardner outlines his theory that all people possess multiple intelligences and therefore "learn, remember, perform and understand in different ways." Individuals differ in the degree to which they use each of these types of intelligences and in how they combine them to solve problems, perform tasks, or otherwise apply themselves.

According to Gardner, there are nine major styles of learning, the optimal ways that we learn—visual, auditory, kinesthetic, verbal, interpersonal, intrapersonal, linguistic, logical-mathematical, and musical. Knowing which type of learner you are is not meant to show you the best or only way to learn; it is intended to teach you how to learn how to learn, a concept known as *metacognition*. This can assist you with increasing your self-awareness about learning strengths and weaknesses so that hopefully you will try out variety of modes of learning, rather than simply staying with your preferred methods.

o **Visual learning** involves taking notes, imagining pictures, seeing someone or something in person, watching a film, or reading a text. Visual learners, at parties, tend to withdraw into the background and observe people. As students, they tend to need to write things down in order to remember them. Visual learners thrive by watching television, reading, reviewing flashcards, or seeing PowerPoint presentations.

o **Auditory learning** involves hearing things, memorizing lectures, or paying attention to conversations. Auditory learners, at parties, tend to listen to conversations or have very in-depth conversations with somebody who is a good conversationalist. As students, auditory learners prefer to hear verbal descriptions of things, such as what they hear on the radio, in a conversation, or on the phone. Auditory learners thrive by attending lectures (even recording them for future review) and paying attention to the speaker as well as having conversations with fellow students about the subject matter.

o **Kinesthetic learning** involves actively engaging with materials, such as drawing, demonstrating things, or physically touching something. At parties, kinesthetic learners typically enjoy dancing, games, and getting involved in the action. As students, kinesthetic learners like to work on projects or tasks, draw pictures, or engage in or watch demonstrations. Kinesthetic learners thrive through activities, experiments, or field trips.

o **Verbal learning** involves learning with words, either through reading or speaking, such as reading a book, engaging in a debate, or having a conversation. At parties, verbal learners typically engage in intense conversations or have loud arguments or debates. As students, verbal learners like to engage in role-playing activities, make recordings of lectures and play them back, or even record themselves reading study notes for playback later. Verbal learners thrive through debates, note taking, reading, and talking.

o **Interpersonal learning** involves learning through social interactions, either by working in a group or simply with other people. At parties, interpersonal learners are typically the life of the party. They socialize and engage with others at every opportunity. As students, interpersonal learners like to share their ideas with others, form study groups, or actively participate in group projects. Interpersonal learners thrive through group work, discussions, or visualizing people doing things.

o **Intrapersonal learning** involves learning in solitude, using self-study and reflection. At parties, intrapersonal learners tend to keep to themselves, or perhaps have a few one-on-one conversations. As students, intrapersonal learners like to be left alone to read, study, take notes, and reflect in private about the material. Intrapersonal learners thrive through being left alone to process and contemplate information.

o **Linguistic learning** involves using words effectively by using highly developed auditory skills and thinking in words. At parties, linguistic learners tend to focus on reading, playing word games, and making up poetry or stories. As students, they prefer to say and see words and read books with others. Linguistic learners thrive by using computers, games, multimedia, books, tape recorders, and lecture.

o **Logical -Mathematical learning** involves reasoning and calculating, thinking conceptually or abstractly, and being able to see and explore patterns and relationships. At parties, logical-mathematical learners tend to experiment, solve puzzles, and ask cosmic questions. As students, they prefer to learn through using logic games, conducting investigations, and solving mysteries. Logical-mathematical learners thrive by forming concepts before dealing with details.

o **Musical learning** involves a high degree of sensitivity to rhythm and sound. At parties, musical learners love music but are also sensitive to non-musical sounds in the environment. As students, they study better with music in the background, may turn lessons into lyrics, and speak rhythmically, tapping out time. Musical learners thrive by using voice and lyrics, musical instruments, music, and other multimedia.

Which one are you?

Journal Assignments

1. This book will question you just as you should question it. But let's begin here: Who are you? What are your dreams, aspirations, passions, desires, commitments, obstacles, barriers, concerns, and worries? Make a list. What skills and abilities do you bring to the classroom? *Courage to Learn* will try to respond by posing and answering questions like: In what context are you, you? What is the historical flow, the cultural surroundings, the economic reality? It will offer strategies on how to handle family life, how to identify obstacles to educational freedom and empowerment, and how to drive, to move, against those obstacles that hold you back. Describe yourself.

2. One method people use to find out who they are becoming, before others do, is to keep a journal where they log what attracts their attention, along with some commentary. In this way, when you go back and read it, you get to listen to yourself instead of listening only to others. List the things you want to learn: everything, not just in school, but over the course of the rest of your life. Make it exhaustive. Also, add some comments: why do you want to learn each thing on your list? Then, look over your list and try to identify patterns in your goals. What do some of the items have in common? Can you group them into related categories? Finally, briefly describe what the list says *to* you *about* you.

3. Reread the section of this chapter that describes the nine types of learning styles: visual, auditory, kinesthetic, verbal, interpersonal, intrapersonal, linguistic, logical-mathematical, and musical. In a brief reflective journal entry, describe which type or types you believe describe you. How can you make use of this information to grow and succeed as a college student?

Chapter One

Proactivity and Managing Your Identity (Online and in Real Life)

Student Learning Outcome:
Students will foster the ability to integrate academic persona—throughout their education, and between campus and community life—with personal identity in order to direct existing intellectual skills, individual purpose, values and ethics to achieve personal success, social responsibility, and civic engagement in today's global society through imaginative writing that redefines the self.

"We can spend our lives letting the world tell us who we are. Sane or insane. Saints or sex addicts. Heroes or victims. Letting history tell us how good or bad we are. Letting our past decide our future. Or we can decide for ourselves. And maybe it's our job to invent something better."
—Chuck Palahniuk, *Choke*

"Never be bullied into silence. Never allow yourself to be made a victim. Accept no one's definition of your life, but define yourself."
—Harvey Fierstein, playwright

Upon entering college, many students compare themselves to other students; this can have a damaging effect on self-esteem. Other students may seem better prepared, more well-adjusted, more confident, better suited to the college environment, more popular, and so on. It's important not to fall into that trap because comparing yourself to others can lead to feelings of inferiority or amplify feelings of unpreparedness. All people throughout their entire lives grow and change differently. Arthur Chickering in *Education and Identity* (1969) proposed what he termed the seven vectors of identity which he claimed were cyclical.

The seven stages of identity development are still the most widely recognized model for the psycho-social changes that college students go through. College student support services today are still modeled after his theories. The seven vectors are:

19

- **Developing Competence:** an individual develops competence in three ways: intellectually, characterized by the ability to reason and think critically; physically and manually, characterized by developing health, artistic ability, and athletic ability; and interpersonally, characterized by developing the ability to communicate effectively and work cooperatively.

- **Managing Emotions:** an individual develops competence in his or her ability to manage emotions and reactions to events.

- **Moving through Autonomy toward Interdependence:** an individual grows independent and self-managing yet also realizes that successful relationships (both personal and professional) are based on interdependence.

- **Developing Mature Interpersonal Relationships:** an individual develops intercultural relations, and an appreciation for—as well as tolerance of –others different from them, which involves accepting, respecting, and appreciating differences and commonalities in others.

- **Establishing Identity:** an individual progresses through his or her identity with a healthy whole-self concept in all aspects of identity.

- **Developing Purpose:** an individual has a strong, goal-oriented outlook on life, deliberately makes meaning within his or her life, and establishes positive meaningful relationships with other people.

- **Developing Integrity:** an individual develops and is able to articulate humanizing and personalizing values, and to develop congruence between values and living. *Humanizing values* are values which merge the concerns of institutions, family, and self with those of others (to enable flexibility, balance, and change). *Personal values* are those values which an individual adopts from humanizing values as a personal code to live by. Developing congruence suggests using your values to determine your actions, so that what you do aligns with what you believe.

Furthermore, Chickering specified that the stages or vectors above are not arranged in some sort of hierarchy. In other words, being at one level is not somehow superior to being at another level; in fact, we all develop at different rates, at a different pace, and in different areas at different times in our lives. This development never stops; it is ongoing and cyclical, meaning that we go through these various stages of development at various times in our lives over and over in a never-ending cycle.

So observing other students or people in your life and comparing yourself to them may just illustrate that they're developing in a different way than you are. One stage of development is not better than or higher than another. We don't advance through the stages of development; we just move around in them. Chickering arranged his stages of development not in a numbered list which would imply a sequence or stages of progress through which we might advance to the final level, but in a circle to imply a continuous flow throughout our lives within one vector of development to another and without them being in any particular order.

We all develop at different rates, at a different pace, and in different areas at different times in our lives. This development never stops; it is ongoing and cyclical, meaning that we go through these various stages of development at various times in our lives over and over in a never-ending cycle.

For example, another student who appears supremely confident may have developed a lot in the area of autonomy but perform poorly in group situations, or another student who seems to be very popular with friends and on the dating scene may have little integrity or congruence between values and actions. In other words, just because somebody is in one stage of development and you're in another doesn't mean that they're better than you or more advanced than you; it simply means that they're at different stages of development. There's no better and no worse.

Therefore, it's normal to constantly be in continuous development and continuous growth. Looking at someone who appears to be more popular or better adjusted to the college environment as compared to you simply means that they are in a different stage of their development than you are. It's natural and normal to be different from other people; that's why we refer to ourselves as *individuals*. People are not machines that follow specific patterns. We are unique and we grow and change in unique ways. You've probably met very young people who were extremely mature and very old people were extremely immature and everything in between.

In most cases, identity development happens unconsciously. We generally don't actively choose to manage how we grow or how we develop; we typically have experiences that impact us in certain ways and enable us to grow in certain areas.

This is normal.

However, understanding a bit about identity development theory can help you be a little bit more deliberate about your own growth. Rather than allowing yourself to grow and change randomly or simply in response to your environment or situation, you can deliberately address growth in certain areas as identified by Chickering.

Take a moment to assess yourself in the areas of identity development identified by Chickering above. If there are areas in which you feel you have room to grow, you can of course choose to do activities that might stimulate growth in those areas. This is sort of like taking charge of your own life. Often times we are *reactive*, which means that we primarily do things in response to what happens to us or what others do. However, successful people tend to be more *proactive*, which means that they initiate action or change deliberately with a purpose in mind.

Proactive Approaches to Identity Management

Have you ever felt that bad things always seem to happen to you? That nothing ever seems to go your way? That other people always seem to have all the luck? While there is no certain way to prevent negative things from happening to you, there are ways to manage your life proactively so that rather than things happening to you, *you make things happen.*

By taking control of and making a deliberate attempt to manage your own development, identity, and future, you will be proactive and initiate change by making yourself into the person that you want to be rather than being made into a person shaped by society, other people, or other outside forces by your circumstances. You will make *good* things happen to you.

As discussed previously, college is a good first step toward making yourself into a different person. You are becoming a college student in order to become a college graduate in order to become a working professional. That is change. And that is proactive. So you are already doing this. By using this book, by going to college, by setting up a career pathway or an educational pathway and following it, you are *already* being proactive.

You are becoming a college student in order to become a college graduate in order to become a working professional. That is change. And that is proactive.

College is a place where you can erase who you were and rebuild yourself into who you are—and who you will be. You can re-invent yourself and create a future for yourself. This is best done by taking charge of your life and your future proactively, by making things happen for you, not letting them happen to you.

To be proactive is to consciously *think ahead* and to *act ahead* of events or outcomes that you anticipate. Proactive thinking can help to avoid potential disasters and to avoid creating additional work for yourself. It involves planning ahead, thinking ahead, anticipating outcomes and consequences, and seeing that what you do today will determine what happens tomorrow. Take the initiative. Instigate change; create the future.

Here are some tips for leading a proactive life, which work in situations as broad as life-planning and as narrow as your workplace:

1. **Develop self-awareness:** frequently reflect on who you are, what you want to happen, and who you want to be.

2. **Think critically about how you might achieve your goals or perform certain tasks more effectively or efficiently:** carefully plan out the events in your life and activities in your day. Manage your time. Get help with urgent or time-consuming, difficult tasks; gather information about what you have to do before you do it so you will know what you are doing and why; create a plan, to do list, or checklist each day; look for steps in your plan that can be shortened or consolidated or eliminated and do so. Follow your plan.

3. **Prevent problems from ever arising:** anticipate outcomes and always take precautions or develop contingency plans in case things don't go as planned. Be ready for anything. This can prevent unintended outcomes from derailing you.

4. **Develop a problem-solving, success-oriented mindset:** frame your goals and ideas in terms of problems to be solved or how to succeed. Rather than dwelling on the problem *as a problem*, look at it *as a challenge*. Rather than feeling intimidated by the *difficulty of succeeding*, focus on *how to succeed*.

5. **Prioritize what you have to do, but don't procrastinate non-urgent tasks and activities:** just as it's better to do preventative maintenance on a car by changing the oil regularly so the engine lasts longer and you don't wind up pulled over on the side of the freeway with your engine on fire, it's better in life to do *preventative maintenance*—like buying food ahead of time before you run out, or reading ahead in textbooks when

you have time, rather than postponing the reading and finding that you don't have time to do a thorough job.

6. **Eliminate unwanted unnecessary tasks (and people) in your life:** we have all been roped into doing things we don't need to do or don't want to do. Oftentimes, this happens out of a sense of guilt or because other people are making you feel responsible for doing what they should be doing themselves. Don't allow guilt or burdensome friends run your life. You have your mission. Stick to it. You have your values and goals. Let them drive what you do, how you do it, and how you spend your time.

7. **Practice continuous self-evaluation:** periodically, spend time reflecting on your progress whether in life, at work or in school. Evaluate how well your planning process is and whether you are getting the desired outcomes you want and need. Look for ways you can adjust what you do and how you do it in order to more effectively manage your time, create success, and be in charge of your own destiny.

Managing Your Online Identity

Just as we each have our own personal identity in real life, most of us have online personas or online identities. And online, we leave fingerprints, meaning that things we do online remain there and leave traces for others to find, much like a skip tracer or detective might trace you in real life. Managing your online identity, just like managing your real life, requires planning and deliberate, intentional actions, but your online identity presents a special case.

Employers and people who do hiring for career-oriented jobs will often Google prospective employees' names or phone numbers or both to see who they are. As the world progressively becomes virtual, our online identities are becoming increasingly important. If you have ever tried to Google yourself, you might be surprised at what you find. You can also Google your own phone number or old phone numbers to see what "fingerprints" you left behind.

This brings up two points: one, you may have left fingerprints that are not very flattering for others to find; second, however, you can manage your online identity much like you can manage your real-life identity.

First, you should research yourself. If you discover that you have many unflattering blog comments, old MySpace pages from high school, Facebook profiles that you no longer use, an Instagram with a whole bunch of pictures of you partying, or something similar, you may want to consider deleting the old profiles and accounts.

Additionally, you may have left comments on various social networks in moments of passion, drunkenness, or anger which don't represent you in a professional light. To delete comments you made on other people's posts, you can often simply delete them yourself; if you can't, you can contact the author of the profile or owner of the site, and politely ask them to remove your comments or photos. Most people tend to be compliant with these sorts of requests. You can also contact Google, Instagram, Facebook, or any other social media network, and request that they delete your profile in the event that you forgot the password and can't do it yourself.

Second, you can take a proactive approach to building an online identity that *is* flattering. After you delete obsolete references to yourself, comments you have made, or pictures you have posted, you can set out to build an online identity that creates a flattering and professional online identity. As discussed elsewhere in this book, employers like to see prospective employees who are similar to what an ideal transfer student might look like: that is to say, employers are looking for employees who are socially conscious, politically active, involved in the world, involved in student clubs or organizations, members of professional organizations in the field, participants in a wide range of activities, and basically just people who make a contribution to their school, workplace or community outside of merely being a student or doing a job.

Therefore, if you still want to have fun online, then make sure that you create a separate professional online identity. You should have two different accounts on your social network sites: one for fun; the other, professional.

Use your fun account for fun. Socialize, party, make jokes, start arguments, insult people, have fun! Do what you do. *But use a fake name.*

In your professional account, however, you should deliberately build an online identity that is impressive to prospective employers. Colleges have not yet begun to research student applicants for admission using social network profiling, but this may happen soon. And some smaller private organizations that grant scholarships or clubs or other organizations that are exclusive about their membership may. But most importantly, your future employer, when you go to look for a career-type job, is very likely to search for you online and in the more popular social networks. And they will be looking for your history, so you should have one. Jobs that tend to attract people not looking for careers probably won't research you very thoroughly, but a professional career job that has a vested interest in hiring the right people and paying a high salary and keeping employees for the duration of their career probably will. Subway is not going to Google you, but Apple might. And Apple would be looking for a historical perspective on you, not a brand-new Facebook profile that has only been active for two weeks. Therefore, even though applying for a job that you intend to make your career may seem like something that's not going to happen for a long time, it is crucial that you begin building your professional online identity now.

There are several ways you can go about doing this.

Begin by first erasing who you were (if it doesn't represent you in the way that you would want to be represented to others when applying for your dream job) as described above.

Then, start creating alternate professional social networking profiles using your real name. As of this writing, the more popular social networks are Facebook, Twitter, and Instagram. The social network LinkedIn is also becoming very important in the professional working world.

When using your professional social networking sites, you can be deliberate about what you do in order to build a history of a professional online presence.

You can join or start groups related to your major or desired job on any of the major social networks. This will enable you to keep up-to-date with current changes in the professions or majors and the current concerns and controversies. Often members of groups or pages on social network working sites will share articles from professional journals that have generated interest among people in that field. You can get involved by also reading some of the same professional journals and sharing articles of your own and by commenting on posts and articles shared by others.

Google:
You can also make a donation to a nonprofit organization preferably in your field. Or you can sign petitions supporting a political action or protesting inequality or something unfair. When your name is Googled, then, Google will typically place petition signatures and donations that have been recorded online publicly at the top of the search results, creating an easily accessible identity for you as someone who is politically and socially engaged.

Facebook:
Facebook tends to be more social but depending on people you make friends with and the groups you join, it can be used to share information widely. There are many clubs and many organizations that have Facebook pages which you can follow or join and which will help keep you up-to-date on current trends and breaking news in your future profession or your major.

Twitter:
While Twitter can be primarily social, it is the social networking site that can stimulate political action and responses quickly. You can start a group by creating your own hashtag (#) or by searching for hashtags that interest you. Several of my students have reported that tweeting complaints about a bad experience at a business has generated an immediate response. Twitter is, as of this writing, the premiere site for organizing people, taking action, and creating social change. It has even been used to mobilize full-scale protests!

Instagram:
Instagram is primarily a photo sharing site and as of this writing does not seem to have much use professionally.

LinkedIn:
LinkedIn is a special case. It is currently and rapidly replacing the paper resume as *the* professional document for job applicants. Many students, instead of asking instructors and supervisors for letters of recommendation, now ask to be endorsed on their LinkedIn profile. LinkedIn is an extensive online resume. Building a network of friends on LinkedIn can help your professional resume become more impressive. You can network with people who have similar interests as you. If you are interested in becoming, for example, a lawyer, you can befriend other

lawyers or law instructors or legal professionals on LinkedIn. You can endorse others in your field of interest and receive endorsements from them. It is becoming progressively more and more important to create an extensive LinkedIn profile for prospective employers. Therefore, you should spend a lot of time using LinkedIn to keep track of those extracurricular activities that you do, your other online involvement, blog posts that you have written, and activities you participate in.

This is time-consuming. That's why you should start now, so that after you transfer to a university, graduate, and enter the job market looking for a career (as opposed to merely a job), you will have had several years to build an online identity that is flattering and impressive. Having no online presence would arouse suspicion in a prospective employer. So build one deliberately starting today.

Deliberately and proactively managing both your online and the real-life identity is a crucial part of taking charge of your life.

Journal Assignments

1. In your journal, evaluate yourself in each of Chickering's seven vectors. Where are you strongest? Where are you weakest? Create an action plan to proactively develop yourself in areas that you feel need development. (And be proud of the areas in which you have grown).

2. Google yourself and your phone number, and inventory all of the sites that come up in the search results. Separate desirable ones from undesirable ones. Delete those that you do not want to remain.

3. Build an online professional profile. Open new profiles (or modify your old ones) to reflect yourself as a professional on Facebook and Twitter. Search for groups which you can join or pages you can like or websites you can subscribe to updates from which relate to your professional or academic interests. Additionally, many universities have clubs that may interest you. If you know what universities you are considering applying to, you can search for student organizations on Facebook or Twitter, and join them ahead of time. That's a great way to get a sense of what student life is like at a university that you haven't visited.

4. Build a LinkedIn profile. Treat this like your resume: in other words, begin to build it carefully and be as inclusive of all your activities, honors, club and group memberships, as well as education and work experience. Look for other people's profiles that you can endorse or befriend so that you can begin to build a professional network of colleagues on the LinkedIn site.

Student Success Profile:

Reyna Urena

Describe yourself briefly in a short biography (hometown, birthplace, high school experience, family, education).

I was born in a small town in the state of Jalisco, Mexico. I lived there with my parents and 7 siblings during my first 18 years. I was very lucky to finish high school there since many of my older siblings weren't able to study more than elementary school because my parents weren't able to afford it and they had to start working very young. It was after graduating from high school that I decided to come here to Los Angeles, California, where two of my older brothers and my sister lived. I decided to come, like my siblings and many other immigrants, to work and help my family.

What was your background before coming to community college?
Before coming to community college, I attended high school at my hometown in Mexico. After that, I moved to LA and studied English as a Second Language (ESL) for about a year at Inglewood Community Adult School. It was there where I heard of Los Angeles Southwest College where I studied ESL for another year before I started taking my regular college level classes.

What, if anything, prompted your decision to attend community college? What were your goals upon entering community college (why did you go)? Did they change after you started college? If so, how?
What prompted me to attend community college was my need to learn English. Coming from Mexico, when I first got to this country I didn't speak any English, and this made it very hard for me to look for a job or to communicate with others. My first goal was to take ESL classes to learn English, but later as my professors advised me to talk with a counselor and take some of the regular classes to get a degree or certificate, to do something more with my education, that's when I decided to talk to my counselor, and he explained to me what my opportunities were and guided me through the process of what I needed to do. After realizing that I had the opportunity to continue with my education, I felt very excited and eager to take the challenge. I saw the opportunity not only to learn the language or prepare for a better job, but also—as the first one in my family to attend college— I saw the opportunity to make my family proud of what I was achieving.

Describe your experience as a community college student. What were the highlights? Were there any special programs or extracurricular experiences that were memorable or inspiring?
My experience in community college was hard but very rewarding at the same time. I found it to be very challenging since my English skills were very limited. On top of that, I have always been a shy person and that made it harder for me to make friends or talk to other people to practice the language. I was very shy to seek help as well. Little by little, I started to realize it wasn't that bad. It required a lot of work and dedication, but I soon began to see the results of it. I started to be more fluent in English, to communicate better, and surprisingly for me, I was even getting good grades; that made me very happy and helped me realize that attending college was something that I could and wanted to do. I feel very grateful for the opportunity and for all the help that I got during my time in community college. One of the programs that I owe the most to is the Puente Program. In Puente, they made sure I had access to a counselor to guide me to the courses that I needed to take; they also taught me about how important it is to get an education and how to make the journey easier. At Puente, I was able to improve my English writing skills, I learned about the educational system here in the US, they also gave me exposure on how it is to be in a four year university, and they helped me with the process of transferring. Sometimes I think I would have not been able to do it without their help and support. Another of the programs that really helped me a lot was the opportunity to do work study. As a student worker, I had the

opportunity to work with very nice people, helping students and getting experience on the job. It is a very rewarding experience when you can help others and give back something of all that has been given to you. I loved working there, and now that I graduated from community college, I feel very grateful that I was able to get a job with them and continue doing something that I love.

How much time went by between high school and community college for you? What were the biggest challenges that you faced when you began attending community college?
After graduating from high school in Mexico, I moved here to Los Angeles and one of the first things that I did was to look for a school to learn English. I studied ESL for two years before starting to take regular college classes, and as I said before, I would say that my biggest challenge when I began attending community college was the language. Sometimes it was a lot of work for me to spend hours of reading, looking for the meaning of words that I didn't understand, translating, or searching on the internet to learn how to write a sentence correctly to write my essays. That was something I wasn't used to, and on top of all that I also had to work which made things even harder.

Did you work while attending community college? If so, how did you balance your time between work and school? Do you have any kids or other family responsibilities? If so, how did you balance your time between home and school? Did you have all three? How did you handle that?
Yes. While attending college as a full-time student, I worked at a Subway Restaurant for about 30-36 hours per week. Besides that, there was a time when I had to manage between classes, work, and my work study. I was going to class in the mornings, then doing 2-3 hours of work study, and then going to work in the afternoon. Then, I got home to do my homework. I would also work and finish whatever homework I had left over the weekend. I have no kids, but at home with my siblings I also had to help with the housework. That's how I was able to balance it all. It is not easy, but it is possible once you learn to prioritize and manage your time accordingly, knowing how long it will take you to finish each task.

Community colleges generally have a high attrition rate, meaning a large percentage of students drop out. Why do you think this happens? What motivated you to persevere through college and transfer to a university?
I think many students drop out because they don't know about the many opportunities and all the help they can get in college. I know there are many who are struggling economically and they have to work to help their families or support themselves, but there are also many others who work and go to school at the same time. For me, what motivated me to persevere through college was that I love learning, but also that I know how important it is to have an education. I didn't want to work at Subway forever; I wanted to do something better with my life. I know accidents happen and that I could be fired from my job, but what

nobody will be able to take away from me is my education. I know that's what will open the door for me to better opportunities.

Of all the reading assignments you completed in college, which one had the greatest impact on you? What's your favorite book and why?
One of my favorite books is *Enrique's Journey*. I read this book for one of my English assignments, and I really like it because it is about this little kid traveling from Guatemala to the United States. Although the circumstances were very different, I was able to identify with some of the things that he went through during his process of adaptation in the US. This book helped me to see that what I was going through was a blessing; I was living with my family, had food and shelter, I had a job, I was going to school, I had what many people didn't. This book taught me that I have to be grateful for what I have and that I have to take advantage of the opportunities that life gives me because not everybody is that fortunate. This kid became for me an example of courage and perseverance.

Of all the writing assignments you had in college, which are you most proud of and why?
The writing assignments during community college that I am most proud of are my outlines for my speech class. This makes me proud because speech was a class which I was afraid of because I have always been shy. I felt embarrassed to talk in front of everybody with my bad English, but the instructor had given us the format for how she wanted us to do our speech, and that made everything a lot easier. I remember getting As for all my outlines and the instructor congratulated me in front of the whole class for my good job. This was very important to me because I thought that class was going to be the worst class of all, but it ended up being one of my favorite classes from community college.

Attending a college or university can be extremely stressful for many students. Does any particular thing stand out as being the most stressful aspect of going to school? What was it and why was it stressful? What coping skills did you use to overcome stress in order to succeed?
To me one of the most stressful things was not knowing the language very well. Another very stressful thing was time. I was often stressed out because I used to procrastinate a lot, and that stressed me out because I would be thinking all day about the assignments that I needed to do. What I used to do in order to overcome this stress is rest. I tried to sleep well to be prepared for my assignments. I also learned that I should not procrastinate. Thinking ahead and organizing my time were some of the skills that helped me to be better prepared. Also, thinking positive and visualizing what I wanted to accomplish with my assignment and what I wanted to get out of the class helped me to be more motivated and encouraged me to do a better job.

Many community college students give up when faced with adversity or challenges or barriers. You, however, didn't. What was the biggest challenge you faced and how did you overcome it? What advice would you give to a

student who feels like he or she just can't do it, has too much going on in his or her life, or is just struggling academically and feels like maybe college isn't the right place?

I think I had to overcome many challenges while attending college. As I said before, I was struggling with my English skills; economically, I didn't have money and I had to work full time to contribute at home; I had a very tight schedule and was going through an adaptation process, being away from family and friends. Those were hard times, but fortunately I counted on the help and guidance that I needed to continue pursuing my education. The advice that I would give to those students who are going through hard times and think they cannot do it is: Do not give up! Look for help, talk to your counselor, make friends. Think about the rewards that come with getting an education. Work hard, do your assignments, ask as many questions as you can. Don't be afraid. When I was about to start my college education, I was hesitant because I wasn't sure I was going to be ready for it, that I wasn't smart enough, but soon I realized that if I do what I need to, if I complete my assignments, if I ask and make sure I understand, that's all I needed to do well. When you're in class, be in class 100%, pay attention and make sure you understand. Successful people are not those who are smart but those who work hard until they achieve their goals.

Were there any memorable faculty, counselors, other students, administrators or staff (at your community college or university) with whom you established a rapport and who made a difference? Is establishing relationships with people on campus important? Tell a brief story about someone with whom you became close and who was supportive.

Someone who made a difference in my educational experience was my counselor. He helped me to see the opportunities I had; he told me about the different resources available; he encouraged me to continue studying; he guided me though the process of what I needed to do, from what classes to take to what people I needed to talk to when applying for financial aid. He reminded me when it was time to apply for admission at the university, helped me to review my application and personal statement, and helped me with my recommendation letters. I believe building relationships on campus is very important because they can help you make everything easier. They can provide you with the information and help that you need. Even if your relationship is with other students, they can help you understand class material better, or they can help you decide what classes are better than others or about professors that they thought were really good based on their own experiences. Building good relationships with faculty or staff can also provide you with a wide range of different resources to help you succeed in college. A good example, as I mentioned, was the relationship that I established with my counselor. He referred me to really nice people and really good professors, and as of today we are still in contact every once in a while.

Courage to Learn **discusses building social capital, meaning developing relationships and skills that are like an investment in your own future. What social capital have you gained since entering community college?**
I think I have gained the skills to manage my time better, to communicate better with people and to express my opinion. I have also built good relationships with people at college, which has helped me obtain a job there, and that gives me the opportunity to know and work with other people in the field of education. I have gotten very helpful advice from them, I have access to more educational resources, and I am constantly learning something new.

What was your social life like in college? How important was it to you personally and educationally?
I'm not a very friendly person when it comes to getting to know new people, but I never had any problems with anybody. I didn't talk much with my classmates because I was very shy, but when we had to work in teams, we usually got along very well. I think I was just very busy focusing on school and work and spending the little time I had left with my family and friends that I already knew. Nevertheless, I was able to keep a good relationship with key people who helped me get along easier; people at the library, at the financial aid office, my counselor, a few professors, and people at Bridges to Success Center where I used to do my work study and where I currently work.

Deciding what university to transfer to is difficult. What factors did you consider when deciding where to apply and where to attend?
All of the schools I applied to were public schools because I didn't think I could afford to attend a private school, but I also wanted to go to a recognized university and one that offered the classes/major that I wanted. Some of the factors for which I decided to attend to UCLA were its outstanding reputation, the majors they offered, and that it was a local school. UCLA had everything I was looking for in a university. It has recognized faculty, the campus is beautiful, and I love the fact that it is local. It is perfect to enjoy the weather of Southern California, and at the same time, it allowed me to stay at home with my family and friends and to keep my job.

Universities are expensive. Many magazine and newspaper articles highlight the fact that attending a university is an investment that frequently doesn't pay off or isn't worth it. Perhaps you've seen stories about students graduating from various universities under mountains of debt and unable to find jobs. How did you handle the financial burden of attending college and a university? Is it worth it? Are you buried under mountains of debt?
The way I have been able to cover my school expenses at UCLA is through financial aid and scholarships. I am very proud to say that as of today, I haven't had the need to borrow any money since my educational expenses all get covered. Besides, I am also working part time to cover my personal expenses. This has helped me to lower the amount of hours working and to spend more time doing homework and studying to get the good grades I need in order to keep my

benefits. The way I see it is as if I am getting paid for going to school. Of course it's worth it. Education is the best investment anyone can make, especially when it's free.

If you are working (while still a student or after having graduated), what is that experience like?
My experience at work has been really good. I love what I do and enjoy helping other students. Moreover, I have the opportunity to work with great people, who I now consider my friends, and on top of all that, I have a very flexible schedule that allows me to continue going to school while working.

How did you manage the transition from a community college to a university? Did you feel prepared or underprepared? What were the biggest challenges that you faced during the transition?
At first I was scared that I might not be well prepared to attend such a prestigious university like UCLA, but since this wasn't the first time that I experienced those feelings, it helped me realize that I am just like the other students, that if I was there it was because I was prepared for it. At first it was a little hard to adapt to the fast pace under the quarter system compared to the semester system that I was used to and to the bigger workload. I think those were my biggest challenges during my transition to university.

What plans for the future do you have (educationally, socially, and professionally)? When and how did those goals emerge?
In the future, I want to get a master's degree in social work and plan work at an adoption agency to help kids to have a family and to become active members of society. Before coming to this country, I never thought I was going to be able to get a degree, so I never thought about what I really wanted to study. These goals emerged during my first year of community college. At that time, I was taking a personal development class, which covered many aspects about education, and that was when I realized that I wanted to pursue a career. In this class, we took a personality test, which was very helpful to identify my interests, my strengths, my and weaknesses. That's when I decided that I wanted to be a social worker.

Looking back, what advice would you give to first year community college students today (i.e. if you could go back in time and talk to yourself on your first day of college, what would you say)?
Don't be afraid. You are a smart, capable person that can achieve everything you truly want. It is not going to be easy, but it'll be worth it. Work hard, but not too hard. Organize your schedule to allow some time to have fun. Don't stress too much. Take care of yourself, sleep, eat well. Be responsible, as long as you do what you are supposed to you will be fine. Try to enjoy what you do. Visualize your goals and what you want the outcome to be. Ask questions. Be nice to others, and, finally, utilize the resources out there to make your life and educational

experience as easy and enjoyable as possible. Remember that if others can do it, so can you.

Chapter Two

The Structure and Purpose of a Community College

> ### Student Learning Outcome:
> Students will be able to justify their academic, career and personal goals, and propose a pathway to attain those goals.

"We have an obligation and a responsibility to be investing in our students and our schools. We must make sure that people who have the grades, the desire and the will, but not the money, can still get the best education possible."
—Barack Obama

Overview

A community college is a two-year school: it introduces you—the student—to your first two years of college coursework. The first two years of college are known as your freshman and sophomore years, similar to when you were a freshman and sophomore in high school. Only now, you are in college, but the terminology remains the same. During these two years, you will take classes that pick up where your high school classes left off. Here, you will take your math, history, English, foreign language, political science, biology and other courses that relate to your general education requirements. General Education, or GE, courses give students a broad introduction to the world in which we live. GE classes are not related to your major. Your major will be the set of classes that you take in order to earn a college degree in a particular discipline. However, at a two-year community college, there will not be as much emphasis on courses in your major as there will be at a four-year college or university. After you have enrolled in a community college, it is imperative that you meet with a counselor who can guide you through the process of picking courses for your particular major.

Goals: Degrees and Certificates

The community college student has several goals from which to choose. Firstly, at the community college you can earn an AA degree. An AA degree is an Associate of Arts degree. It is a two-year college degree which requires 60 units to complete. Each community college will offer different fields or disciplines in which it awards a two-year degree. Fields typically included within the AA degree are English, foreign language, psychology, sociology, history, and fine and performing arts. This is why it is important to check with your particular school to find out what the requirements are to earn an Associate of Arts degree at your college.

The second option for the student is to earn an Associate of Science degree or AS degree. An AS degree is also a two-year college degree. It requires roughly 60 units to complete but will be in one of the sciences; thus, it's named an Associate of Science degree as opposed to an Associate of Arts degree. This degree might require several more units to complete compared to an AA because you will be taking more science and math courses to complete it. Fields typically included within the AS degree disciplines include computer science, mathematics, and some of the earth sciences.

The third option for community college students is the Career Certificate. The Career Certificate is a diploma awarded to students upon completion of a set number of courses related to a particular occupational discipline. It is not a college degree because these are typically courses designed to train you in a specific field, such as computer programming, pilot training, or auto mechanics, but it is formal recognition that you have successfully completed a training program and can make you eligible for a skilled job.

> *Whatever your background, whatever your situation, the community college experience can be a wonderfully fulfilling time of your life.*

Transfer to a Four-Year Institution

Thus, many students are able to complete their two years in a community college and get all the education they need in order to enter their particular fields. Many students do quite well after completing only two years of community college coursework. Nurses, for example, are only required to earn a two year degree as are people in certain other fields and occupations such as computer specialist, dental hygiene, fashion design, environmental engineering technician, radiology, and paralegal and legal assistants—among others. However, in your particular field you might need a four-year college degree, commonly known as a Bachelor of Arts (BA) or Bachelor of Science (BS) degree. In this case, you will need to transfer to a four-year university because community colleges award only two-year degrees and career certificates. Many students find that they need a Bachelor of Arts or a Bachelor of Science college degree. We will discuss those degrees and their requirements in Chapter 3 and subsequent chapters. The purpose of the community college is to give you, the student, a sound and solid grounding in college coursework, to expose you to the different disciplines encompassed in general education classes and the liberal arts, and to give you the career or vocational degrees and certificates you require in order to be successful in your career.

It is important to make the most of your two years at a community college. Some students may require more than just two years. For instance, you might need to work in order to help support your family, or you may have a career already and choose to take classes during the evenings in order to advance your career. Whatever your background, whatever your situation, the community college experience can be a wonderfully fulfilling time of your life. There you will find dedicated professors, caring staff, and especially the other students with whom you will be interacting and forming long-term friendships.

Units: What Are They? How Many Should I Take?

As a beginning college student, you may wonder, "What is a unit?" A unit is one hour of lecture time per class per week. For instance, a three-unit history class will meet for three hours of lecture time per week. A five-unit biology class will meet for five hours of lecture time per week. This may include laboratory time. You may want to plan accordingly when you choose your schedule. How many hours can you devote to being in class lecture per week? As mentioned, many students who attend community college already have many outside commitments and can only devote a set number of hours for college lectures and for study and homework. It is a good idea to buy an inexpensive planner so that you can begin to organize your time and your study hours to manage your time effectively while you attend the community college of your choice. Most students find that taking 12 units and a part time job combined with family (and other) relationships is challenging; therefore, effective time management and planning can help prioritize what little time you do have to ensure your success.

In our educational system, twelve units are considered full time attendance for a community college as well as a four-year college and university student. Not surprisingly, six units are considered half time attendance in a college. It is important to know this distinction because the financial aid providers for some students may need to know how many hours, or units, you are taking in order to allocate money proportionally for students in need. Speaking with your college counselor about how financial aid is impacted by the number of classes that you take and managing your work schedule a very important part of your educational planning.

One tip that may help you become a more successful student is to avoid taking classes that are similar in nature in each semester. Thus, it would not be a good idea to take two math or two biology classes in one semester because the style of thinking and learning is similar in both classes and other styles of thinking would be neglected, thus less enriching. It is best to take classes in different disciplines so that you can allow your mind the variety that it will require in order to be challenged more effectively. For instance, you may want to take a history class together with a math course as well as English and music. That would be a stimulating variety of courses for you to take during your first and second semesters.

In addition, if you are not comfortable writing essays and doing research, it is not a good idea to take two writing- or research-intensive courses in the same semester, like Speech 101, and/or History 101, and/or English 101 (or their equivalents). For students who are taking math or biology classes, there are typically tutoring labs on campus for you to utilize in case you might need some tutoring. The staff there is usually very helpful, kind, and understanding of students who might need a little extra help with their studies. Math and science courses can be especially difficult and tricky.

Therefore, it is a good idea to become familiar with the math and other tutors on campus who might be able to help you with your studies. Most campuses have a writing lab or writing center and sometimes even a tutorial center. These resources are provided free, so making yourself aware of them on your campus will enable you to take advantage of these needed resources. You will also find ads posted on campus of people who will work as your tutor, for a fee, in their or your home. While paid tutors are often more available than those in tutorial centers, remember that they may not be affiliated with the school, and therefore they may not have the same degree of contact with campus resources and your instructors, so their teaching methods or problem-solving techniques may be different.

The most important thing to remember is to get the help you need to succeed!

This is not necessarily bad—in fact, if you have difficulty with a particular subject or instructor, you may wish to actively seek out someone who teaches the subject matter in a different way. However, just be careful and research the tutor before paying someone who ends up not being worth your investment of time and money. Ask your friends for recommendations; ask the tutor for references and then call the people on the reference sheet. Prefer former or current students from your campus or from a nearby university to the unknown. *The most important thing to remember is to get the help you need to succeed!*

General Campus Resources for Success

Getting the help that you need means accessing the services and support that your campus offers, and using those campus resources. Student services—which provide academic, counseling, personal, and other non-academic support—vary from campus to campus, so check your campus to see what services are offered and which available services might be helpful for you. In almost all cases, the services are free of charge. Here is a list of the types of support services that your campus might offer:

Academic Support / Tutoring Center
Tutoring centers provide assistance to students in many academic, personal or social aspects of student success. Services include: tutoring, academic and student success workshops, online tutoring, and online student success tutorials.

Admissions and Records
The Admissions and Records Office admits and registers all students; maintains, retrieves and distributes student records and transcripts; serves as the final evaluation of all graduation applications; reports attendance data to appropriate agencies; and provides information and supportive contracts to students, faculty, administrators, and the community.

Assessment/Orientation Center
The Assessment/Orientation Center offers required assessment tests for enrollment in Math and English courses.

Associated Students Organizations
Associated Students Organizations (A.S.O.) are composed of elected and appointed members of the student body who serve as representatives; offices include the A.S. President, Vice President, Treasurer, Recorder, Senators, Inter-Club Council (I.C.C.) President, Commissioners and Senate Members. Student representatives may also serve on college committees. The A.S.O. provides student activities, clubs, events, and access to resources.

Bookstore
Most college bookstores offer a complete selection of the textbooks and course materials required or recommended by faculty. In addition, extensive classroom and office supplies, study aids, college clothing, giftware, books, magazines, and snacks are sometimes available.

Cultural Centers
Many colleges have multicultural centers to serve as a central location for student events and activities and/or to provide support, literature, and information for students, faculty, and staff about serving the needs of AB540, undocumented students, LGTBQI students, as well as students from historically underrepresented groups such as African American, Native American, Latino/a, Asian/Pacific Islander, low income, or former foster youth. Generally, activities and services are available to the entire campus community. Some cultural centers sponsor guest speaker events, resource libraries, field trips, cultural celebrations, opportunities to collaborate, safe spaces to study, or areas and events for dialog on diversity issues and self-empowerment.

CalWORKs
The CalWORKs Program is designed for students who are receiving (or applying to receive) AFDC/Welfare. CalWORKs Counselors provide students with the

guidance and support needed to meet both their academic goals and the requirements mandated by their County Social Worker. A team approach is used to advocate for student rights. Services include academic, career and personal counseling; child care grants; emergency assistance for bus passes, parking permits and books; referral to both on/off-campus resources for basic needs and emergency support services (housing, utilities, mental health, shelter, etc.); and referrals to other on-campus programs.

CAFYES: Cooperative Agencies Foster Youth Educational Support
For current and former foster youth, CAFYES programs offer additional educational support. The program requirements are that students must be current or former foster youth between the ages of 15 and 25, be eligible for services from EOPS and Chafee (or have a "Ward of the Court" verification letter), and be enrolled in at least 9 units. Services include: priority registration and tutoring; personal, academic, and career advisement; workshops on student success, financial literacy, and independent living; referrals to support services for housing, mental health, and childcare; and financial assistance with books, supplies, parking, and (depending on eligibility) gas cards, parking and transportation.

CARE: Cooperative Agencies Resources for Education
CARE, a program through EOPS, provides specific support services for single parent students who receive cash aid and are in the CalWORKS Program or deferred. Assistance is provided to ensure the opportunity for students to succeed and attain their educational goal. CARE offers financial assistance for auto repairs, books, bus passes, educational supplies, and gas cards—as well as referrals and information on child care; life, occupational, and academic counseling; social services; and tutoring.

Career Center
Career Centers provide students with career/life planning and development resources, such as counseling for career decision-making or life and career transitions, computer and internet access to research job opportunities, occupational assessment tools, reference materials, and career planning and workplace readiness workshops.

Child Development Center
Some colleges have Child Development centers which serve multiple purposes, providing student-parents with on-campus child care services and serving as a classroom for students majoring in Child Development and Early Education.

Computer Labs
Most colleges provide open-access computer labs for students to do research, type and print out assignments, or access online instructional materials.

Counseling and Student Development Office
Counseling departments offer a full range of services to students on a walk-in, by appointment, or online basis, as well as courses in personal development. Counselors are available to assist students with orientation, course placement, career goals, educational plans, and life management issues. In addition to providing information and/or advisement on college policies, transfer and major preparation, general education requirements, transcript evaluation, progress checks, and referrals to other support services on campus.

Disabled Student Programs and Services
Disability Support Services (DSPS) offices offer a variety of support services beyond what is available to the general student population for students with documented disabilities. Services and educational accommodations are provided in compliance with state and federal legislation. Eligible students can receive reasonable accommodations are determined by the DSS counselor/specialist on an individual basis. Services and accommodations are based on the educational abilities and limitations unique to each student, but may include: testing accommodations, specialized counseling, DSPS student orientation and assessment, access to alternate media, notetaking or interpretive services, access to adaptive or assistive technologies, and courses and workshops on assistive computer software and learning strategies.

EOPS: Extended Opportunities Program and Services
EOPS is a support services program designed to provide entry, retention and transition services for educationally and economically needy students. The support services are designed to assist and contribute to the student's success in college. They provide: counseling services on campus policies, financial aid, scholarships, campus, and community referrals; financial aid assistance for students in locating and applying for appropriate types of available financial aid and in completing the various financial aid forms; and outreach services to prospective students.

Financial Aid
The Financial Aid Office supports students and their individual financial needs with monetary assistance to students who may benefit from higher education; it is the central location for assistance with applying for federal financial aid, work-study awards, and scholarships, and determining eligibility for financial assistance.

First Year Experience
The First Year Experience (FYE) program is a student success program for first year students. Participating students receive guaranteed English and Math classes for the year. Benefits include: guaranteed enrollment, early registration, enrollment assistance, academic advising, smooth transfer pathways, tutoring, and career counseling.

Honors Program

Honors Programs offer a variety of courses that fulfill the general education requirements of most majors with innovative classes that encourage participants to do additional exploration of course materials beyond that of a traditional, standard course.

Health Services

The Health Center provides the health care, wellness care, and personal counseling to students similar to the services you might find in a medical clinic. The health center professionals can also make referrals to off campus medical centers for services not provided on campus.

International Student Center

International Student Centers offer services designed especially for international students on the F-1 student visa and those seeking an F-1 student visa, supporting international students both academically and personally. Services and programs include: international admissions, academic and personal counseling, immigration advisement, orientation, living and employment resources and advising, cultural activities, and mentorships.

Library

College libraries assist students, faculty, and staff to attain their educational and informational goals by offering traditional services such as: access to the book and audiovisual collection, periodicals, interlibrary loan service, reserve materials and reference and research assistance; access to technology both on campus and off campus via the library's website, including the library catalog, online databases for periodicals and in-depth subject resources, as well as Internet searching and documentation assistance; and onsite assistance for students with their research needs. There are often computers with Internet connections for student research use and word processing capabilities and printing services available as well.

Math Lab

Math labs are designed to provide students with resources and support to assist students in math courses. Services may include: individual tutoring, CD and DVD lectures, computer tutorials, online homework programs, individual and group study locations, and access to textbooks.

MESA

The MESA program supports students to successfully transfer to four-year universities in science, technology, engineering and math (STEM) majors. This support is especially crucial to students who come from low-performing high schools. MESA programs usually offer: orientation, academic workshops, academic advisement and counseling, transfer assistance and counseling, career development, professional networking opportunities, field trips, professional development, and internships.

Puente Program

The Puente Program assists educationally underrepresented students who wish to enroll in four-year colleges and universities, earn degrees, and return to their communities as leaders and mentors to future generations. The program is open to all students, and provides English and Counseling courses with a focus on transfer, mentors, off campus travel, networking opportunities, and academic and counseling support from acceptance in the program through graduation.

Service Learning Center

Service learning centers provide the opportunity for students to connect the classroom to the community. Real-world experiences result in active, enhanced learning, civic engagement, commitment to helping others and helping provide solutions regarding issues that affect the community and world.

STEM Program

STEM programs are designed to increase student participation, persistence and success in the fields of Science, Technology, Engineering and Mathematics (STEM). Programs often include: counseling and supplemental instruction, transfer support to a university, peer mentoring, guest speakers, STEM workshops, networking opportunities, and student clubs and support groups.

TAP: Transfer Achievement Program

The Transfer Achievement Program (TAP) is a comprehensive program designed to encourage and support students in their goal of transferring to a four-year university. Some of the benefits of the program include: priority enrollment, additional personal and academic counseling and guidance, opportunities for peer networking, personal development courses and workshops, and field trips to colleges and universities.

Transfer Center

Transfer Centers help students prepare to transfer to four-year universities with support in areas ranging from college exploration to college selection, major exploration to major preparation, and the entire application process. Services and activities include: field trips, access to university and college catalogs, transfer counseling and advisement, contact with university transfer representatives, financial aid information, transfer application assistance, and workshops and events about transfer opportunities.

TRIO

TRIO Programs are federal outreach and student services programs designed to identify and provide services for individuals from disadvantaged backgrounds. TRIO programs serve and assist low-income individuals, first-generation college students, and individuals with disabilities to progress through the academic pipeline from middle school to postbaccalaureate programs. Services offered frequently include: counseling, tutoring, workshops, field trips, mentoring, transfer guidance and counseling, and ongoing support.

Veterans' Services
Veterans, service members, and their survivors and dependents maybe eligible to receive support and assistance at a Veterans Resource Center to assist with collecting their benefits as well as a full range of student support services aimed at providing for the specialized needs of veterans.

Workforce Center
Workforce centers educate students on the skills, attitudes, and experiences required to succeed in the workplace with up-to-date information on employment opportunities, job-seeking techniques, employability skills, business etiquette, and job placement. Workforce centers often provide: postings of employment opportunities, assistance with resumes and cover letters, workshops on interview techniques and employment skills, job search resource materials, computer access, and job fairs.

Writing Center
Writing centers provide tutoring on writing projects, assistance with academic writing projects such as transfer letters and scholarship applications. Often, walk-in and by-appointment tutoring are offered. Frequent workshops on a variety of topics related to academic writing are held in writing centers.

Campus Life: Get Involved
While you are attending a community college, it is a good idea to become as involved as possible in campus life. You will find that your experience in college will be much more rewarding if you become actively involved in student clubs and campus events. Most community colleges have a Homecoming event every year, as well as sports events, games, carnivals and festivals. Many of these can be quite colorful and fun to experience. There, you will find food from all over the world and multicultural music as well as other live entertainment. Become involved in these activities. Or, you may want to join one of the many student clubs that exist at community colleges. For instance, you may want to join a sports club, such as a tennis club, or, if you are religious, you may want to become familiar with the campus ministries at your school. Joining a club on campus will enable you to meet and network with people who have interests similar to yours as well to gain marketable experiences that will look good on a transfer application or a resume. In today's job market and with colleges and universities severely impacted with far more applicants than they can accept, the more you do *beyond* earning good grades, the better your chances of distinguishing yourself from the other applicants and getting hired to a competitive job or accepted into a competitive university.

Another reason that it is useful to become involved on campus is that you will be able to develop various skills that you will later use in the workforce. Students who become involved in the Associated Student Body, or ASB [sometimes called the Associated Student Organization or ASO], are later able to use the leadership qualities that they gained during their stay at a community college in whatever career they choose to follow. Thus, if there is a position open in student government, such as student senator, or student body president, try out for one of those positions. Flex your leadership and public speaking skills. Become used to making decisions that affect other people. This invaluable and highly transferable skill can be used later in your career. Student body organizations often function as the students' representatives for campus policies, planners of campus events, council for student organizations, and clearinghouse for other student opportunities. Therefore, getting involved with your campus's student body representatives will not only make you look good on your university and job applications and increase your networking skills, but also provide easy access to other beneficial opportunities.

Familiarizing Yourself with the Campus Layout

The topography of community college campuses is usually very appealing. They are usually smaller than a four-year college or university and have a very cozy feel to them. You will find that the architecture of community college campuses is very picturesque and might evoke Gothic or Spanish Colonial architectural styles. As soon as you become involved in a community college, purchase a copy of the *Schedule of Classes*. The *Schedule of Classes*, published every semester, will list the times and locations where the classes will be held for that semester. Class times and classrooms change every new term, which is why the *Schedule* is published a couple of months before the start of every new term. The *Schedule of Classes* will also have within its pages a map of the campus. Become familiar with the campus layout, and get to know where the major buildings are located, such as the Admissions and Records building, the Financial Aid offices, the Math and Science buildings, the Liberal Arts buildings, the Counseling Office, the Track and Field areas, and so on. You may find that some of the buildings are named after major benefactors to the school. So, a major building on campus may be called Smith Hall, for example, or the Johnson Plaza. Many of these buildings will be large and have several floors to them, so it is a good idea to visit the campus before the semester begins so that you will know where your classrooms are located. Also, be aware of the fact that at the last minute, the college may change the building or room number where a class was supposed to meet. If this happens, a notice will usually be posted on the door where the class was originally supposed to be held. The notice will direct students to the new building or room number. Arriving to campus early enough to react to last second changes will help you avoid being late to class.

Enrolling in Classes

As you flip through the *Schedule of Classes,* you will find that different classes have different section numbers. Thus, a math class may have a dozen different sections depending on the level of math and the type of math. So, for instance, the Algebra classes may have a certain numeration that is different from the Geometry or Trigonometry classes. Look closely at the section number of a class you want to take. Many of these are printed in small numbers and are grouped together, so it may be easy to make a mistake when you begin planning your schedule and get ready to sign up for your courses. You certainly will want to avoid the stress of sitting in class on the first day only to have the professor walk in and announce that this is a completely different class than the one you expected!

These days, community colleges are highly sophisticated in their enrollment procedures. You will find that you are most likely able to enroll on-line through the Internet or through a touch-tone telephone. The exact procedures for enrollment, either on-line or by telephone, will be different at different colleges, so become very familiar with the enrollment procedures of the school you wish to attend. If you are still confused, do not hesitate to ask somebody at the Admissions and Records office or to call the office by phone and ask a staff member to guide you through the system that is used.

One of things that will probably happen when you decide to enroll at a community college is that you will be asked to take an Assessment and Placement test. This test gauges your strengths and weaknesses when it comes to different academic areas, especially those related to math and English. You will be assigned a test date, and it is very important that you show up for the test. When you take the test, do not get stressed or worried. This placement test is designed merely to measure your math and English skills. Afterwards, once you get the results of your assessment test, you will be told which classes you should take in math and English. You should not see this as a pass or fail exam. You will not flunk if you get a low score, but you will be placed in classes which are appropriate for your skill level. Afterwards, it is advisable that you make an appointment with a college counselor to discuss your scores and the score placement system of the school you attend. Naturally, all community colleges will have a different testing and placement system.

Most *Schedules of Classes* will illustrate a diagram that will show the family tree, if you will, of the math and English courses at the college. This will show the degree of difficulty and how many semesters you will need in order to get to the level of English and math required for your major or vocational coursework. Information such as this can be very helpful for planning your course of study.

Working with Counselors

As you begin making trips to the counseling offices with your questions regarding classes, get to know the different counselors. Each one will have a different personality, working style, and philosophical viewpoint. Yet, they are all there to help you adjust and be successful in college. As you become more and more familiar with their personalities, choose one whose style appeals to you and whose advice you find easy to understand. Try to stay with this counselor the entire time you are attending college. Build a friendship and alliance with a particular counselor. Make your counselor your ally as you progress through the community college system. Most counseling offices will have the different certificate and degree plans posted on a wall and provide copies for you to take home where you can see all the classes required for a particular college degree or certificate. Thus, if you plan to get an Associate of Science degree in Automotive Mechanics, the planning sheet will show you all the math and science classes you need to take in order to get that particular college degree.

When you examine these sheets, it is important that you become familiar with the time necessary to complete all of the college classes required for your goal. If you are planning to get a two-year college degree, keep in mind that this will take roughly 60 units to complete. Even if you were attending full-time, that is, enrolling in twelve units every fall and spring term, and taking up to six units during the Summer term, it will still take roughly two years of your life to complete. So, plan accordingly.

Most counselors have a good amount of training in psychology and personal counseling. Thus, if you feel the need to talk to somebody regarding a personal matter or an emotional problem, feel free to talk to counselors. You will find that they are very caring and empathic listeners, and they will be able to help you gain some knowledge or insight into your problem. However, if the problem you present to them is difficult enough that it may exceed their training or background, they may refer you to a community clinic where you can receive low-cost counseling on a sliding-fee scale. In any case, you should never feel shy about opening up to college counselors: it is their job to help you get through school, no matter what that entails.

Many college counselors begin to generate quite a loyal following among students who wish to see them on a regular basis, and their schedules can become booked very quickly. Thus, it is important that you call early on a Monday morning to make an appointment with a counselor that you prefer. Depending on the caseload and the time of year, a counselor's schedule may become booked even by midweek. Establishing a personal relationship with your preferred counselor will often enable you to make a regular, standing appointment or exchange phone numbers, email addresses or other contact information, so that you can get the help you need as easily as possible.

Keep an Open Mind

During your first visit to your counselor, he or she will develop your Educational Plan, or Ed. Plan. On an empty grid sheet, he or she will list all the courses needed to complete your degree, certificate, or transfer requirements. Study it closely, become familiar with how many units each semester will require, and plan your life accordingly. Even if you can only afford to take one class per semester, due to lack of time or financial constraints, then take your time and enjoy that class to the fullest. Make the most of your classes. Get to know your professors. Make friends with your classmates. Take as many notes during class as possible. Keep your mind open as you listen to the lectures. Many of us come to college with preconceived notions, ideas, or assumptions, already hardened in our minds about various aspects of life. While most teachers will respect and value the opinions of their students, it is also important to keep an open mind as you attend your classes; allow other students to express their opinions without prejudging them, and be open-minded enough to consider changing your mind about topics you may have thought you had made up your mind about. Allow yourself to be challenged but don't be afraid to challenge others. Be able to take criticism since this is what strengthens your knowledge, and don't be afraid to give criticism or express your opinion—even if it is different from that of others— for that is what demonstrates your own unique original thinking.

Journal Assignments

1. Imagine that you are planning your future and that money, family obligations, location, and other responsibilities are *not* barriers. Then, set some goals. If you had no barriers, what would you want to do with your future? Where would you go to school? What would you study? What degree would you earn? What job would you apply for? Where would you live? Don't make excuses or put limits on yourself here. The idea is to find out what you would do if you could do anything you wanted to do without worrying about money and time.

2. Write 3 one-paragraph descriptions of yourself: Who you were, who you are, and who you will be.

Fieldwork Journal Assignment: Visit at least three different student services/programs and do the following:

- Collect literature from every program (i.e. flyers, brochures etc.)
- Describe the programs missions' and student benefits
- List eligibility requirements to qualify for the Program

Chapter Three

Financial Aid for College

Student Learning Outcome:
Students will gain knowledge and understanding of the requirements for and process of applying for financial aid and apply knowledge to their own personal experience.

"The lesson I learned was: When in doubt, build your own damn truck. It's a lesson we all need to learn. You need to educate yourselves, learn every language you can. You need to not be a slave to the credit system and gain economic independence. You need to build your own damn truck rather than wait for someone to give you one."
—Luis Valdez, playwright

At some point during your decision to advance your college education, you, among countless others, will have to figure out a way to finance your education. Some students are fortunate enough to be born into wealthy families. However, for the great majority of working-class students, finding a way to finance college becomes a necessity. There are several options open to you to obtain the money to pay for your tuition: grants, work-study, scholarships and loans.

Federal and State Financial Aid Programs: Overview

The following is a brief overview of financial aid options that you should investigate by speaking with your counselor and visiting the financial aid office at your community college.

Free Application for Federal Student Aid (FAFSA)

The primary tool to apply for the federal financial aid is the Free Application for Federal Student Aid (FAFSA). Although the FAFSA is still available in paper form, it is also now available online at www.fafsa.gov and can easily be submitted through the step-by-step online tutorial. The FAFSA needs to be submitted no matter what your financial situation may be. You may receive any combination of financial aid; for instance, you might be granted both a subsidized and an unsubsidized loan for the same academic year. If your university is a member of the Federal Direct Student Loan Program, your federal loans will come straight from the federal government, and not through a private lending institution. In short, this should be your starting place.

Most importantly, there is no fee attached to this form. It is easy to fill out, and you need only do this once per academic year. Approximately three to four weeks after you file your FAFSA, you will receive a Student Aid Report (SAR) in the mail. Another copy will be sent to school(s) of your choice. Then, about two weeks after receiving your SAR in the mail, you will receive a letter from your college informing of the amount and type of financial aid you are qualified to receive. As of this writing, there is a March 2nd deadline to submit the FAFSA to the Federal processor. Thus, make sure that you heed the deadline, and submit your form in a timely manner. Also, keep abreast of deadline changes to make sure that you are not blindsided by changes of when these forms are due.

Community college students if eligible after submitting the FAFSA application may qualify for different forms of financial aid. These include **Federal Pell Grants, Federal Supplemental Opportunity Grants, Federal College Work Study,** student and parent loans, private grants and scholarships. Each will be discussed below.

Basic Eligibility Requirements for Financial Aid
· Be a U.S. citizen or an eligible noncitizen
· Have a valid Social Security number
· Maintain satisfactory academic progress
· If you are male and between the ages of 18 and 25, you must register with selective service
· Must have high school diploma or recognized equivalent (GED) certificate or home school setting under state law
· Be enrolled, working toward a degree or certificate in an eligible program
· Not be in default on a federal student loan and do not owe money on a federal student grant
· Be enrolled at least half-time to be eligible for direct loan programs

Satisfactory Academic Progress Standards
The term "satisfactory academic progress means that students must:
• Maintain a 2.0 or higher Cumulative grade point average
• Cumulative non-grades (Withdrawals, Incompletes, No-Credit) are less than 33%
• Have fewer than 90 attempted units
• Not have an Associate degree or higher

Selective Service
Most male students must be registered with Selective Service to receive federal student aid.

🔲🖲 You also must register if you are a male and are not currently on active duty in the U.S. armed forces.

🔲🖲 You can call Selective Service toll-free at 1-888-655-1825 for general information about registering, or register online at www.sss.gov or via the FAFSA.

Pell Grant

- Awarded to undergraduate students who have exceptional financial need and who have not earned a bachelor's or graduate degree.
- In accordance with the Consolidated Appropriations Act of 2012 signed by President Obama, the maximum lifetime eligibility for Federal PELL Grant is six full-time years (600%)
- Annual Award (subject to change) is up to $5,730
- To apply online visit www.fafsa.ed.gov

Federal Supplemental Educational Opportunity Grant

- Awarded to undergraduate students who have exceptional financial need and who have not earned a bachelor's or graduate degree
- Federal Pell Grant recipients receive priority
- Funds depend on availability at the college; apply by your college's deadline

Federal Work Study

Federal Work-Study is awarded subject to funding availability to students who indicate an interest on their FAFSA and who demonstrate need. FWS enables students to earn a portion of their financial aid award through part-time employment either on or off campus. If your financial aid Award Letter includes FWS, you must attend an orientation, and there is a six (6) unit minimum enrollment requirement. You will need to consult regularly with your federal work-study coordinator on campus.

Federal Grant Resources

To learn more information about federal grants:

- www.studentaid.ed.gov
- www.fafsa.ed.gov

State Grants

A grant is a block of money that is awarded by the state, in this case California, for the purpose of paying for college. A grant is different from a scholarship in that a grant does not have to be repaid; both, however, represent available money for you to use for tuition and other school-related expenses. They are awarded through the California Student Aid Commission (CSAC). State grants include the Cal Grants, the Chaffee grant, the Child Development grant, the Dream Act for AB540 students, and the Board of Governors (BOG) fee waiver program.

Cal Grants

One choice for you if you will need extra money for college is to apply for a **Cal Grant**. In order to apply for a Cal Grant, you must complete the FAFSA. As mentioned previously, you can use either a paper-copy FAFSA from the financial aid office of your community college or use the form on-line.

Following is a brief description of the different types of Cal Grants:

1. **Cal Grant A Entitlement**. You need to demonstrate financial need and meet the grade point average and family income requirements. These grants can only be applied toward four-year colleges and universities.

2. **Cal Grant A Competitive**. You need to demonstrate strong accomplishments and have a financial need to be in order to qualify. These grants are not guaranteed every year. These are intended for transfer students.

3. **Cal Grant B Entitlement**. In order to qualify, you need to show financial need, demonstrate the grade point average necessary, as well as have the family income as outlined by the California Student Aid Commission. These grants can be applied toward the tuition of a community college and four-year colleges and universities.

4. **Cal Grant B Competitive**. You need to show academic promise, and your family income has to be no higher than the limits specified. These grants are also not guaranteed. These can be applied to defray the cost of tuition at a junior college as well as a four-year college or university.

If you do qualify, you will be notified by mail, in the form of a Cal Grant notification letter, informing you of your award.

Chafee Grant

- The California Chafee Grant is free money for current or former California foster youth to help pay for college or career and technical training
- Chafee Grants don't have to be paid back
- Chafee Grant is a federal and state funded grant subject to yearly availability of funds
- To qualify, you must:
    - Be a current or former foster youth
    - Not have reached your 22nd birthday as of July 1 of the award year
    - Have financial need

- To apply:
  - Submit the California Chafee Grant Program Application online at www.chafee.csac.ca.gov
  - Submit the FAFSA application online at www.fafsa.ed.gov

Child Development Grant

The Child Development Grant Program is designed for students who:
- Are attending California public or private two-year or four-year postsecondary institutions
- Intend to teach or to supervise in a licensed children's center in California

The program provides benefits to selected applicants who:
- Are enrolled in approved coursework leading to Child Development Permit
- Maintain at least half-time enrollment
- Maintain satisfactory academic progress
- Demonstrate financial need

Dream Act

The CA Dream Act Application is used by undocumented students who meet the eligibility requirements of AB 540.
AB 540 students may include:
- undocumented students
- students who are U.S. citizens, but are not CA residents
- dependent students whose parents are not CA resident

AB 540 students are those who:
- Have attended a CA high school for at least 3 years or graduated early from a CA high school with the equivalent of 3 or more years of credit, AND
- Graduated from a CA high school, passed the California High School Proficiency Exam (CHSPE), or obtained a Certificate of General Education Development (GED), AND
- Enrolled in an accredited and qualifying CA college or university, AND
- If applicable, have completed an affidavit to legalize immigration status as soon as you are eligible.
- To confirm your AB540 eligibility, you will be required to submit affidavit and provide supporting documentation to the Admissions Office.
- Dream Act Application and Certified GPA Verification deadline March 2 of each year.

- To learn more about the California Dream Act and to apply online visit www.caldreamact.org

Board of Governors (BOG) Fee Waiver

- The BOG Fee Waiver waives enrollment fees
- You are eligible to apply for a BOG Fee Waiver if you are:
    - A California resident or are classified as an AB 540 student, and
    - You are enrolled in at least one unit
    - *Students are encouraged to apply using the FAFSA or California Dream Act Application (for AB 540) so they are considered for all available financial aid programs*

Scholarships

The other very attractive option for you is to start a search for a **scholarship** based on your academic strengths or other talents. Scholarships are similar to grants in that they do not have to be repaid. Once you are awarded a scholarship, it is yours to keep. The many scholarships and fellowships that are awarded each year to deserving students are drawn from the scholarship funds of private corporations and foundations. Traditionally, scholarships were awarded to the top-performing students in high schools who had the highest marks. Now, the criteria have expanded to include awards for artistic abilities, such as a musical talent or athletic prowess. In addition, students in a particular academic track might be qualified for scholarships, as are students from certain minority groups who have traditionally not attended college in very high numbers. Students might quality for a scholarship for living in a certain geographic area or even for being a southpaw (left-handed)!

One way to begin your search for suitable scholarships is to use some of the on-line databases that use information that you provide to match you with a suitable scholarship category (see list below for links).

As mentioned previously, the traditional way of earning a scholarship is to show a strong academic merit. Each sponsor who has established a scholarship fund will select and publish the criteria for winning it. Your challenge, therefore, is not only to demonstrate substantial academic merit, but also to tailor that merit to the sponsor's criteria.

The web-based FastWeb scholarship site is very popular and easy to use. The site will find the right matches for your background. With FastWeb, you can even transmit your application on-line to scholarships in their database. The site can also help you locate a particular college for specific scholarship information.

Think of these scholarship search companies as your "matchmaker" in regards to scholarships, and they will find the most suitable "matches" for a scholarship. Finding a foundation that awards scholarships based on criteria that you meet greatly increases your chances of eventually winning a scholarship. There are numerous scholarship search sites on the Internet. Beware of some sites that charge fees in order to do their search for you. This is usually a waste of your money as the information found on these sites is more or less the same as that found on the free scholarship-search sites, such as FastWeb. Even if you are not a 4.0 student, it is still worth the time and effort to research a scholarship since not all are based solely on grades. Some are based on other skills, such as extracurricular accomplishments. Furthermore, be wary of scholarship scams on sites that promise a scholarship if you send them your money first. Never send money in order to win a scholarship. If you do decide to search for a scholarship, check in with your school to ask about its scholarship policy, to avoid conflicts with any financial aid you might already be receiving. Another thing to keep in mind is that if you win a scholarship, the money used for tuition and related fees are not taxed, but the rest could be. Thus, play it safe and know the reporting requirements of your scholarship money so that come tax-time, there are no further hassles regarding your scholarship money.

As mentioned previously, the traditional way of earning a scholarship is to show a strong academic merit. Each sponsor who has established a scholarship fund will select and publish the criteria for winning it. Your challenge, therefore, is not only to demonstrate substantial academic merit, but also to tailor that merit to the sponsor's criteria. Different sponsors will have different objectives when establishing a scholarship fund. For some corporations, it may take the form of community investment. Other companies may award scholarship money in order to keep certain top employees or to attract potential employees. Universities may award scholarships in order to attract outstanding athletes or to attract women and minorities into majors where they are underrepresented, such as the sciences. Other organizations may award scholarships as a way to advertise their sector of the economy. Finally, a scholarship foundation might be created in order to honor a prominent person in a particular field and maintain the legacy of his or her mission and life's work.

Begin your search early for the scholarship that is right for you. Pay close attention to the grade point average requirements as well as other criteria listed by the sponsor. Because these sponsors receive a high number of applications, any given student portfolio will be considered *only if* the student meets the specified requirements. If you find a scholarship that appears to suit your needs yet you do not have the requisite qualifications, then you may challenge yourself to improve your grades, or otherwise meet the qualifications, well in advance of the time at which you plan to apply. This is why you need to begin your search early, so that you can give yourself plenty of time to bolster your credentials and maintain a competitive edge. If anything, you should plan to make yourself *overqualified* for these scholarships. One good way to ensure that you will be in good standing for a scholarship is to stay as active as possible in extracurricular activities during your high school and community college years. The activities which will count the most are those which develop and promote leadership qualities. As mentioned previously, maintaining an active role in student government in high school or the Associated Student Body at your community college will go a long way to impress scholarship sponsors.

Scholarship Resources

- www.fastweb.com
- www.finaid.org/scholarships
- www.finaid.org/websearch
- www.finaid.org/scholarshipscams
- www.scholarships.com
- www.ftc.gov/scholarshipscams
- www.finaid.org/taxbenefits
- www.irs.gov/pub/irs-pdf/p970.pdf

Loans

Loans are money that is borrowed by students to help finance their education. They have to be repaid to the institution that loaned it to you, so this may be a last resort. There will usually be interest added to the loan as well, so effective financial planning is crucial. However, while loans may seem to be the least desirable option for getting financial assistance with college, they are certainly better than not attending a university. Many times, students will decide to attend whatever university offers them the best free financial aid package rather than the best school for their major or career plans. That's not the best way to decide where to attend college. Taking on a loan, while daunting, can mean the difference between attending a mediocre university as opposed to a top tier one. Since the college you graduate from has a huge role in determining your future earning potential and will establish your credentials in the job market as much, if not more than, all other factors, this is not the place to be cheap and stingy. So, for many reasons, loans can be appealing. You, in consultation with your family and counselor, will determine the best plan for you, but before you dismiss loans as an option, consider them as an investment in your future. If borrowing money that has to be repaid will lead to a higher-paying job for the rest of your life, then it's probably worth it! Yes, you will have to make payments toward the loan after you graduate, but that's a small price to pay relative to a lifetime of higher earnings. There are four principal categories of loans:

1. Student loans (**Stafford** and **Perkins** loans)
2. Parent loans (PLUS loans)
3. Private student loans (Alternative student loans)
4. Consolidation loans

Student loans usually carry low interest rates and will not require a credit check or any type of collateral. They also carry with them several deferment options and flexible payment plans. The main federal student loan is known as the Stafford loan.

Stafford Loans

There are two types of Stafford loans:

- **Federal Family Education Loan Program (FFELP)** These types of loans are given by private institutions such as banks, savings and loan associations, and credit unions. This type of loan is backed by the federal government against default.

- **Federal Direct Student Loan Program (FDSLP)** These types of loans are awarded through "Direct Lending Schools" but are principally from the U.S. government.

All of the **Stafford Loans** fall into one of two categories: subsidized or unsubsidized. If a federal loan is subsidized, the government will pay the interest while you are attending college. If a federal loan is unsubsidized, you will have to pay all the accrued interest. The upside of this is that you can defer your payments until after graduation. If you choose to defer paying off your unsubsidized Stafford loan until after you graduate, you can do so by capitalizing the interest. This means that the interest payments are added to the principal loan balance that will compound the size of the loan as a matter of course. All applicants—no matter what their financial status—are eligible to receive an unsubsidized Stafford loan. If you are a family dependent and applying for college and choose to take out a Stafford loan, you may be able to borrow the following amounts (as of this writing):

- $2,625 for your freshman year
- $3,500 for your sophomore year
- $5,500 for each remaining year

Note that students who are independent as well as students whose parents were ineligible for a PLUS loan can receive an additional unsubsidized amount of $4,000 for their freshman and sophomore years, and $5,000 for the junior and senior years of college. Students in graduate school may borrow $18,500 per year. However, of this amount only $8,500 is subsidized. There are also caps on the combined four years of college, as well as a $65,500 cap for combined undergraduate and graduate loans. Also, note that for students that are independent as well as those whose parents were turned down for a PLUS loan, the cumulative amounts that can be borrowed are: $46,000 for the total undergraduate tuition, and $138,500 for the combined undergraduate and graduate tuitions. Quite a few college students use both subsidized and unsubsidized loans to maximize the amount they can borrow. The federal Stafford loans have interest rates that are variable and are capped at 8.25% interest. All the institutions that provide the Stafford loans offer the same rate; however, some provide incentives such as reduced rates if payments are timely or made electronically.

Perkins Loans

Another worthy option for both undergraduate and graduate students with economic constraints is the **Perkins Loan**. This loan is comprised of money from the federal government which is administered in and given by a university. By some accounts, it is the most attractive option open to students. The Perkins loan is a subsidized loan, which means that the federal government will pay the interest during the time that you are in school, as well as during the nine-month grace period after graduation. Another benefit is that this loan carries no origination or guarantee fees. The Perkins loan carries a 5% interest rate. Should you choose to utilize the Perkins loan, you will have ten years in which to repay it. The financial aid office of your university will mediate the allotment of money you are loaned. The loan caps are $4,000 per year for undergraduate students. The cap for graduate students is $6,000 per year. There is a total limit of $20,000 for undergraduate student loans, and a $40,000 cap for undergraduate and graduate loans combined. Some colleges and universities have what is known as an Expanded Lending Option (ELO) in which they may offer more money in the Perkins loan package. In order for a school to have an ELO program, a college or university must not have a default rate higher than 15%. Another benefit of having a Perkins loan is that it carries easier cancellation features than either the Stafford and PLUS loans. In order to see if you qualify to receive a Stafford loan, you must submit your FAFSA.

Parent (PLUS) Loans

A second type of loan that families can utilize is Parent Loans. These loans are designed for parents of students who are still dependents in order to further cover the cost of tuition. Under the federal **Parent Loan for Undergraduate Students (PLUS)**, parents can receive a loan to pay for any remaining expenses not accounted for by financial aid. This can amount to the full cost of tuition. Similar to the Stafford Loan, the PLUS Loan can be of two varieties: FFELP, in which private institutions administer the money; or Direct in which the loan is administered through the government. The interest rate on a PLUS loan is variable and capped at 9%. Parents must begin to pay off the money 60 days after the funds are completely disbursed. The period to repay the loan can be up to ten years. Remember that PLUS loans are your parents' responsibility so you will not be held accountable for this debt. You may decide to make the payments on your parents' behalf on the PLUS loan, but should you fall behind, your parents would be held accountable. Usually, parents who take out a PLUS loan also weigh the option of a home equity loan.

Private Education Loan

Another option open to you is to take out a **Private Education Loan**, also known as an **Alternative Education Loan**. These loans help cover the balance between the amount that the government will lend you and the remaining costs of your tuition and expenses. Because these loans are administered through private institutions, you will not have to fill out any federal forms. These loans can become an attractive option when the money loaned through federal programs is clearly less than what is needed to cover the cost of college tuition, or when a family desires more flexibility in the repayment plans. For instance, the federal loan programs do not allow you to defer payment until you graduate; therefore, many parents choose Private Education Loans. Private lending institutions will allot monies depending on your educational plans; however, these private loans are usually more costly than federal loans. If your parents are weighing the benefits of an alternative education loan, they may also want to think about a home equity loan or a PLUS loan.

Consolidation Loans

Another option to consider is loan consolidation. Also known as a **Consolidation Loan**, with this option multiple loan amounts are lumped into a single loan from one lender. This single amount can then be used to make payments on the balances of the other loans within the lump sum. Consolidation is available for most loans from the federal government, which includes FFELP (Stafford, PLUS, and SLS), FISL, Perkins, Health Professional Student Loans, and NSL, HEAL, Guaranteed Student Loans, and Direct loans. Some financial institutions offer loans that consolidate private educational loans. The process of loan consolidation extends the life of the period during which you make payments on your loan debt, lengthening the period beyond the standard ten-year life of the loan. This extension, based on the amount of the loan, can be made for up to 30 years, if need be. The smaller amount paid each month may make this an attractive option for some families. Yet, this period extension increases the amount of interest that is paid.

Journal Assignment

Research scholarship opportunities using the websites listed from this chapter and any other sources that your instructor suggests. Check what the requirements are for each that you think you may qualify for (i.e. criteria you have to meet, letters of recommendation you have to get, and essays you have to write, etc.). Investigating scholarships requires that you spend a great deal of time and should be done in consultation with your counselor; however, most scholarships have similar requirements. List the instructors, mentors, friends, relatives, co-workers, employers and former employers that you think could write you a good letter of recommendation because they know you well and like you.

Then, write—in letter form or email form—a request to the person whom you will be asking for a letter of recommendation. Include: who you are and how you know the person; what you are applying for; what things about you that you'd like the recommendation letter to include (like specific assignments you've completed, volunteer service, community involvement, family obligations, work history, personality traits, other outside interests, your *strengths*—whatever is relevant); and the contact info for the school or program that the person writing your recommendation letter should include (name, address, phone number) for the institution to which you are applying.

Chapter Four

General Education and Transfer Requirements for Universities

Student Learning Outcome:
Students will gain knowledge and understanding of the requirements for and understanding of the process of completing a university application including the application websites, deadlines minimum transfer eligibility requirements, academic reporting requirements, and the university notification timeline.

The object of education is to prepare the young to educate themselves throughout their lives."
—Robert M. Hutchins (American Educator and Writer)

What Are General Education Classes?

In order to fulfill your goal of acquiring either a two year Associate of Arts or Associate of Science degree or to transfer to a California State University, a University of California, or private college or university, you will have to complete a number of General Education classes. You might wonder, "What are General Education classes?" General Education classes are designed to give you a broad exposure to different fields, disciplines and philosophies.

For those of you who want to transfer, many questions must be on your mind. You may be wondering if you want to transfer to a California State University campus, a University of California campus, or to a private college or university. First, some important distinctions must be made between each of these three systems so that you know the differences between the three systems and can make the most informed decision possible.

California State University

The **California State University** schools, of which there 23, offer a curriculum-based education which emphasizes the different ways in which that knowledge can be applied. The degrees awarded by the CSU schools are bachelors, masters, and doctorates that are "joint program" doctorates. This means that the CSU schools may collaborate with each other or with another school to offer a doctoral degree. If you are among those who are eventually accepted and admitted, you should be proud to know that the CSU system admits the top third of California's high school graduates. As of this writing, you need a minimum Grade Point Average (GPA) of 2.0 if you are transferring from a community college. With 23 campuses spread throughout the state of California, it is America's largest four-year university system. Most of the campuses use the semester system in their academic years. This means that your fall semester will begin in late August or early September and continue into December. Then you will enjoy a winter vacation and begin again in the spring. The spring term begins in January and continues until May. The semesters typically last for 16 weeks. The only CSU campuses that operate on the quarter system are Bakersfield, East Bay, Los Angeles, Pomona, San Bernardino, and San Luis Obispo.

Some of the schools are well known for certain programs, such as California State University, Long Beach, which has an excellent curriculum for preparing future teachers for their certification credentials. It is a good idea to visit the website www2.calstate.edu which has links to all of the campuses and offers both general and specific information about the campus system. One other caveat to keep in mind, not as a deterrent but rather as something to prepare you for your possible journey to the CSU campus, is that certain programs are *impacted*. What this means is that the program is full due to the high number of applicants: there are more students applying to the program than can be smoothly accommodated. You should not worry if you find out that your major is an impacted major. But do try to decide on a major soon so that in case your major is impacted, you can give yourself plenty of time to take any prerequisites for your major at your community college. Additionally, if you find out that the major to which you are applying is impacted, fill out the application early because the impacted majors have a shorter application period.

> *It is a good idea to visit the website www.csumentor.edu which has links to all of the campuses and offers both general and specific information about the campus system.*

If you feel certain about the particular campus you would like to transfer to, then another good idea is to log into the school's official website. Keep in mind that the California State Universities are large, commuter campuses. There are students living on campus, but the proportion is very small compared to the amount of students who commute by car, bus, or bicycle. You will definitely feel the size and scope of these campuses by visiting one or more them. It is generally recommended that you visit these campuses before you even apply so that you can get the general "feeling" of the campus and decide whether the atmosphere is right for you. If you are planning to transfer to a California State University campus, keep in mind that you *must* apply early. The filing period for the Fall semester is October 1-November 30. The filing period for the Spring semester is August 1-31. The period for filing for the Summer term is February 1-28. Finally, the filing period for Winter term is June 1-30. These dates may change, so you are strongly encouraged to check on the school's website or to ask a university representative. The website to apply to the Cal State Universities is **CSUApply: www2.calstate.edu**.

The University of California

The other major system to which students apply is the **University of California** system. This system has nine schools, each of which has the UC designation attached to them. The University of California schools are research-based and award doctorates in different fields. This would be a good choice for you if you want to go into a research-based discipline, such as medicine or anthropology. As of this writing, you need a minimum Grade Point Average (GPA) of 2.4 if you are transferring from a community college. These schools choose students from the top eighth of all high school seniors. Undergraduates can only attend full-time and during the day. There are no part-time or evening classes for undergraduates. Concurrent enrollment, when you are attending classes at two schools simultaneously, can only occur during summer school at the UC campuses. While at the CSU schools the majors with more applicants than can be accommodated are referred to as *impacted*, at the UC schools they are referred to as *screened*. Students in these majors must complete certain classes at a community college or other university before they transfer to a UC school.

If you plan to transfer to any of the seven University of California campuses which utilize the quarter system, be prepared to do your college coursework at a faster pace than what you have been used at your community college.

Another thing to note is that the University of California, with the exception of UC Berkeley and UC Merced, uses the quarter, rather than the semester system. You will have three 10-week terms rather than the more common two 16-week semesters in the fall and spring. The California State University system uses the semester system, and the University of California the quarter system. Thus, if you plan to transfer to any of the seven University of California campuses which use the quarter system, be prepared to do your college coursework at a faster pace than what you have been used at your community college. Most community colleges utilize the semester system, so your first semester at a University of California campus will be a bit of a jolt. Many community college students hold jobs that are either part-time or full-time, and if you are one of these, be prepared to adjust your financial plans, as well as your work schedule, because the University of California schools will leave less room for off-campus working hours. In this case, you may have to take out a loan or apply for a scholarship, which will then give you the freedom to pursue your coursework with less of a strain on your schedule. Chapter 4 will deal with Financial Aid and will give you many ideas on how you can finance your education.

If you do decide to pursue your education at a University of California school, as of this writing, these are the requirements you will have to meet:

1. You need to complete 60 semester (90 quarter) units of transferable college credit with a Grade Point Average (GPA) of at least 2.4. You cannot take any more than 14 semester (21 quarter) units as Pass/Not Pass.

2. You must complete the course pattern below, and get a C or better in each class:
   - Two transferable college courses (3 semester or 4-5 quarter units each) in English composition;
   - One transferable college class (3 semester or 4-5 quarter units) in mathematical concepts and quantitative reasoning;
   - Four transferable college courses (3 semester or 4-5 quarter units each) chosen from at least two of the following subject areas: the arts and humanities, the social and behavioral sciences, and the physical and biological sciences.

Also, if you meet the requirements of the Intersegmental General Education Transfer Curriculum (IGETC—see below) before you transfer to the UC school of your choice, you might be able to take care of Part 2 of the above requirements. The IGETC requirements do not have to be completed at only one community college. If you move, or decide you do not like the community college you are attending and that you want to attend another community college, you may then pick up where you left off with your IGETC requirements to satisfy the transfer requirements for your major before you go on to a four-year college or university.

If you applied and were admitted to a UC school immediately after your high school graduation, you are qualified for transfer even if you have a C (2.0) average in your transferable classes. Or, if you met the Scholarship Requirement while you were in high school, but did not meet the Subject Requirements, you must complete transferable classes in the missing subjects. You must get a C or higher in each required class and have a C average in all transferable classes to qualify for transfer.

If you plan on transferring to a University of California school, keep in mind the filing dates for admission. Applications can be accessed beginning in August. The filing period to submit the application for the fall quarter is November 1-30. The filing period for the winter quarter is July 1-31. Finally, the filing period for the spring quarter is October 1-31. As stated above, these dates may change, so do your homework and check with the school to which you are applying to double-check the dates. The website to apply is **UC Application: https://admissions.universityofcalifornia.edu.**

Transfer Requirements

Within both systems, different schools and programs inside those schools will all have different entrance and transfer requirements. This is why it is so important that you research the requirements for your particular field before applying. There are certain fields and programs with so many applicants that university officers must use the process of comprehensive review. Simply put, comprehensive review is an evaluation procedure whereby the university will look beyond a student's grades and satisfaction of mere entrance requirements and weigh other factors that will impinge upon a student's qualifications for admission. The following factors are the criteria for comprehensive admissions review:

1. Completion of a specified pattern or number of courses that meet breadth or general education requirements.
2. Completion of a specified pattern or number of courses that provide continuity with upper division courses in your major.
3. Grade point average in all transferable courses.
4. Participation in academically selective honors courses or programs.
5. Special talents, achievements and awards in a particular field, such as visual and performing arts, communication or athletic endeavors; special skills, such as demonstrated written and oral proficiency in other languages; special interests, such as intensive study and exploration of other cultures; experiences that demonstrate unusual promise for leadership, such as significant community service or significant participation in student government; or other significant experiences or achievements that demonstrate your promise for contributing to the intellectual vitality of a campus.
6. Completion of special projects undertaken in the context of your college curriculum or in conjunction with special school events, projects or programs.
7. Academic accomplishments in light of your life experiences and special circumstances.
8. Location of your college and residence.

IGETC and GE Transfer Requirements

Transfer students have two basic patterns that allow them to complete their requirements for lower-division general education classes. At the California Community Colleges, one pattern is known as the **Intersegmental General Education Transfer Curriculum (IGETC)**. This is a plan that allows students to fulfill their General Education requirements before they transfer to either the

California State University system or the University of California schools. The following are the five areas that are listed in the IGETC requirements:

Area 1 – English Communication
- Area 2 - Mathematical Concepts and Quantitative Reasoning
- Area 3 – Arts and Humanities
- Area 4 – Social and Behavioral Sciences
- Area 5 – Physical and Biological Sciences
- Area 6 – Language Other Than English (UC Requirement Only)

Under the IGETC plan, students must complete no fewer than 37 semester or 49 quarter units in lower division coursework and earn a C or higher in each of those classes.

The second pattern or option for transfer students is the **GE (General Education) Breadth Requirement** plan. Under this plan, you will complete 39 semester units of lower division general education classes in the following categories:

- Area A – Communication in the English language and Critical Thinking
- Area B – Physical Universe and its Life Forms
- Area C - Arts, Literature, Philosophy, and Foreign Language
- Area D – Social, Political, and Economic Institutions
- Area E – Lifelong Understanding and Self-Development

You can have up to 39 of your lower-division courses certified by a community college. This means that the community college you attend will sign off on your completion of 39 units of lower-division coursework, none of which will have to be repeated once you successfully transfer to a four-year college or university.

An important detail to note is that there is a maximum of 70 transferable units that can be applied towards your transfer to the California State University or the University of California systems. So, you must be careful not to take more than 70 units of transferable coursework; otherwise, you are spending more time, energy and money than necessary at a community college when you could have transferred already. Each of the 114 California Community Colleges have different courses that satisfy the different categories of classes listed above. Keep in mind that there will also be a minimum number of units that must be completed in each of these categories. It is your responsibility to make sure that the community college you are attending will certify your completion of the classes that satisfy the California State University GE breadth requirements. Your community college can either give you certification for a specific subject area, or it can give you certification for the entire pattern.

Another term that you will encounter when you begin your college education is Upper and Lower Division coursework. This refers to the level at which any particular course belongs. A class can be a "pre-major" course, and thus would be taken along with other general education classes, and would not count toward your major. Lower division coursework is taken during the first two years of college coursework. Freshman and sophomores are usually busy taking their lower division classes at community colleges. Even if you start your education at a four-year college or university, you will still have to take lower division coursework before progressing to upper division classes. If you look at a college catalog and look at a specific discipline, such as math, you will find that the courses are listed in a certain numerical series, such as the 100-level courses, and the 200s and later the 300s, and so on. Most universities will have their numbering systems on their catalogs organized so that a certain number series is lower division, like 100-299, and the rest, from 300 and up, are upper division. After you have completed 60 or more transferable units, or 90 or more transferable quarter units, you will become an Upper Division transfer student.

Private Colleges and Universities

The third option for transfer students is a private college or university. A private university is one that does not rely on the State of California for its support. Whereas the University of California and the California State University systems both get funding from Sacramento, private universities are independently run. They get all of their money from the tuition they charge, from businesses and corporations, and from the alumni who make donations.

The typical advantage of private universities is that they are usually smaller in size, so you get more time with your professors. For those of you of strong religious faith, some universities have faith-based curriculums, and chapel or Mass services on campus. These universities may be more expensive. They can

Additional information on transfer opportunities is available from your counselor; you may also want to look at the websites listed at the end of this chapter for additional information on schools, programs, and requirements—but as admission requirements change frequently, be sure to consult with your counselor for the most up-to-date information and most recent updates to the IGETC, CSU Breadth requirements, and other articulation agreements with private universities and colleges.

charge whatever they want because, as a privately run institution, they can write their own rules. Literally. Some of the better-known private universities include the University of Southern California, commonly known as USC, as well as others, such as Loyola Marymount University, Chapman University, Mount Saint Mary's College, and Occidental College. Research and visit these universities to find out whether a private university is the right option for you.

The nation's accredited independent colleges and universities provide many options at the undergraduate, graduate, and professional level for students planning to continue their education beyond the community college. Admissions requirements vary widely among institutions. Students who transfer to independent colleges and universities may be given credit for most, if not all, of their community college work. Some, but not all, private colleges and universities in California may accept credit for general education courses and for most other courses designated by the community college for transfer. Since each independent college and university has different general education and major preparation requirements, it is important to consult with a counselor for proper course planning and transfer information.

Additional information on transfer opportunities is available from your counselor; you may also want to look at the websites listed at the end of this chapter for additional information on schools, programs, and requirements—but as admission requirements change frequently, be sure to consult with your counselor for the most up-to-date information and most recent updates to the IGETC, CSU Breadth requirements, and other articulation agreements with private universities and colleges.

The Quarter System vs. the Semester System

Typically, colleges will divide the academic year using either the semester system or a quarter system. The two are very different, and if you're not ready for the switch, it can be difficult to adjust. Most high schools use the semester system: you receive one set of permanent grades after the first semester ends (around Christmas) and one set of permanent grades at the end of the school year. Between semesters, you might switch a few classes around. However, some colleges opt to use the quarter system instead. So what's the essential difference between the two? Is one better than the other? The quarter system is much more fast-paced, but aside from that, choosing which system will best suit you depends on your study habits as a student and your own preferences.

71

Here's a brief breakdown of the differences:

Semester System
• The academic year is divided into two large blocks, called semesters. One semester is usually about 15 weeks long plus one week for finals, so that puts you in school for 32 weeks.
• In one semester, you generally take approximately five classes. With two semesters in a year, you will complete about 10 classes a year.
• Most colleges on the semester system start earlier — around mid-August — and get out earlier as well. You'll usually have a major break around Christmas.
• The length of a semester gives you more time to make up class work and get the hang of things. It also means if you don't like a class, you're stuck with it for a lot longer; plus if you like to procrastinate, the amount of time makes it even easier.

Quarter System
• While colleges offer four quarters in a year (fall, winter, spring, summer), only three are actually needed to make one academic year. Therefore, even though they are called quarters, your year is actually divided into thirds instead of fourths, unless you choose to take summer classes.
• A quarter is usually 10 weeks long plus one week for finals, keeping you in school for three quarters that last a total of 33 weeks (about as long as your semester friends).
• With only ten weeks, if your class meets only on Tuesday and Thursdays, then you're only in that class twenty times.
• What this means is that the pace is MUCH faster. In those few meetings, you have to cover a whole topic. Missing a class can leave you way behind. If you have a lot of work, you will need to work hard to get it done in time. The quarter system is much less-forgiving and, as a whole, more challenging than the semester system.
• However, because the length is less, if you hate a class, you don't have to suffer through it as long as you would on a semester system.
• In one quarter, you'll usually enroll in three or four classes. With three quarters, that ranges from 9 to 12 classes in a year.
• Colleges on the quarter system tend to start later — mid-September — and stay in school until around mid-June. Typically, you'll have a nice break in December and a brief break in late March.

Ideally, this chapter has given you a glimpse of the many requirements and considerations you need to be mindful of when you begin preparations for transferring. The process of transitioning from a community college to a four-year college or university may seem daunting, but with careful planning and a spacious amount of time to get everything completed and all the paperwork turned in, it should all proceed smoothly. My only major adjustment after I transferred from East Los Angeles College to UCLA is that I had to walk a longer distance to class!

Resources for this Chapter

The websites below will assist you in locating universities and colleges nationwide, admissions information, and potential financial assistance.

Association of Independent California Colleges and Universities
www.aiccu.edu
The AICCU includes information on the 78 member institutions. Click on "Key Facts" for a list of all participants.

Assist
Assist.org
California Community College articulation agreements with CSUs and UCs.

Higher Education: University of Texas
http://www.utexas.edu/world/univ/state/index.html#accred
Search for colleges and universities nationwide by state

Hispanic Association of Colleges and Universities
www.hacu.net
Information on member institutions, including admissions, transfer and financial aid.

Historically Black Colleges and Universities (HBCU)
http://hbcuconnect.com/
Information on member institutions, including admissions, transfer and financial aid.

National Collegiate Athletic Association On Line
http://www.ncaa.org/
Information on eligibility for athletes.

Study Abroad Programs
http://www.studyabroad.com/
This site provides listings for thousands of study abroad programs in more than 100 countries throughout the world.

Virtual Tours Online
Take a virtual tour of campuses across the US
http://www.campustours.com/

Useful Planning Tools

The Transfer Degree: AA-T and AS-T

One additional benefit of going to a California Community College is the ability to take advantage of Senate Bill 1440, the Student Transfer Achievement Reform Act. SB 1440 is an agreement between the California State Universities and the California Community Colleges which is intended to streamline the transfer process for community college students. When community college students complete an AA degree specifically designed for transfer, the AA-T or AS-T degree, they are guaranteed admission to their local California State University as juniors and are given priority status as applicants to programs of study similar to that of their transfer degree work in community college. More information can be obtained from your counselor or this website: www.californiacommunitycolleges.cccco.edu/Students/AssociateDegreeforTransfer.aspx

TAG Agreements

Some community colleges have agreements with universities in the UC system which are similar to the transfer degree program above; these are called TAG agreements, and they are prescribed lists of community college courses to take which will result in guaranteed early review and admission to the sponsoring UC university as long as the student completes the required coursework and maintains a specified GPA. Six UC campuses offer TAG agreements to students from all California Community Colleges. Students who are interested in applying to the UC system must meet campus-specific requirements in order to qualify. After consulting with a counselor, students should complete an online TAG agreement and submit it during the filing period, which is in September for the following fall semester. Once submitted, students are responsible for completing all coursework indicated, maintaining their GPA above the required minimum, and applying for university admission during the appropriate filing period. (See universityofcalifornia.edu/apply.) Additional information about TAG agreements, including which campuses offer them and what the requirements and restrictions are can be found here: uctap.universityofcalifornia.edu.

The Transfer Alliance Program (TAP)

Some UC universities, such as UCLA, also offer a TAP program, the Transfer Alliance Program. This is an honors-based program which, in partnership with designated community colleges, enhances students' chances to transfer to the university. This program provides additional counseling, honors courses, and links to the UC campus, such as invitations to events, campus tours, and expert guidance.
More information is available here:
http://www.admissions.ucla.edu/Prospect/Adm_tr/ADM_CCO/tap.htm.

Transfer Admission Planner

The UC system also offers the TAP (Transfer Admission Planner), a handy planning tool, which is located at the URL indicated below and allows students to enter courses as they take them at community colleges and track their progress toward meeting the admissions requirements. This tool is extremely helpful to keep track of your progress as you advance toward completing your degree requirements. I highly advise that you use it!

http://admission.universityofcalifornia.edu/transfer/transfer-admission-planner/index.html

Journal Assignment

Choose one or more of the websites listed above and begin to explore your choices. Then, write a brief explanation of what you found. Did you find a few good schools for your intended major? Any scholarships you might be eligible for? What else did you learn from your preliminary exploration? Finally, discuss how you will proceed differently. What does your research prompt you to do next? Set some goals. Using your earlier journal entries and this one, identify goals that you want to pursue, and then list the steps you think you need to take to implement them.

Student Success Profile:

James Butler

Describe yourself briefly in a short biography (hometown, birthplace, high school experience, family, education).

I am a 23-year-old father. I was born and raised in Los Angeles, California. Growing up, my parents made sure I was in the best situation to learn and grow. They put me in extracurricular activities: football, marching band, and basketball. I also attended a private school when it was affordable for them. They both did not graduate from college, so they only had an idea for raising an educated, black male, and I am grateful for their effort. But, once I got into high school, I was on my own. I had to figure out what I wanted to do with my life. Most of my family barely got diplomas and worked regular jobs or went to the military. I was never

77

encouraged to go to college. Once I graduated, I figured I would just work and make money.

What was your background before coming to community college?
I worked two jobs: JCPenney and Security. Both were dead end jobs. I was young, working to buy new clothes and video games.

What, if anything, prompted your decision to attend community college? What were your goals upon entering community college (why did you go)? Did they change after you started college? If so, how?
I realized I was selling myself short by not putting my knowledge to work. I felt I was too smart to not be doing something productive with my time. Once I enrolled in CC, I had no real direction. I just told myself whatever I decide to do, I will do my best at it. I wanted to transfer to the best college I could and get the best grades I could. My goal was to take advantage of every opportunity that I could. I take this mind frame in whatever I do now because the amount of pressure I put on myself to do well has always been a successful formula for me.

Describe your experience as a community college student. What were the highlights? Were there any special programs or extracurricular experiences that were memorable or inspiring?
I had a great experience as a community college student. A friend recommended me to join the Puente program my first semester, and it was probably one of the best decisions I made to listen to her. In the program, I learned about how to maneuver in life and in college. I also discovered my strengths and weaknesses educationally, which helped me discover what I wanted to major in: English.

How much time went by between high school and community college for you? What were the biggest challenges that you faced when you began attending community college?
I was out of school for three years before I started going to community college. My biggest challenge was managing my time and figuring out how to find all the resources that were available to me. I also had a hard time realizing things are different than high school. Yes, the teachers still care, but they do not have to hold your hand through everything, and they will make it obvious that they aren't going to.

Did you work while attending community college? If so, how did you balance your time between work and school? Do you have any kids or other family responsibilities? If so, how did you balance your time between home and school? Did you have all three? How did you handle that?
I worked on and off while going to community college. If you are serious about your studies, I feel it is definitely a difficult task to do both. I would try to study while working and I've been written up for doing so, but I had a bigger goal to accomplish than working a job. I also had a daughter while I was in school. I had to take a semester off and work to make sure I had enough money for her and

myself. There was a time where I was working, going to school, and had my
daughter at home waiting for me. It was one of the hardest times in my life. I
always felt tired and rushed. I usually work well under pressure but this was just
overwhelming. I saved up enough money to quit my job eventually.

**Community colleges generally have a high attrition rate, meaning a large
percentage of students drop out. Why do you think this happens? What
motivated you to persevere through college and transfer to a university?**
I think the reason community colleges have a high attrition rate is because most of
the students are non-traditional or students who face different circumstances than
University students. The pressure college places on you—in comparison to the
appeal that working a full time job or living a content life—doesn't seem
worthwhile. I've met many students who said they would rather do something else
than putting up with the rigors of college. I realized from the start of me going to
school that it was going to be a long and tedious process. Luckily for me, I am
addicted to learning new things so I never got tired of school or ever considered
dropping out.

**Of all the reading assignments you completed in college, which one had the
greatest impact on you? What's your favorite book and why?**
I had an African-American literature class that really helped me out. Being an
educated black male, there is a time confusion I think we all go through. A time
where you realize most of the people you have always learned about were Old
White Men. You lose a sense of worth and belonging after a while, because you
are trying to figure out where you belong in the equation. In my African-American
literature class, I learned so much about my people and the culture we are creating
in a place that has oppressed us for so many years. People like Fredrick Douglass,
W.E.B. Du Bois, and James Baldwin were creating something to look to and build
from. That is one of my goals now: to continue create a legitimate black culture in
America so we do not have to feel lost anymore.

**Of all the writing assignments you had in college, which are you most proud
of and why?**
I had to do a cultural ethnography for my Anthropology class. That was one of my
favorite assignments. I chose to go to the Occupy LA protest. I was a very
interested in the protest and the cause of it, but I have never been the type of
person to go out and protest. This assignment forced me to go out of my comfort
zone. The day I went was the last day of the protest. I was in the middle of the
police raid of the encampment. It was like nothing I have ever experienced. I
finally stepped out of my shell and I wrote a great paper on my observations.

**Attending a college or university can be extremely stressful for many
students. Does any particular thing stand out as being the most stressful
aspect of going to school? What was it and why was it stressful? What coping
skills did you use to overcome stress in order to succeed?**

The most stressful time for me was during finals. I am an English major and I took mainly writing classes, so there were times where I had to write multiple 3+ page papers and have them in around the same time. Writing a good paper is a process so I had to take these processes and break them down for multiple papers just to make sure I had enough time to get my ideas out eloquently. I literally stayed up until about 4 am researching and writing for at least 2 weeks. I cut myself off from anything that wasn't beneficial to me succeeding in those classes.

Many community college students give up when faced with adversity or challenges or barriers. You, however, didn't. What was the biggest challenge you faced and how did you overcome it? What advice would you give to a student who feels like he or she just can't do it, has too much going on in his or her life, or is just struggling academically and feels like maybe college isn't the right place?
My biggest challenge was finances. I missed 2 semesters because of money. I couldn't afford to pay for my classes or I needed money to take care of my family. My only advice to people going through any adversity is don't lose sight of your goal. People get overwhelmed and forget what they're in school for. I always kept my eye on the prize, and when things got hard I would break down my goal into tinier goals that I could accomplish. In return, by doing that it gave me a sense of worth even though I was struggling.

Were there any memorable faculty, counselors, other students, administrators or staff (at your community college or university) with whom you established a rapport and who made a difference? Is establishing relationships with people on campus important? Tell a brief story about someone with whom you became close and who was supportive.
There were a few people who I established a rapport with. Dr. Ortega, my counselor, was one of the most helpful. Whenever I had an issue, he always made time in his schedule to help me out. I'm a big worrier and Ortega was that relatable figure I needed to let me know that everything I wanted to do was possible. I think it is very important to establish relationships with the staff at your college. They have been through what we're going through, and they can be great assets in you college career. I've had teacher and staff offering to write letters of recommendation. When people get to know you, they will more than likely be willing to help you because most of them want to see you succeed.

Courage to Learn **discusses building social capital, meaning developing relationships and skills that are like an investment in your own future. What social capital have you gained since entering community college?**
Since being in community college, the skills I gained that I treasure the most are my communication and understanding skills. I, now, have the ability to have a conversation with anybody and be able to communicate clearly and objectively with them. I can see and I am able to understand different points of view. I became more open minded. I feel this contributes greatly to my social capital.

What was your social life like in college? How important was it to you personally and educationally?

Usually I am a quiet person until I get to know a person; then I'll open up. In college I realized this is not an effective way of making friends and meeting new people. I always try to make a few friends in every class I am in. I build a network of people around to ensure that we can pass a certain class and help each other. I also did this because you never know what people have to offer you unless you open up and communicate with them. There was a time when I was unemployed for a long time and my daughter's mother was pregnant. My classmate—whom I became friends with—was a manager at a retail store and gave me a job so I could start saving money up and preparing to be a father.

Deciding what university to transfer to is difficult. What factors did you consider when deciding where to apply and where to attend?

This was not very difficult to me. I told myself once I start going back to school, I want to transfer to the best college possible. I knew Cal Berkeley was that school, and I knew I belonged there. So, that was the school I wanted to go to.

If you are working (while still a student or after having graduated), what is that experience like?

When I was working and going to school, it was not easy. Your job demands time from you and your classes demand time from you—in and out of class. Sometimes it is necessary to do both, but you have to be willing to sacrifice time and be able to manage a tight schedule.

What plans for the future do you have (educationally, socially, and professionally)? When and how did those goals emerge?

I plan on finding and meeting more people once I start attending Berkeley. I want to be more involved with the campus and community around me. I am starting to understand that college is more than just learning from books, but learning from the people you encounter is also important, and sometimes you can learn more from the people you encounter and befriend than in a class you had to take. To me this is all to build my social capital.

Looking back, what advice would you give to first year community college students today (i.e. if you could go back in time and talk to yourself on your first day of college, what would you say)?

Never lose sight of your goal. It is not going to be an easy path to take and that is why so many people don't finish college. But, perseverance is key. I know you have issues outside of school that seem like they will never go away or get better, but they will. Take your time. Do not put more on yourself than you can handle and realize humility is not a weakness. Being a student is a humbling experience, and you will gain so much from it.

Chapter Five

Career Planning and Development

Student Learning Outcome:
Using reflective self-assessment tools and aptitude test results, students will design educational goals and a plan that works backwards from career and degree objectives to major pathway.

"What is the recipe for successful achievement? To my mind there are just four essential ingredients: Choose a career you love, give it the best there is in you, seize your opportunities, and be a member of the team."

—Benjamin Franklin Fairless, U.S. Steel Company Executive

"You just have to keep trying to do good work, and hope that it leads to more good work. I want to look back on my career and be proud of the work, and be proud that I tried everything. Yes, I want to look back and know that I was terrible at a variety of things."

—Jon Stewart, actor

Deciding on a career is a very important decision in one's life and should not be taken lightly. There are many factors that need to be considered when you are making a decision about what career path you want to follow. To choose the a major and a career path that will result in happiness—or at least career satisfaction—you should take into account your personal values as you discussed in your values clarification journal, since they are what ultimately inspire and motivate you and since they are how you will measure your level of satisfaction. Additionally, you will want to use the tools in this chapter, as well as some self-reflection, to determine where your aptitude lies, what you feel passionate about, and what types of environments you feel most comfortable in. Moreover, as a community college student, there are additional factors you may need to consider, specifically: what major are you going to study and what is the educational preparation required for your chosen career path?

Just as universities are looking for well-rounded students, employers are looking for well-rounded employees. As I have been emphasizing throughout this book, academic preparation is only a part of your college experience and transfer preparation. The extra-curricular activities that you participate in matter, and universities look at the whole student, not just grades. Employers, similarly, seek out prospective employees based on a combination of **hard skills** and **soft skills**. Hard skills refer to the skills or technical proficiency needed to do a job. Generally, that would mean academic preparation or job training, like the minimum qualifications for a job. However, keep in mind that virtually every applicant will meet the minimum qualifications to do a job, so employers increasingly are looking beyond minimum preparation and hard skills to a job applicant's soft skills.

Soft skills are less tangible than hard skills; soft skills include: working effectively on a team, motivating others, communicating effectively and professionally, solving problems effectively, being flexible, taking criticism constructively, and managing time effectively. Many, but not all, workplaces expect that successful job applicants will possess soft skills, and especially once you are working in your career, those employees who demonstrate excellence in both hard and soft skills are more likely to be candidates for promotions. Several of the most important soft skills are explained below:

- **Teamwork.** Good team members know when to lead and when to participate, as circumstances dictate. A team player will share responsibility with others for both successes and failures.

- **Effective communication.** Good communicators can articulate their thoughts clearly in writing and in speaking as well as read or listen to the thoughts of others.

- **Interpersonal skills.** Having good interpersonal skills means being able to interact with people with empathy and without judgment.

- **Problem solving.** Effective problem-solvers use their critical thinking skills to identify problems and develop appropriate solutions using logic and reasoning.

- **Time management.** Scheduling tasks in a way that will allow projects to be completed by established deadlines and prioritizing time to ensure that the most important things get done first are qualities of efficient time management.

- **Flexibility.** Being flexible and having an adaptable mind-set enables a flexible person to respond positively to changes and be depended on for leadership for stressful situations.

So, as you plan out your college and career pathways, remember that there are numerous factors—feelings, soft and hard skills, that you may want to emphasize on a resume or consider as you narrow down your list of potential careers to maximize your potential future career satisfaction.

Self-Defeating Narratives

Often times, community college students may be undecided on their major or have a hard time relating their major (if they have one) to what they want to do for a career if they have chosen a career path prior to enrolling in community college. Also, one must be cautious not to fall for the myths and self-defeating ideas about choosing a major, such as the following:

- There is only one right major for me, and true happiness is impossible to achieve until I find it;

- Once I choose a major, I am stuck with it and cannot change it;

- If I really had my act together, I would know exactly what I wanted to major in;

- To become a doctor or lawyer, I have to major in a natural science and be pre-med or pre-law;

- I'll never find a major that fits me perfectly;

- Choosing a major means giving up on all others;

- If I choose the wrong major, I am a failure.

None of the above statements is true; these statements—and those like them—form part of a self-defeating narrative "script" that can be very discouraging and lead to feelings of being overwhelmed or giving up. Don't give up! The negative messages that we receive from others are discussed in the chapter of this book entitled "Fear of Success and Fear of Failure." Briefly, though, between the media, our negative friends, and our own self-doubt, these messages creep into our brains and make themselves right at home. It is natural to move forward in your life, especially as a new college student or recent graduate, with some degree of uncertainty. Unfortunately, the days when community college was free to everyone—which enabled students to explore all sorts of courses at their leisure to see what felt right—are over. Therefore, it's important to be a bit more strategic in your approach to college, to choosing a career path, and to choosing an appropriate major. However, this does not mean you can't change your mind. You can change majors. You can create options and flexibility for yourself by selecting broad majors, switching to another major after you transfer to a university, or majoring in a different field in graduate school. In fact, those are all pretty common things to do, so don't let self-defeating myths stop you before you even get started.

Donald Super's Theory: Career Maturity

As part of what is called the life-span and life-cycle approach to career development, the Australian career theorist Donald Super has viewed careers in stages. Basically, he argues that based on our age range, we pursue career pathways that align with our personal development. It makes sense that when we are young, we are exploring various jobs, and that as we grow older, we seek out more stable careers. In addition, it makes sense that as we change and as the workplace changes, we tend to change. It is a natural process of growth to adapt to the world and to our changing selves, situations, and environments.

Super has identified five stages of career development, listed below. Unfortunately, there is not industry-wide agreement about the age ranges that each stage applies to, but the approximate age range is indicated:

- **Growth (Youth, birth to age 14):** In the growth stage, we fantasize about what sorts of careers we could have, like our dream jobs; we explore our interests; and we entertain our curiosity to imagine having jobs in fields that we think we will like. As we grow, we develop our initial sense of self--who we are--as well as our attitudes, our desires, our needs, and general feelings about the workplace.

- **Exploration (Early Adult, age 15-24):** In the exploration stage, we begin to narrow down the jobs and careers that we have explored or imagined in the growth stage. Typically, this stage involves crystallizing our job and career choices to ones that are realistic and which we have a solid interest in pursuing—and perhaps beginning to work in those fields. In this stage, we may take classes in the field, apply for internships to "try out" a career, or pursue hobbies related to our future careers in order to develop useful skills.

- **Establishment (Adult-Middle Age, age 25-44):** In the establishment stage, we have entered a career and are stabilizing ourselves within that career. This stage may involve building our entry-level skill sets and gaining experience, becoming frustrated with our choices and contemplating a mid-life career change, and/or advancing within our careers. At this point, those happy with their career choices begin to thrive and advance rapidly while those unhappy consider returning to school for additional education, retraining, or a career change.

- **Maintenance (Maturity, age 45-64):** In the maintenance stage, we are generally in a holding pattern, updating our experience and skill sets, possibly beginning to feel as if we are stagnating, and/or innovating within our fields. At this point, we are continually adjusting—working hard to advance our careers and gain promotions, or seeking newer, improved careers.

- **Decline (Approaching Retirement Age, Age 65+):** In the declining stage, we tend to decelerate, reduce the amount of work that we complete, slow down and begin to think about planning for retirement.

[Super and Thompson, cited in Abernathy, C.A. (2000) Career Development Theory. Retrieved from: http://taracat.tripod.com.careerthrory1.html]

The guide to Super's stages is presented only as a guide; we all develop at different rates, so the 5 stages above are intended to show how we tend to progress through life in terms of our relationship to work. Many factors influence how we develop. First, on a personal level, our individual psychological makeup plays a part in how and when we make work-related decisions and at what pace we advance. Additionally, biology plays a role too: we all grow and mature at different ages, most likely due to our genetics. Second, there are situational determinants. Our personal and family history combined with our socioeconomic status may affect our rates of development and advancement. And finally, there are environmental factors. The labor market, at any given time and place, may differ, and employment practices may change over time as well.

Thus, the main "take-away" from Super's theory is the idea that our self-concept changes over time. We don't always grow up to be what we fantasized about when we were kids, but this is natural. Our lives change; our values change; what we want changes. When we become parents, for example, we may realize we want a higher paying job than we did when we were single. Sometimes our relationships or family circumstances change, so we go from a living situation where we could count on multiple incomes from roommates to supporting ourselves with a single income. Other times, the workplace itself changes, and careers that were once popular and stable go into decline. Often, in mid-life, we realize we aren't happy with our choices, so we opt for a change. Of course we do! All of this is natural.

Super argues that because we grow and because our life situations change, it's natural that our occupational preferences will change over time. We adapt, and career development is a lifelong process. To begin, it helps to think about values.

What Are Values?

Values are what people believe to be important in how they work and live their lives in general. We use values, whether we are self-consciously aware of it or not, to determine our priorities and to measure how successful or unsuccessful we are at living our lives the way we want to live them. In other words, when we live our lives in a way that aligns with our values, we feel satisfied; however, when our values don't match what we are doing with our lives, we tend to feel discontent.

What Are Your Values?

Being aware of what your values are plays an important role in your personal satisfaction. By making decisions and formulating plans that match your personal values, your life will be far more satisfying. Why? Because you will be doing things that you value. For instance, if you value your relationship with your family or value having a lot of alone time to read or listen to music, but find yourself in a demanding job that requires you to work 60-70 hours a week—like a lawyer—you'll be too drained of energy and have too little time to spend with your family or alone with your books and music. That will inevitably lead to stress and unhappiness because your job interferes with what you value most dearly.

Live your values! When you are aware of your values and use them to make decisions about what career to pursue or how to live your life, you are far more likely to be happy and stress-free. Obviously, not everything is a life-changing decision, so basing every daily decision you make on personal values would be ridiculous; however, some decisions do impact the rest of your life, such as: what job to pursue, what career path to follow, what schools to attend, who to start a long-term relationship with, where to live, and so on.

Our values inevitably change over time. Generally they are stable: they often stem from our upbringing, parents, religious faith, and life experiences, yet they aren't rigid or unchanging, nor do they always have limits or boundaries. When we enter the workforce, for example, we often prioritize and value our income. We work hard and strive for a promotion and to make as much money as possible, but when we start a family, often our priorities change and we value family time more than we do money.

Since values are intangible and since they often change over time, they can be difficult to define. Even if you feel you have a strong sense of your personal values, it is a good idea to periodically reassess your personal values to see if anything has changed, especially before making a major life decision or when something in your life changes in a major way. Your personal values are a key part of who you are, so use them to inform your plans for who you want to be. Often, when we are facing choices and there seem to be several reasonable options available, values are reliable sources to assist you in making the best decision. Use your values as a guide to make decisions. And live your values!

Here is an activity to help you identify (or reassess) your personal values. As you read through the questions and list of values, try to create a self-portrait that defines you in terms of your values. First, consider when you have felt most happy; then consider when you have felt most proud. These are the times in your life when your life aligned most strongly with your values. Also, you might also consider the opposite: the times you felt most unhappy or the times you felt the least proud. Those are the times in your life when your life was least aligned with your values. Finally, consider what other people find valuable by reading through the list below. Sometimes it is difficult to put your values into words, so the list might help. Look for patterns. Once you know what makes you feel happy and what makes your life fulfilling, you can actively seek out a life and career that will make you feel happy and satisfied!

- **Happiness:** At what point in your life were you most happy? Where were you? What were you doing? Who were you with? What else contributed to your happiness?

- **Pride:** What times in your life did you feel the most proud? Why? Who else, if anyone, shared your pride? What else contributed to your feelings of pride?
- **Explore Yourself:** Author and blogger Steve Pavlina has identified over 400 values, 100 of which are listed below. In order to explore your values, read over the following list and try to identify your top 10 values. You may add words if you don't see ones that match your feelings. As you make your list, look for patterns; some values may be combined. If you value charity, generosity and volunteering, these each suggest that perhaps "being of service to others" is one of your main priorities. *What do you notice about what you value?*

- Accountability
- Accuracy
- Achievement
- Adventure
- Affection
- Affluence
- Altruism
- Ambition
- Amusement
- Appreciation
- Approachability
- Approval
- Art
- Assurance
- Attentiveness
- Attractiveness
- Availability
- Being the best
- Belonging
- Benevolence
- Bravery
- Challenge
- Change
- Charity
- Chastity
- Cleanliness
- Comfort
- Commitment
- Community
- Compassion
- Competition
- Confidence
- Conformity
- Connection
- Conservation

- Control
- Creativity
- Credibility
- Curiosity
- Determination
- Education
- Empathy
- Enjoyment
- Environmentalism
- Ethics
- Faith
- Fame
- Family
- Fitness
- Freedom
- Friendship
- Generosity
- Happiness
- Health
- Independence
- Inspiration
- Integrity
- Intelligence
- Intimacy
- Justice
- Leadership
- Logic
- Love
- Making a difference
- Marriage
- Nature
- Nonconformity
- Obedience
- Open-mindedness
- Order
- Originality
- Patience
- Passion
- Peace
- Perfection
- Privacy
- Professionalism
- Respect
- Responsibility
- Science

- Security
- Self-reliance
- Self-respect
- Sensitivity
- Sexuality
- Solidarity
- Solitude
- Spontaneity
- Status
- Teaching
- Teamwork
- Transcendence
- Understanding
- Volunteering
- Wisdom
- Wittiness
- Wonder
- Worthiness
- Youthfulness
- Zeal

www.stevepavlina.com

Majors and Career Planning

Ideally, career planning comes first if you are able to select the "best major" for a chosen or given career field. However, realistically, majors are often chosen by interest level or by "default" with little exploration or thought to career implications—and that is definitely not the best way to go about making such an important decision. Frequently, the basic definition of a major is not clear to students. Declaring a major is part of the process that leads to earning a degree: a major is designed for academic purposes rather than for career purposes. The association between many majors and specific career fields is also often unclear. Although there are some exceptions in which the link between major and career is clear, like Nursing or Engineering for example, more often than not that is *not* the case. Thus, once you are able to recognize this, you can begin to ask questions, make assessments, and conduct the appropriate research that will assist you in making connections or relevance between major and a career. This research should consist of assessing yourself through career inventories and identifying your skills, abilities, place in life, goals, values, personality type and preferences along with your interests in order to make an effective and informed decision. So where do you begin? Well, the career-decision making process is similar to that of a scavenger hunt in which you must collect certain information or clues, and then piece them together to map out a guide that will assist you in making an effective decision to both a major and a career.

The most logical and efficient way of developing an educational pathway is to choose a career, and then, after finding out what you have to learn and major in for that career, to choose a major. This might mean talking to people in the field or looking at job advertisements for the positions in the field to see what the hiring qualifications are. In addition, you might consider your experience in college, any volunteer positions or internships you have had, and any commendations for excellence you have received. You might consider factors like your favorite subjects in school, your friends' careers, or the job sectors with the highest pay or most growth, before making a decision, but this is allowing outside factors make a decision for you. You should choose what you want to do. That is not easy, but luckily there are many tools and strategies that can help you.

Aptitude Tests:
Myers-Briggs Type Indicator (MBTI)

A Counseling class, your college's Career Development Center, or your counselor might introduce you to commonly used assessment tests that measure your interests and aptitudes. These tests can serve as a guide to help you identify strengths and weaknesses as well as interests and disinterests, and therefore help you choose a career that is likely to be one that you find rewarding. Career satisfaction comes from knowing who you are and where your passion lies, and finding a career that enables you to use your passion: people who love their jobs are generally happy people! One of the most common of these assessment tests is the **Myers-Briggs Type Indicator (MBTI)**. It is best to take these assessment or aptitude tests with an expert, such as your counselor, because the results do have to be interpreted. Taking assessment tests and having an expert interpret the results for you can help to identify work environments that might be a good fit for you, specific careers and occupations that you might enjoy, and the types of work that you tend to prefer.

The MBTI is basically a personality test which identifies preferences based on your personality traits in four basic areas: being extroverted or introverted, preferring sensing or intuition, thinking or feeling, and judging or perceiving; then, it matches them with types of work. Your results to a series of questions assessing you in each of these 4 basic areas are plotted on a graph; the interpretation, then, is indicative of your personal preferences. This is important, for example, because someone who is extremely introverted wouldn't be happy in a career that required constant interactions with the public, nor would the opposite mismatch make an extrovert happy. The results of the MBTI identify broad, general personality types and align them with a core value system. This can point you in the right direction or at least narrow down types of careers that may be suitable for your personality. Some people are service-oriented; others want to empower others; still others may want to understand mysteries or get things precisely right. Knowing your personality type can help.

The Myers Briggs Personality Types

The Myers Briggs theory measures your personality and preferences, and assigns letter codes, as indicated below. Do you prefer:

91

- People and things **(Extraversion or "E")**, or ideas and information **(Introversion or "I")**?
- Facts and reality **(Sensing or "S")**, or possibilities and potential **(Intuition or "N")**?
- Logic and truth **(Thinking or "T")**, or values and relationship **(Feeling or "F")**?
- A lifestyle that is well-structured **(Judgment or "J")**, or one that goes with the flow **(Perception or "P")**?

According to Myers Briggs theory, for each pair, one concept is dominant over the other. The letters associated with your preferences are combined to obtain your Myers Briggs personality type. For example, having preferences for I, N, F, P gives a personality type of INFP.

- **Extraversion (E) and Introversion (I)** - The first pair of styles is concerned with how you direct your energy. If you prefer to deal with people, things, situations, or "the outer world", then your preference is for Extraversion. If you prefer to deal with ideas, information, explanations or beliefs, or "the inner world", then your preference is for Introversion.

- **Sensing (S) and Intuition (N)** - The second pair concerns what type of information/things that you prefer to process. If you prefer to deal with facts, what you know, to have clarity, or to describe what you see, then your preference is for Sensing. If you prefer to deal with ideas, look into the unknown, to speculate about new possibilities, or to anticipate what isn't obvious, then your preference is for Intuition.

- **Thinking (T) and Feeling (F)** - The third pair reflects your style of decision-making. If you prefer to decide on the basis of objective logic, using an analytic and detached approach, then your preference is for Thinking. If you prefer to decide using values - i.e. on the basis of what or who you believe is important - then your preference is for Feeling.

- **Judgment (J) and Perception (P)** - The final pair describes the type of lifestyle you adopt. If you prefer your life to be planned, stable and organized, then your preference is for Judging (not to be confused with 'Judgmental', which is quite different). If you prefer to go with the flow, to maintain flexibility and respond to things as they arise, then your preference is for Perception.

When you put these four letters together, you get your personality type code. Since there are sixteen combinations possible, there are also sixteen Myers Briggs personality types possible.

As always, however, maintain a healthy skepticism. Don't be discouraged if the career field or occupation you are considering does not appear in your assessment results. It is a standardized test. You are still making the decision; however, it would be a good idea to explore your desired career with an open-mind, especially if these assessment results indicate a complete mismatch; many people are successful in careers that are not typical for their interest patterns and personality types, so the test is not a definitive answer—it's just an indicator. Should you not see your desired potential career in the assessment results, in consultation with your counselor or another professional expert, try looking at the broader patterns represented by the occupations in the results. You may see that certain skill clusters or interest areas emerge. You might want to speak with a career professional to explore the unique perspective you could bring to your work, or to prevent any stress that might arise as a result of your career choice.

In addition to using standardized assessment tests, of course you should also investigate your interests and careers that you believe interest you and for which you are well-suited. Begin with some basic questions, also known as the four Person-Environment Fit questions:

- Who am I?
- Why do I want to work?
- What do I want to do?
- Where do I want to do it?

Exploring these questions, in consultation with your counselor, can help narrow down career choices, and therefore major choices, as well. Thorough responses to the above questions can clarify your interests, but you will also need to explore on your own.

Self-Assessment Tests: Holland's Six Personality Types
According to John Holland's well-known and frequently-cited theory, most people fall into one or more different personality types: **Realistic (R)**, **Investigative (I)**, **Artistic (A)**, **Social (S)**, **Enterprising (E)**, or **Conventional (C)**. These categories are often referred to as the "Holland Codes" or "RIASEC."

Basically, his theory suggests that people of the same personality type cluster together in certain jobs and majors, which creates a particular work environment that fits their type. So, for example, a music studio would attract primarily creative people who value creativity—artistic thinking and behavior—so people who are creative are more likely to thrive in creative environments with artistic co-workers because they can use their strengths and abilities and can value those same qualities in others; on the other hand, someone who is primarily conventional would not be likely to thrive in a creative environment because he or she would feel out of place. Therefore, fitting in to a work environment (or major) can, according to Holland, lead to greater career satisfaction and lifelong happiness.

When deciding on your college major and/or career, taking your Holland personality type into account can help you determine what majors and careers are the best fit for your personality, and ideally this will lead you in a direction best suited for you. Of course, there is no guarantee; however, taking a career key test like Holland's can often guide you in the right direction. Your test results will be coded using the RIASEC letters above, and many people find that their test results indicate a combination of strengths, like "Conventional-Realistic" or "Artistic-Social."

Your personality type is then matched with particular job environments and professions that are compatible or incompatible with your type. In the Holland test, a code is created to show how much you resemble each of the types. The top three characteristics that you exhibit are indicated in the code, while the bottom three are not. The assumption is that your ideal career would involve your top three characteristics, and various occupations that you may explore can similarly be classified according to the same types.

The characteristics of each of the Holland types are described below:

- The **Realistic Type (R)** likes realistic jobs, such as aircraft controller, surveyor, farmer, electrician, or automobile mechanic. A realistic person may lack social skills but will have mechanical ability. Additional personality characteristics include being: conforming, honest, genuine, hardheaded, humble, materialistic, modest, natural, normal, persistent, practical, shy, and thrifty.

- The **Investigative Type (I)** likes investigative jobs such as chemist, physicist, anthropologist, geologist, biologist, or medical technologist. An investigative person has mathematical and scientific ability, but often lacks leadership ability. Additional personality characteristics include being: reserved, precise, introverted, intellectual, independent, complex, critical, curious, cautious, methodical, and analytical.

- The **Artistic Type (A)** likes artistic jobs such as actor or actress, interior decorator, writer, stage director, musician, or composer. An artistic person has artistic abilities such as skill in writing, music, or art, but often lacks clerical skills. Additional personality characteristics include being: original, open, non-conforming, intuitive, independent, introspective, impulsive, impractical, imaginative, idealistic, expressive, emotional, disorderly, and complicated.

- The **Social Type (S)** likes social jobs such as speech therapist, psychiatric caseworker, clinical psychologist, counselor, religious worker, and teacher. A social person has social skills and talents but often lacks mechanical scientific ability. Additional personality characteristics include being: warm, understanding, tactful, sympathetic, patient, responsible, social, kind, idealistic, helpful, friendly, generous, cooperative, and convincing.

- The **Enterprising Type (E)** likes enterprising jobs such as sports promoter, business executive, manager, or sales person. A social person has leadership and speaking abilities but often lacks scientific ability. Additional personality characteristics include being: sociable, self-confident, popular, pleasure-seeking, impulsive, optimistic, energetic, extroverted, domineering, attention-getting, agreeable, ambitious, adventurous, and inquisitive.

- The **Conventional Type (C)** likes conventional jobs such as banker, financial analyst, stenographer, bookkeeper, cost estimator, or tax expert. A conventional person has clerical and arithmetic ability but often lacks artistic abilities. Additional personality characteristics include being: unimaginative, thrifty, practical, persistent, obedient, orderly, inhibited, careful, efficient, conscientious, and conforming.

The Holland test will assign you a combination of three personality types, and suggest sample occupations to pursue in each of the three categories. These recommendations are certainly not meant to be mandates, but rather to be a guide—like suggestions—for you to consider. Above all else, follow your heart and your passion.

A popular and widely used variation of the Holland test is the Strong Interest Inventory assessment. Based on Holland's research, it also identifies which of six work environment-types match best with your interests. The six types of environments are: enterprising (managing, selling), artistic (creative), conventional (data processing, accounting), investigative (analyzing, researching), social (instructing, helping), and realistic (repairing, building). Again, you are asked a series of questions and the results can be analyzed.

Remember, it isn't a final decision; it's your decision for now, but you want it to be as well-informed a decision as it can be. What else do you need to know?

Exploring Career Paths on Your Own

Your campus may have a career or job placement center, which can help you as you begin to identify possible career paths; and, as always, you can also turn to your counselor for assistance. You should, at this point, have taken some the assessment tests indicated, or at least some similar aptitude assessment, and also given some thought to your own interests. Before you begin to make a decision about what career path and major to follow, review the information you have and consider, as is best when making any decision, if there's anything else that you need in order to make a good decision. Remember, it isn't a *final* decision; it's your decision for now, but you want it to be as well-informed a decision as it can be. What else do you need to know? Here are some questions to get you started thinking about your own career knowledge base.

Do you need...
- information on specific types of employers or careers?

- to explore:
    a. different careers?
    b. your own interests, values, skills, etc.?
    c. careers to learn more about them?
- to read more - talk to people - experience a career?
- information about something (major, career, job, company, etc.)?

A crucial piece of the career exploration process is literally exploration, or asking, "What types of careers are there?" Important parameters in the exploration process are to: keep an open mind; don't discount careers because of their title or status; be aware of biases based on incomplete or faulty information about careers (examples: teachers don't make very much money, or retail jobs are about folding sweaters at the GAP); be mindful and reflective as you look at different careers. Why are you choosing to discount or keep careers in the mix?

Exploration can be divided into three categories of action: READ, TALK, and DO. All are important steps in which to engage prior to making decisions about your major or your career path.

- **Read:** Read about different careers: the Library has several books on major and career exploration; see also the Resources for this chapter (and websites listed throughout), or the site mentioned earlier in this chapter, O*Net OnLine <http://www.onetonline.org>.

- **Talk:** It is good to read about careers, but it is also important to talk to professionals in the field. Doing an informational interview can help you delve deeper into a career area. Always talk to a variety of people to get the widest perspective possible. Who should you talk to?
    o Parents, other relatives, and their colleagues
    o Neighbors
    o Professionals
    o Professors
    o Recruiters (see employer presentations in Careercat/MT)
    o Academic Advisors
    o Professional Organizations
    o Alumni
    o Mentors

Combining your MBTI with your Holland types test will yield a list of top occupations that are suited to you based on your personality type and your work environment preferences. The list will often range from careers as wide-ranging as: urban planner, musician, editor, psychologist, attorney, and pharmacist. But the test results will also include typical work tasks and lists of the knowledge, skills, and abilities needed to complete the work, so you can compare what it takes to be a pharmacist or musician and make a decision that way. The U.S. Department of Labor maintains a searchable database of jobs linked to the

MBTI and Holland assessments, so a visit to O*Net OnLine at
http://www.onetonline.org can provide additional details.

Take the information you have collected and synthesize it: put it all
together. You've explored your own personality, your needs and wants, and found
your workplace-type comfort zone. You have aptitude test results to think about.
You've considered your own feelings, career goals, and found a few alternative
career pathways. Hopefully, you've had a chance to research the labor data for
your chosen career on O*Net OnLine (at http://www.onetonline.org) and browsed
a few job listings to see the desired job qualifications in several of your potential
careers. You've consulted others to get some feedback: your counselor, family,
mentors, and professionals in the field. Without being hasty, consider all these
factors, and any other factors that are important to you even if they aren't
mentioned here, and make a decision. If you struggle with this, you might go back
to your values and rank assorted careers on a ten-point scale to see which ranks
highest in potentially satisfying you. Then, work backwards from your chosen
career to choose a major and develop an action plan.

Developing a Plan of Action

Once you decide what direction you want to go in, create a plan of
action, whether that means deciding on a major or a career or both. For instance,
with the major you would look at what major preparation you are going to be
taking to attain the degree, whether it's for an associate degree or for transfer.
With the associate degree, you would have to research what major classes you
need to attain the degree. If you are trying to transfer, you would have to research
what major preparation is needed, as discussed in Chapter 3, and what classes you
would need to complete before transferring to the university of your choice.
Additionally, talk to a Counselor to ensure that you are on the right path, and if
possible take some college tours to the universities you are considering attending
for your bachelor's degree.

Remember that the courses you take for your A.A. or A.S. degree are not
necessarily the same as those that are required to transfer to a university.
Universities set their own admission requirements, so the CSU system has
different requirements for transfer than the UC system and private schools. Often,
even different campuses within the same system have different admission
requirements; this is why it is so important to consult with your counselor in order
to develop an appropriate plan of action, so that your major will help you transfer
to a university and get you the degree you want, so that you can get the job you
want.

One part of your action plan will certainly consist of applying for a job
by writing a resume and cover letter.

Resume Writing Tips

When you go out to look for a job, an internship, or career, the primary
marketing tool you will use is your resume. To begin with, determine an
objective: what is it that you set out to do? Specifically, what job are you looking

for? At this point, it is necessary to know what experience and skills are needed to succeed in that job. Prioritize the content of your resume by listing the most relevant experience and emphasizing the skills that you have for that specific job. It is best to customize your resume for each job you apply for rather than to make a generic, one-size-fits-all resume.

A resume tends to be as brief and focused as possible. The people who review resumes receive many of them and have to work quickly to decide who to interview and who not to, almost at a glance, so treat it like a marketing tool: a commercial for yourself.

There are tons of free templates that you can download online to help you with formatting and style, such as Myperfectresume.com and Resumegenius.com; a quick Google search will give you far more options than you need. Pick one that you like, that is professional, and that represents your personality, style, and objective effectively.

Writing Your Resume

Although your resume is a commercial for yourself, it should not read like a commercial. And in your writing, be concise, factual, and, when possible, state definitive results that you have obtained from previous work. While you do not need to discuss every accomplishment in your life in detail, be aware that companies hiring today are looking for more than just training, education and experience. They want to see a proven track record. Your interview is where you can elaborate on your accomplishments; your resume is just an announcement of them.

Resume Structure

- **Name and Contact Info:** In the top center, indicate your name, mailing address, phone number and email address. Use a professional-sounding email address.

- **Resume Objective Statement:** The resume objective statement is at the top of your resume under your name and contact information. It should state briefly who you are and that you specifically desire the job you are applying for. Think of it as a headline. For example, for a job in business management, you might write, "Experienced, outgoing, achievement-driven recent graduate seeking a position in Business Management."

- **Body:** The body of the resume lists "Qualifications," "Professional Experience," "Work History," "Education," and "Achievements." "Achievements" should probably be last, but otherwise these sections should be ordered by how important, relevant and impressive each one is. Put your strongest section at the top. For instance, if you have a degree in the field from a good school, but not so much relevant work experience, then put the Education section at the top.

- **Ending:** Most resumes indicate "References available upon request" at the bottom.

Additional Resume Writing Tips

Here are some additional tips for writing the body of your resume:

- **Use bullet points**. To structure the body of your resume, use short sentences in bullet points, including the main selling points of your resume at a glance. Don't go to detail about specifics; instead, begin your resume with an objective statement and use the body to offer evidence that you will be a valuable employee.

- **Use action verbs** like implemented, developed managed, prepared, or presented. Emphasize what you can *do*.

- **Include statistics**: Dollar amounts, percentages, and any other hard data will stand out in the body of a resume. Saying that you "balanced a cash register every night" is less impressive than saying that you "accurately rang up $300,000 in cash and credit sales annually."

- **Emphasize your strengths**: Highlight what is *most relevant* since most incoming resumes are reviewed in under 30 seconds. Therefore, make sure to put the most relevant and strongest points—the ones that best support your job search objective—first, where they are more likely to be seen.

- **Match your skills to the need that the hiring position has.** Review online job postings and newspaper job postings for positions that interest you. As each job will generally have a brief description of the company and the position available, use the keywords listed in the ads and match them to the bullet points on your resume.

- **Be positive**. In your resume and interview, above all, you must remain positive. Leave out negative statements and irrelevant points.

- **Avoid overusing the space on the page:** In journalism and advertising, what is called "white space" is important because it attracts attention to the words or images that are surrounded by **white space**. Don't cram so many words into your resume that it looks like a page-long solid block of text. Leave some unused white space. Notice from print ads that the ones that grab your attention most effectively tend to be those that have a lot of blank space in them and include a few keywords—the bare minimum amount of text needed to convey the message.

- **Formatting:** Use a free template that you download, or design your own if you have the skills. Don't use difficult-to-read fonts; stick with Arial, Times New Roman, or some similar easy-to-read font. The font size should be a minimum of 10 point. The words in your name should be the largest words on the page.

- **Revising and Proofreading:** Finally, ask someone at your campus's workforce center, a counselor, an instructor, and/or a friend with professional experience to look over your resume for the overall impression it creates as well any typing errors. It should be perfect!!! No spelling errors. No typos. No alignment errors or other inconsistencies. The page layout should look clean, not cluttered.

Cover Letters

Your cover letter is the next step to complete: it is a letter that basically introduces your resume to your prospective employer, like a letter of introduction that you write to a hiring committee or individual, encouraging the person or people hiring to take a look at your resume and consider you for an interview. Treat it as an opportunity to elaborate on your resume, where you can go into more detail about the bullet points that you have included in your resume—and as an opportunity to personalize yourself beyond the bullet-point list of job qualifications that your resume uses to portray you. Finally, it is also a writing sample, so again it should be perfect.

Here are some tips on writing the cover letter:

- **Don't Repeat Your Resume:** A cover letter enables you to use full sentences instead of bullet points, so use sentences to expand upon your resume points and describe additional details that you weren't able to squeeze onto the single page of your resume. Show off your writing and communication skills at the same time that you tell why you are the perfect fit for the company.

- **Write a Custom Cover Letter:** Again, do not use a generic cover letter that is vague. Write a specific, custom one for each job that you are applying for. Hiring managers can easily spot recycled and generic stock phrases like, "I am interested in applying for a job with your company to advance my career in the industry." That sentence could be applied to any job, in any field, anywhere. It is like announcing to the hiring committee that you don't care about the job. No one wants to hire someone too lazy to write one letter.

- **Begin with a Template:** Like with your resume, there are numerous free, downloadable templates for cover letters to help you with formatting. A quick Google search will provide you with numerous examples. One website that you might use is www.themuse.com/resources.

- **Get Your Readers' Attention Immediately:** Begin with a statement that showcases your passion, announces a remarkable achievement, quotes an expert in the field, which you can apply to yourself, or even something funny.

- **Briefly Share the Story of Why You Want to Work There:** Briefly, in a short paragraph, tell the story of how you came to apply for a job with this company. Did you once have a positive experience with the company? Do you have a passion for banking? What started that? Have you been daydreaming about being a business manager or librarian or lab tech your whole life? Tell the story!

- **Focus on What You Can Provide to Your Employer:** Do not, under any circumstances, explain why you need the job or why the job would be great for you. Focus on how great you would be for the job. You need to be the standout applicant among many other applicants. The job market is competitive. You are writing to someone who has a job to fill and who has to read a bunch of cover letters and resumes all day. What makes you special?

- **Clearly Show Your Capabilities and Potential:** Your resume will show what you've done in the past; in your cover letter, state what you can do in the future. You should already know the key requirements and workplace priorities for the job, so emphasize how your skills, attitude, growth potential, knowledge, education, and/or willingness to learn make you a perfect fit. Devote at least one paragraph to explaining what you specifically can bring to the workplace and job. Expand on the strengths you possess in the key areas required for the job.

- **Emphasize Relevant and Transferrable Skills:** Often you will find that you don't have the exact desirable experience that an employer is looking for; however, you can often borrow relevant experiences from other jobs or internships that you've held to show how they are *transferable skills*. You may not have experience working in a bank, for example, but if you have worked at a fast food job, then you may have handled money, interacted with the public, and resolved customer conflicts. These skills are transferrable and relevant to a banking job.

- **Quote Previous Employers or Co-Workers:** If you can, include a positive, flattering quote from a previous boss, your instructor, or counselor to show that others have observed your passion.

- **Highlight the Right Experiences:** If you are ever uncertain about what sorts of qualities an employer is looking for, copy the text from a job

101

description or from the company's website describing the position or the company itself, and drop the text into a word-cloud program, such as Wordle (www.wordle.net), and see what words stand out. Those words will be the qualities that a hiring manager is looking for most; then, you can be sure to emphasize those same qualities in your cover letter.

- **Don't Draw Attention to Your Weaknesses:** Don't apologize for a lack of experience or anything negative. Why draw attention to that by bringing it up? Keep the focus on what you *can* do. Brag. You should be bragging.

- **Keep the Writing Tone Brief, Real, and Professional:** Avoid exaggerating or overselling yourself, and don't be unnecessarily formal. That's boring. No one likes boring. Be reasonable so that you sound like a real person and someone that people would want to work with. Don't use too much jargon, but do review the company's website to see what sort of language they themselves use. Businesses use business language and a businesslike tone, so your cover letter should also do that. Some other creative workspaces might find that to be too cold, so for a creative job, you'd want to show off your creativity with writing that is more creative and innovative. This shows that you understand the workplace environment.

Good luck. Take this last step of applying for a job seriously! Getting a job in your chosen field—a career—that makes you happy is the ultimate goal of this book. It's why most people go to college and sacrifice years of their lives to learning. The sacrifice is great, but so is the payoff.

Putting It All Together

Planning your major and applying for a job or career is a *recursive process*; that means that while there are steps in the process, they aren't simply done in numerical order and never repeated. Rather, you will go back and forth, repeating the steps and refining your results, as you engage in self-discovery, try new classes, take on jobs and internships, or explore your options. A recursive process is one in which you repeat and refine as you go. It's rare to know what you want to do as soon as you enter college. Therefore, as you finally move toward selecting and finalizing your major, applying for a job, and planning your career pathway, keep in mind everything that you have learned (or will learn) from this book: the etiquette, interview, and professionalism tips from Chapter 7 "Internships"; the advice your mentor gave you from Chapter 9 "Mentors"; everything you read and learned from your experience in the workplace and/or from Chapter 6 "Part-Time Jobs"; your collection of social capital from Chapter 8 "Networking to Build Social Capital"; and all of your planning from this chapter; not to mention, all the advice from your instructors, peers, and counselors. Have an eye toward the future. Be ready for diversity in the workplace since there is a wider variety of personalities and people in the workforce than there even is in college. Finally, be sure to research your goals and career choices frequently enough that you don't miss some important new development: we live in a global workplace, and the world changes so rapidly that you want to be ready for anything that the future may hold.

Chapter Resources

- **O*Net OnLine:** http://www.onetonline.org

- **Department of Labor:** http://www.bls.gov/opub/working/page1a.htm

- **Occupational Outlook Handbook:** http://www.bls.gov/oco/

- **Job Web:** http://www.jobweb.com/

- **America's Career InfoNet:** http://www.acinet.org/acinet/

- **California EDD:** http://www.caljobs.ca.gov/

- **JobStar Central:** http://jobstar.org/index.php

- **ONet:** http://online.onetcenter.org/

Journal Assignments

1. In your journal, follow the steps suggested in this chapter to settle on a potential career path. Take the Holland and MBTI assessment tests, and assess yourself and your own interests. Then, make a chart that lists all potential career options you can think of in the top row and then list all of the qualities that you want in your career (help others, flexible work hours, creative work environment, high pay, etc.) in the left column. Be thorough! Rank each possible career in each of the categories from the left column on a scale from 1 to 10. Add up the scores from each column and see which career ranks highest.

2. This chapter discusses values and the importance they have in our daily lives, our educational goals, and future career aspirations. We discussed how our values are formed and where they come from. Which values do you embrace personally? Write an essay in which you discuss your top 3 values and the roles they play in your life today. Include the following:

- How does each value reflect the person you are today or hope to be someday?

- What makes each value a "top value"?

- Why are these values important to you?

- Did these values play a role in your decision to come to college?

- What roles does each of these values play in your future?

Chapter Six

Part-Time Jobs

Student Learning Outcomes:
Students will apply time management skills to their lives by evaluating their weekly schedules, reorganizing it, and identifying times available for study, work and socializing.

"If there is anything you want in this world, it is for you to strike out with confidence and faith in self and reach for it, wheresoever you may find it in nature"
—Marcus Garvey, "Prophecy"

"Working with great people makes you great; you learn a lot and it also gives you the experience and confidence to move on with your own career."

—Nas, musician

Most, if not all, students inevitably find the need to manage some level of work commitment during their years in college. The chances are good that you will be among these working students. Many students are already working when they enter a community college. For those students, this is the only way they find to finance their community college courses. If you are currently working as a community college student, chances are that you are in an exploratory stage of your development. This is typically a time when many young women will hold part-time jobs waitressing as a means of financing their college education. It is also common to see young

If time permits, especially over a summer vacation, it might be a good idea for you to explore some of these different strengths and abilities as a means of discovering which type of work you are most suited for, and which lines of work definitely do not work for you.

men and women waiting tables or standing behind a cash register in order to foot the bill for school.

Exploration

Being in an exploratory stage of your development means being in a time when you are discovering your strengths and your weaknesses as well as hidden abilities you may not know you possess. If time permits, especially over a summer vacation, it might be a good idea for you to explore some of these different strengths and abilities as a means of discovering which type of work you are most suited for, and which lines of work definitely do not work for you. This will be a time when you may find that you prefer to work as part of a team rather than alone. Conversely, you may find that you prefer to work alone rather than as part of a group. There is no better way to discover the truths about yourself than by performing different types of tasks in different job settings. For instance, you might find that you really enjoy interacting with people. If this is the case, you might want to consider a future career that involves customer service. Alternatively, you might be the more creative or artistic type who needs space and solitude in order to gain your creative insights.

Another benefit to your part-time employment is that you get to discover how comfortable you feel about having a supervisor. Some people feel very comfortable having a boss and being told what to do. It gives them a sense of satisfaction and even pleasure in knowing that they are outstanding employees that have contributed in no small way to a company's success and profitability. However, a real danger comes when an employee feels good about the initial praise that he or she receives, yet begins to delude him or herself into thinking that they are happy working as an employee. This stark realization may come when their formerly, friendly boss is now irate or impatient with the employee, perhaps planting the seed of doubt in the employee's mind as to whether or not he or she was meant to be an employee rather than a self-employed entrepreneur. Much of the initial discomfort you might feel with your first irate boss is because it will be a "breaking in" process of getting used to a temperamental supervisor. On the other hand, this may also have a positive effect in helping to stimulate motivation in an employee to become a better, if not kinder, supervisor than the one with whom they currently work. On a more basic level, you will also be discovering whether you will enjoy doing manual work, or prefer the "white collar" professions, such as office work.

Ideally, the employment you find while in college should pertain to your major; thus, if you plan to major in accounting, a good idea would be to find a job where your bookkeeping skills will be honed. If you are just starting out in your freshman year of college course work, you may not have much to worry about if you are working in a job that is unrelated to your area of concentration. However, by the second year of college, you should begin to formulate a plan to begin working in the field that corresponds to your major.

Finding a Job that Relates to Your Major

One good way to find a job that relates to your major is to visit your school's Career Counseling, or Development, office. These offices are designed to help students find and keep a job pertaining to the different fields of study offered on campus. The counselors at these offices can also help you with writing good resumes and cover letters, as well as teach you effective interview skills and offer workshops designed to give you sound advice in your career development, such as how to dress appropriately for the workplace. Many of these services are provided at little or no cost to the students. You would do well to take advantage of these freebies to learn as much as you can about the keys to success in the workplace. Therefore, after reading this, you will gain valuable knowledge if you take note of your personal working style regardless of what job you happen to have. Even if you work at a fast food restaurant, when you walk in tomorrow to that job, take notice of whether you actually enjoy interfacing with the customers, or whether you find a genuine interest in handling the money at the cash register (which may point to a future career in finance), or whether it is the manual work of preparing the food which interests you (which may suggest to a future career in the culinary arts).

Balancing Work and School

Because of the financial necessity of work, many students end up taking courses at night or on a part-time basis. This can present certain challenges which must be addressed. If you are majoring in one of the sciences, you may want to reconsider your work schedule; indeed, the more difficult math and science classes, especially those that require lab time, should be taken during the day. The reason for this should be immediately clear: if you work all day, then rush off to school to take a calculus class at night, chances are you will be dozing during the lecture. One should not be sleeping through any college class, no matter how easy the course may be, but when it comes to a subject like upper division math, it then becomes especially important to leave yourself time and energy for sufficient study and practice.

However, due to the financial strain that college places on families, working while in college may not be by choice but by necessity. Some advice from the website www.thedigeratilife.com:

1. **Optimize your time.** Why not spend some of your leisure time working and making money? If you really want to keep up with all of the latest gossip or socializing, then maybe you should try getting a job at the same place where your friends work.

2. **Watch out for good work opportunities.** If you've decided not to work because you've had no luck finding the "right" kind of job, don't feel bad. You may be looking in the wrong places, or may need to do more with your job hunt. Consider some of the suggestions in this chapter. If your job interferes with your

education, quit your job and find another.

3. **Prioritize your activities.** Schoolwork should always come first. Don't work if you have an exam the next day or a ton of homework. There are only two times during a semester where taking time off from work seems reasonable: during midterm exams and final exams. Make sure to focus 100% on your studies during these periods.

4. **Seek balance.** The trick is to try to find time for everything — and I mean everything. This includes school, work, family, friends, the significant other, and whatever else adds value to your life. Notify your friends that you will be extremely busy on certain days of the week *and* that there are evenings or weekends when you can spend time doing fun things.

5. **Reward yourself.** As much as saving money and being focused is of the utmost importance, everyone deserves a break occasionally. Go out on a date. Travel—even if it's local. Spend a weekend out of town, visit relatives, or go to a concert.

6. **Keep your mind on the bigger picture.** Think about the bigger picture. There are going to be nights during the school year when you don't get enough sleep and there will certainly be some parties that you will miss. Even so, realize that you'll be able to complete college with no debt and with enough money saved to allow you the freedom to be selective about the first job you take after you graduate. There are, of course, some college programs that are so intense that students in these courses are really way too busy to do much else besides study.

Students are drowning in debt like never before. People in their 20s are making financial decisions that are setting them on the wrong path in life. Young people are working at jobs that they don't like because they feel that they are stuck without any options. Don't feel this way or let this happen to you! You can work and go to school and be part of a family: it just takes planning and time management, a few sacrifices, and informed decision-making. In the

> *You can work and go to school and be part of a family: it just takes planning and time management, a few sacrifices, and informed decision-making.*

long run, you will emerge from your college experience with a degree that will open a pathway into better employment, so while you may feel left out at times during college, you won't feel that way for the rest of your life.

(http://www.thedigeratilife.com/blog/index.php/2009/01/19/how-to-work-full-time-college-fulltime-student/)

On-Campus Employment

If you must work while attending college, then one option you may want to consider is to work on campus. This has several advantages: first, all your daily activities remain localized on campus, eliminating the need to commute long distances to go to work. Remember, these will be years when every hour of the day must be accounted for, and you will really need to hone your time-management skills.

There is no better way to save yourself time, energy, and expensive gasoline, than to hold a part-time job somewhere on campus where your supervisor can work around your class schedule. A very noble and reasonable job on campus is the tutoring center. You may want to consider applying for a job tutoring in a subject you know like the back of your hand; however, if the tutoring center on your campus does not assist students in that subject area, then you may want to consider offering your skills to the tutoring center coordinator. The college may have had a need for a history tutor, or a Chinese language tutor, but may never have filled that position with a qualified candidate. You might very well be the candidate for whom they were searching.

One other good part-time employment opportunity will be to work in the library. College libraries are almost always in need of part-time student employees that can re-stack the shelves, check books out, and organize their multimedia equipment, such as projectors, and so on. Visit your college library and ask them if they have any openings for part-time student positions. An added advantage of working in a library is that you will be exposed to the books that you will be later using for your term papers, theses, and dissertations.

Students typically look for part-time jobs where there are long lulls during which they can pull out their textbooks from their backpacks and keep up with their reading or review their notes in preparation for exams; therefore, you may want to follow suit and search for a quiet clerical position on campus or near campus. Another opportunity for part-time employment, which some lucky students are able to get at the beginning of every term, is to grade papers for a teacher at the college. Professors are typically loaded with term papers to grade and multiple-choice exams to review. They will probably choose to grade essay exams on their own, as they will feel only they have the experience and expertise to grade an essay exam. They are looking for very specific information on these essays or blue book exams. But this should not dissuade you from approaching your professors and asking them if they need a grading assistant. If you are one of the lucky few who are chosen, you will most likely be assigned to grade multiple-choice exams.

If you have a specialized skill, such as working with computers, you might be able to find employment in your college's IT, or Information Technology, department. These departments typically run the computer networks, maintain the servers, and monitor all the electronic traffic of the computer terminals throughout the campus. Or, if you have worked in a copy and print center, such as Staples or Kinko's, you might be able to get a job on campus at your school's bookstore copy center. If the bookstore on your campus does not have a print and copy distribution center attached to it, then you may want to ask where on campus it is located and apply for a job there. These centers, which are usually small, can become quite busy due to the high volume of photocopying and printing needed by all the departments of the college campus. College professors are always running off hundreds of copies of their class syllabi (schedules).

Internships
[Note: Internships are discussed in depth in Chapter 7]

Another great opportunity to make the most of your skills as they relate to your education is to get into an internship that relates to your particular field. Scan the online employment companies, such as Monster.com, to look for openings for college interns. An internship can become a vital part of your education. You will actually get to see first-hand how people perform their jobs in your chosen field of study. There might be instances in which you find that the actual day-to-day functions of the job are not as exciting as they might seem when described during a classroom lecture. Keep in mind that college internships typically do not pay very well, and that you might even have to consider doing it on a *pro bono,* or unpaid, basis. You will have to weigh this decision carefully. As mentioned, the choice of many students to work is not really a choice at all but rather a financial necessity.

Some community college students might already be married or have children. Thus, an unpaid internship is a luxury they cannot afford. If you happen to be in this category, then make the most of your day job by keeping it tied to your ultimate career. The fortunate thing about the working world is that many skills are transferable from one job to the next or from one career to another. Thus, if you are waitressing in order to pay the bills and go to school, you are, by the very nature of your work, gaining invaluable customer service skills, often referred to as "people skills." If you wish to become, for example, an attorney, you will have already gained a lot of experience in dealing with people, something attorneys have to do every day. Someone who works at a cash register might gain

111

the mathematical skill of monetary transactions which are transferable to careers in accounting, banking, and finance.

On-Campus Internships

Internship opportunities on campus can become valuable experiences, even if they are not full-on internships. For example, if you are majoring in journalism, you could begin polishing your writing skills by contributing weekly articles to the college newspaper. Almost all colleges and universities have their own newspapers. Some of the larger universities carry more than one. For instance, California State University of Long Beach has its daily newspaper, *The Daily 49er*, which is published by the journalism department, as well as *The Union*, which is an independent university newspaper. It is probably a good idea to become associated with the official newspaper of your campus to be able to reap the benefits of the tutelage of the faculty and staff associated with its publication. These student newspapers have their own staff with a regular turnover due to the inevitable graduations that occur each year. Therefore, if you plan to enter a field that requires good writing skills, you should make every effort to contact your school's newspaper and inquire about any openings.

The Competitive Job Market

While you consider which type of job to apply for, keep in mind that the competition these days can become very stiff, in almost all fields. So, if you wish to set yourself apart from the competition, one set of areas that can be sharpened would be: cover letter and resume formatting, interview etiquette, and on-the-job behavior. The library or counseling center may offer free workshops on these skills to students. Take advantage of these presentations as they can give you invaluable advice and guidance, plus a competitive edge in areas such as those mentioned above. Potential employers will definitely look for a professionally written resume, which highlights the importance of not only gathering work place experience, but of the need to document it in an elegant manner.

Business Etiquette

All too often, young people who enter the work place are not given guidance as to how they should present themselves in an interview or how they should behave properly in a business environment. The number of lawsuits related to sexual harassment would be reduced to zero if people only understood the rules of proper behavior in a business office. The behavior that they have been enjoying in high school cannot be carried over into a place of employment. It is an unfortunate reality that many young people are never taught proper business etiquette; no one mentored them or showed them the proper way to react to different situations in a corporate setting. Sexual harassment is only one of many different types of harassment. This is why these workshops and seminars relating to finding and keeping a job are so important. They will show you what every employee needs to know about getting ahead by demonstrating the right behavior. Once employed, the employees should study the employee handbook as diligently as textbooks are studied in college.

There are proper ways to behave in any social situation, and work is no exception. Just as in any formal social situation—a wedding, a funeral, meeting your girlfriend's or boyfriend's family—behavior in the workplace and during an interview for a job or internship has certain rules governing what you are permitted to do and not permitted to do. When it comes to business, you're a reflection of your company. If you meet with a prospective employer and you're wrinkled, unkempt, loud or have a foul mouth, the chances are good that this employer will want nothing to do with you. Similarly, when you work for a company, those same expectations exist when you interact with your company's clients or customers. You don't want to be the person who drives business away! Even if you don't deal with the public, there are general guidelines to follow. For instance, if you spend half your time gossiping about other workers, arriving late, or talking on the phone, not only will you look bad, but your co-workers will view you with resentment, causing bad morale. When it comes to the workplace, *always* represent yourself as a professional.

Below are some ways you can practice good workplace etiquette from the website *Essortment: Information and Advice that You Want to Know.* It applies equally well to job interviews and general behavior on the job:

- **Pay attention to your appearance** – If you show up to work every day with a wrinkled shirt, uncombed hair or dirty fingernails, it will be noticed. Who do you think your supervisor is going to choose to represent the company on a business trip or in a meeting? The person wearing sneakers and T-shirt, or a co-worker who always shows up for work with well-groomed features and freshly ironed clothes?

- **Unclutter your desk or work area** – Your work area, cubicle, or desk should be an extension of yourself. If it's messy and cluttered, you'll probably have difficulty locating necessary items. In addition, your co-workers will not regard you in a favorable light due to the untidiness of your workspace. No one likes to wait while you attempt to unearth a missing item from under a mound of papers. It's best to keep desk clutter to a minimum.

- **Be on time** – If you're late on a regular basis, people notice. While everyone has the occasional tardy morning, it's not fair to your co-workers to feel the rules don't pertain to you. If you have trouble leaving the house on time, or seem to always be missing connections, perhaps you should wake up earlier to remedy the situation. The same holds true for business meetings. It is never a good idea to arrive late for a business meeting. Someone has taken time out of his or her busy schedule to meet with you; the least you can do is show up on time. If you are late because your train is delayed or there's a traffic jam, call ahead to explain your tardiness. Never intentionally keep a client, or anyone else for that matter, waiting.

- **The greeting** – There's a saying, "You never get a second chance to make a good first impression." Nowhere is this more true than in the office. When meeting people for the first time, it's good practice to use eye contact and a firm handshake and tell the other person how nice it is to meet him or her. If you already know the person, but others in your environment don't, it's necessary to make the proper introductions.

- **Pay attention** – Whether in a meeting, on the phone, or sitting in a co-worker's office, pay attention. It's very bad form to be caught with your mind wandering, playing with your cell phone, or to have no clue as to what actually took place. Be a good listener and take notes. Don't interrupt unless you absolutely have to.

- **Telephone etiquette** – Just as they would resent someone who's constantly tardy, coworkers also have issues with those who spend most of their time on personal phone calls. Not only are they disruptive, but it's unfair to have pleasant chats while those around you are working. It's good business to keep personal phone calls to a minimum and to keep cell phones turned off during business hours. In addition, there are ways to conduct yourself on the phone when you're speaking with clients. Never talk with food in your mouth, use foul language, or leave the party on the other end hanging on eternal hold. No matter whom you're talking to, try not to talk so loud that everyone in the office can hear every word of your conversation. This is distracting and inconsiderate, as is the use of a speakerphone. Try to avoid this as much as possible.

- **Other things to take into consideration:**
    - **Use cologne or perfume sparingly.** Not everyone enjoys your favorite scent.
    - **Avoid the use of profanity.** Not only does it make you look bad, it makes others uncomfortable as well.
    - **Avoid sharing in office gossip sessions.** Gossip hurts and there's a good chance it may not even be true.
    - **Respect the privacy of those around you.** Don't read memos or faxes on other people's desks and don't make comments about overheard phone calls.
    - **Be respectful** to all, no matter what their title.
    - **Return messages, emails, and letters.** It wastes less time for all involved to make a short phone call to say, "No thank you" than to keep avoiding a person's call.
    - **Don't borrow money.** It can lead to a very uncomfortable situation.

- o **Stay awake.** If you're prone to nodding off during business meetings or at your desk, bring in some coffee.
- o **Groom in Private:** It's great to practice good hygiene, but not so great to do it in public. Save the flossing, hair brushing and eyebrow plucking for the rest room during your lunch hour.
- o **Don't slouch.** It's a poor reflection of yourself if you're slumped over your desk all day. When working at any job, the key is to be courteous and polite, pay attention to your appearance and treat others with respect.

Follow those simple rules, and you should go far.

(from http://www.essortment.com/career/officeetiquette_sfkm.htm)

Business Attire

Another unfortunate reality regarding the modern work place is that young people fresh out of college do not seem to fully comprehend the necessity of dressing properly in a business office. An office is an office, and therefore you should pay heed to how you dress and select your clothes to make the best impression possible for your supervisor. There have been countless reports of young employees arriving to work in jeans and sneakers, or without the benefit of a shave or even a shower. The carefree nature of personal grooming, or lack thereof, of one's days as an undergraduate can no longer be adhered to once inside an office at a job. Fortunately for us Americans, we can find very inexpensive dress shoes, slacks and sport coats. You can never go wrong with black-colored clothing for any of these three items. Black is a highly respectable color for business attire and can even double as elegant eveningwear or be used for after work events out on the town. Another secret advantage to wearing black is that it never goes out of style, and of course, it hides the stains well.

Punctuality

Another area, often overlooked with almost reckless disregard by young employees, is punctuality. In most professional business environments, business begins at 8:00 in the morning, and lasts until 5:00 in the afternoon. While far from being a universal rule, it is still the norm. If you wish to make a positive impression upon your employer, you need to make every effort to be punctual every day. All too often, young people do not realign their body clocks, or circadian rhythms, after college, and are still on the old schedule of burning the midnight oil and waking up close to noon. Of course, this may present a very big problem for your punctuality while you are working and going to college. Keep in mind that an employer will ultimately be *paying* you to be on time every morning, in contrast to a university professor who may only mark you down for tardiness. That is not to say that being late for class or missing lectures is a great idea either. You are *paying the college* for your education, so if you choose to be late for class lecture and you end up missing valuable information, you will be cheating yourself out of the education you have worked so hard to finance. Therefore, in both scenarios, tardiness represents a waste of your time and money, and a waste of time for either your professor or your employer.

Studying and Time Management

Successfully managing a part time job, your education, and your personal obligations is not easy, but it is possible: success requires most of all that you manage your time effectively. Each unit a class carries represents an hour of class lecture time, per week. Thus, a three-unit history class will take up three hours of lecture every week. So as you begin to organize your work and study schedules, remember this rule of thumb: at most colleges and universities, a twelve unit *semester* load is considered full time. This is also important for financial purposes. Naturally enough, six semester units is considered half-time attendance. A final rule of thumb is to allow two hours of study time for every hour of lecture time. So, if you are taking twelve units, that will translate into twenty-four hours of study time every week, or a little over three hours per day, every day of the week. Therefore, be very careful as you plan every semester. Many students successfully work full- or part-time while going to college—and statistics often indicate that students who work tend to have a lower or slower graduation rate than those who don't work. However, it's also possible that students who work while going to school deliberately take fewer classes and therefore are just progressing at a slower pace. There is no reason why you cannot have a successful blend of classes, study time, work, and even time with friends. The trick lies in managing your time effectively.

One last consideration: as reported in the *Los Angeles Times*, "Students attending California State University may be in for a dose of tough love as they are asked to choose majors more quickly, be more disciplined about attending class and be willing to sacrifice family time and outside activities to earn their degrees" (Source: Carla Rivera. "Cal State Will Push Students to Graduate." *Los Angeles Times*. Thursday, January 28, 2010. A5). In the article, author Carla Rivera reports that the Cal State Universities are working on a plan to be implemented by Fall 2010 to prevent students from remaining in college for too long because those who "dawdle" reduce opportunities for others to enroll. Albert K. Karnig, president of Cal State San Bernardino, provides the following advice: "There are tremendous sacrifices to winding your way to an undergraduate degree, and advantages and benefits to making those sacrifices…We have to communicate to students the importance of staying in, of persisting, and it may mean doing without some things." This is why planning and time management will continue to be of the utmost importance to your success.

116

Journal Assignment

Make a sample schedule for typical week of your life. On a calendar for one week, list *everything* that you have to do (like work, go to class, take your grandmother shopping, pick up your little brother from elementary school, etc.) and everything that you want to do. Then, observe where the available time is, and schedule some time to study and some time for yourself. Look over your schedule. Briefly write a journal entry in which you compare what your week feels like as you live it to what your life looks like on a schedule. Is there time for everything? Is studying going to suffer because there isn't adequate time for it? What, if anything, on your schedule could you do without? What would change if you had to live your life (or one week of your life) without that activity?

Chapter Seven

Internships

Student Learning Outcome:
Students will apply the practical and analytical skills necessary to obtain an internship by writing a letter of interest to prospective employers.

"Giving kids clothes and food is one thing but it's much more important to teach them that other people besides themselves are important, and that the best thing they can do with their lives is to use them in the service of other people"
—Dolores Huerta, Labor Organizer and Activist

In the middle ages, the most common form of learning, as well as the most noble, occurred between a master and a student, known as an apprentice. Families would send their child—normally a young boy—to study with an expert in one of the trades. This could be any of the trades that had been historically practiced in Europe. This included blacksmiths, silversmiths, carpenters, dyers, or anyone else who knew a skilled trade thoroughly. It was a privilege and an honor to study beneath a master. At about the same time, or perhaps even before, there arose a group of scholars from the clergy in the monasteries who likewise had become very learned men. Soon, these learned clergymen began to attract students of their own. The students who came to listen to their lectures formed unions of their own, and the clergymen who gave these lectures formed their own associations. These associations would later give rise to the first universities in medieval Europe. As with the tradesmen, families began sending their sons to study under these men and to become learned in theology, and in later centuries, the fields of law and medicine. Because of the fact that these learned clergymen were no less masters than the specialized tradesmen, the diploma awarded to students who studied under a master was later to become known as the master's degree.

Finding Internships

As you prepare to make the most of your education, you will have the chance to benefit from the kind of guidance granted to medieval students. The modern equivalent of studying under a master is to obtain an internship. It is a

118

good idea to plan how and where to find the right internship for you. At its most basic level, the ideal internship will allow you to see the everyday practice of the particular discipline that you will eventually study as a major. Furthermore, the ideal internship will not interfere with your study time and possible work hours. A good way to find out about internships is to inquire at your school's employment office or career development center for leads to follow. Employers such as major corporations will typically leave flyers and announcements at colleges precisely to attract students. Of course, the Internet now has several good sites devoted to helping students find internships. [See the Resources section at the end of this chapter for a list of promising websites]. If no sites are readily available, then do a Google search by merely typing the word "internships" as the query word followed by the name of the city where you live. You may then want to narrow down by the type of industry you wish to study. Thus, you might write "internships forensic studies Denver" and see what Google or Yahoo digs up. One good way to use the Internet to find internships is to go to the websites of the types of employers for whom you would like to work. Search these sites and begin collecting names, telephone numbers, and e-mail addresses of all the contact persons who would know of internship possibilities for you. Do not hesitate to contact people in charge of a department in which you would like to work, and ask them if they would be willing to grant you an internship. Mention the fact that you are attending college and that it would mean a great deal to you to be able to set aside a few hours each week to study all the aspects that make the business successful so as to one day become part of the team of employees. Because economics is what it is, you might have to settle for an unpaid internship, but note that the experience will pay off later in other ways.

Another good place to search for internship ads will be local newspapers. Begin with your college newspaper. You may also want to scour the employment section of the major newspapers of your city, just in case there might be ads for internships. These ads come and go rapidly since the positions are filled quickly with qualified candidates, so if you see an ad for an internship which looks promising, do not hesitate to apply for it. Apply for internships as earnestly as you would for any other job opening. Similarly, you need to have your resume and cover letter ready, updated, and formatted elegantly so that when these ads do appear, you will be ready to apply immediately. Another good idea is to have a portion of your wardrobe specifically set aside for interviews. Have a pair of coats or business suits and dress shoes ready for a last minute appointment.

Being Prepared for Your Interview

When called in to interview for a possible internship, you should, as stated above, dress professionally and appropriately. Here are a few more tips:

- Take a writing tablet on which to take notes during the interview or on which to write down your questions before the interview.
- Take a good pen which you trust not to leak ink onto your nice business attire.
- Be courteous and respectful to the interviewer.

119

- Greet him or her with a firm handshake and make eye contact.
- Smile when possible. This is important, although you might be the best "brainiac" a company could train, you also want to create the impression that you are affable, that is, congenial. However, don't overdo it and begin laughing too much; although you want to appear congenial and easy going, you also want to convey that you are mature and serious enough to be able to take on something as weighty as an internship.
- Also, bring along a few spare copies of your resume, as well as a typewritten list of professional references. If possible, include the name and telephone number of your current employer, if you have one. You can even put this list of professional references at the end of your resume, in the same document.

Approaching Your Internship: The Virtual Classroom

Assuming that you get hired, or at least brought on board for an internship (as it may be unpaid), take with you the same type of notebook you used during the interview so that you can take notes each day. Think of the internship as a kind of "virtual classroom" in which you will have to take notes, learn, and memorize no differently than you would in a traditional classroom. Furthermore, do not fool yourself: you will be evaluated and "graded" on your performance. A potential employer's decision to hire you will be based in part on how well and how quickly you are able to learn all that you are meant to learn during an internship.

Sometimes, it is necessary to go through the effort and expense of an experience, such as an internship, in order to fully appreciate the nature and complexities—even tediousness—of a given profession.

In the end, you might decide that you would not enjoy performing the type of work which you are learning about in the internship. Do not write this off as having been a waste of your time; on the contrary, it was a valuable investment of your time and energy. Sometimes, it is necessary to go through the effort and expense of an experience, such as an internship, in order to fully appreciate the nature and complexities—even tediousness—of a given profession. You may very well end up having two or three internships under your belt by the time you graduate from college. If you do, count yourself among the fortunate; not everyone is given the privilege of glimpsing into the day-to-day operations of, for instance, a newspaper or a hospital, and receiving modest pay while glimpsing!

Education and Your Internship

During your internship, you may be taking courses in college which correspond to the same field. If you are, alert your professors to this fact, as you may be given extra credit or perhaps the opportunity to speak about it in class. Even if you are not fortunate enough to receive bonus points from your professor, you should nevertheless incorporate your experiences back into your classes. Make a PowerPoint presentation on your internship or distribute some of the material, such as literature, from the internship to your classmates. Additionally, you should give your classmates all the relevant contact information so that if they show the same level of interest as you did initially, they might have the same opportunity to have this kind of experience. Thus, you should write on the blackboard the name, address, telephone number, e-mail address, and fax number of the internship contact.

What to Do If You Cannot Find an Internship

In case you are unable to lock down an internship in the field you wish to study, your professors might know of opportunities for internships offered by different organizations and companies. Therefore, you should approach your professors and respectfully ask where you might be able to secure an internship. Again, keep in mind that these internships may not necessarily be paid positions. Remember, at this point in the game, what you are after is experience, not necessarily a high rate of pay—that will come later. One major benefit of pursuing an internship is that you are beginning the process of building a professional network of contacts. This will help you throughout your career; nothing can be so useful as to have a network of people with whom you can share ideas, constructive criticism, as well as employers' names, telephone numbers, and websites!

If you cannot, despite your best efforts, find a good internship, then at least try to work as close as possible to the field you are studying so as to be able to gain as many *transferable skills* as possible. These transferable skills can then later be applied to the actual field in which you wish to have a career. For example, a friend of mine wants to become a big-time movie director. However, given the competitive and highly selective nature of that profession, he has been unable to find a job directing a film. Never one to be discouraged, he has since found part-time employment videotaping bar mitzvahs. At first glance, this might appear to have absolutely nothing to do with the fine art of movie making. Yet, upon closer examination, there is a hidden genius in his decision. Movie directors have to study lighting, spatial relationships, coloring, backgrounds, and camera angles. They also have to be skilled at capturing a powerful moment and giving it a certain tempo and fluidity. By going to one bar mitzvah after another, this friend of mine is actually learning to capture these different elements on film. No matter that it is on a camcorder, he is still fashioning his skills at capturing all of these aspects of movie making in these celebrations. This is precisely what I mean by developing your transferable skills. Thus, if you want to become a world-class chef and are not lucky enough to get an internship at the Waldorf in New York, you might very well benefit greatly from working at a sandwich deli. There, you will learn about different types of breads, a wide variety of cheeses, meats, dressings, and other condiments, as well as drinks. Additionally, you will have to learn about ordering wholesale food items, possibly some menu planning, pricing, and last but not least, some cooking and use of the proper cooking utensils. Not only that, but you will also end up learning how to operate an oven, freeze and thaw food, practice sanitary food handling practices, and even deal with county health codes and inspections. Therefore, even a "simplistic" part-time job can become quite an education! It all depends upon your attitude and eagerness to learn.

Institutional Internship Coordinator

Some schools will have an employee known as the internship coordinator, whose job and specialty is to find internships for students. Most likely, this person will be working in the career center. If your school has such an employee, get to know him or her well and begin a series of meetings with this person to begin the proper planning and strategizing to find you a quality internship. Try to befriend this person and to see him or her as an ally—someone who will be working alongside you to help you to gain the most out of your college experience. Additionally, you may want to become familiar with all the literature that your career center offers. A well-supplied career center will have books for you to borrow, perhaps some videos and magazines aimed at college students, as well as dozens of flyers. Make good use of all of these materials, take as many as you can, and thumb through them to search for internship ads.

Even if you are still attending a community college, you may want to take a trip to the nearest state university and head to the central office of the department relating to your field of study. Thus, if you are majoring in engineering, head to the engineering department's main office and ask the receptionist if there are any postings for internships. If the receptionist asks you whether you are a student, merely respond in the affirmative, as some university officials may only want to provide these ads to their own students. Remember to take a notebook and pencil and to take copious notes while browsing through these ads. Also, check out the Office of Student Affairs, usually located next to the student union. Scan the walls and message boards of the student union on the chance they might also contain notices regarding internships. Additionally, you should pick up a copy of the campus newspaper to scour the ads for a possible internship opening. If this does not yield the results that you hoped to find, then perhaps you should make a special trip to one of the major universities in your vicinity to make the same kind of search with the hope that it will yield better results. Although one can get as good an education at a state university as at a highly prestigious school, some employers will place ads for internships at these exclusive schools and not at the state universities. That is not to say that an exclusive university is in any way superior to a state university, but perhaps you might find more opportunities for an internship through some of these better-known schools. Thus, as you journey through your years in college, you should count your internship experiences as integral aspects of your undergraduate education. Try to view the internship experience as a kind of "virtual classroom" where you will learn as much about yourself as you will about the internship.

Internships and Self-Discovery

There may be times when this process of learning about yourself becomes the key and integral aspect of a college education. In fact, it may be more important for you to learn about yourself than for you to learn anything else in a lecture or even in an internship. However, it is through the internship that you would learn the most important aspects of your skills, aptitudes, natural talents, predilections, and aversions. You should have a careful blend of temperament features in your psyche as you begin working in your internship. Ideally, you should be both eager to learn, ready to show ambition, and have a natural willingness to do that which is necessary that will ensure success. At the very same time, you will also need to maintain a natural relaxation within you. This relaxation can carry through the most difficult and trying of circumstances, not only in college but also in life. A relaxed attitude will allow you to assimilate more information, keep it for a longer duration of time, and maintain a demeanor that allows you to deal with temporary setbacks and disappointments. Actually, the more internships you are able to lock down, the better you will be able to

Indeed this is your charge—to make the most of every internship and learning opportunity placed in front of you. Internships are a blessing. Think of them as such, and open your mind as well as your heart to all the ways in which you will be able to grow in character, expand your intellect, and mature in your sensibilities.

develop this easy going nature. This is similar to when one becomes a veteran of many job interviews. After a while, they lose their power to scare you. One develops an easy familiarity within interview styles, formats, the lexicon, dress codes, and the general ethos of an office environment. This will be the type of relaxed approach which you will be able to teach yourself as a result of having worked on several internships. Even if you are among those fortunate enough to already know the field in which you will be working and have already declared a major, it is still a good idea for you to work at more than one internship in that field. Different employers might have different approaches to the same field, so it becomes a matter of enriching your mind and experience base with these different positions.

Multiple Internships

Additionally, do not despair if your first internship does not reward you with the kind of enrichment for which you had hoped. Sometimes it boils down to the luck of the draw or even just good timing to be able to lock down a really good and sought-after internship. This underscores the need to maintain your professional network as active and constantly increasing to be able to draw from this network the contacts you need and leads to follow in order to lock down a great internship. You might even have to go through a few of them before you are able to gather the kinds of experiences you should have in order to become a well-rounded graduate. Also, as with the working world, you should not burn any bridges behind you; should you move onto a bigger and better internship and are asked why you left the previous internship, never let your new employer know the degree of dissatisfaction which you felt at your previous site. Speak about your previous internship in positive terms, and tell your interviewer all the things that you learned. Although you may not be interviewing for a job, the person interviewing you for an internship will nevertheless will be pleased to hear of how you made the most of your previous position, and plan to make the most of this new internship. Indeed this is your charge—to make the most of every internship and learning opportunity placed in front of you. Internships are a blessing. Think of them as such, and open your mind as well as your heart to all the ways in which you will be able to grow in character, expand your intellect, and mature in your sensibilities through interning.

Internships are where the "rubber hits the road" and you begin to see the reality of different careers. You may very well end up changing majors as a result of what you see in your internship. But do not despair if you do. This will merely highlight the fact that the internship served its purpose in showing you the less-than-perfect conditions of certain fields. Remember, your years in college should be filled with exploration, testing, and trial and error. The internship will merely be a valuable adjunct to your college classes in helping you to crystallize some difficult career choices.

Resources for this Chapter
Suggested Internship Sites:

- **College Central (www.collegecentral.com)** — a great place for college students and grads to begin job and internship searches. You can post your resume, search for jobs and internships, find job fairs, and get expert job and career advice. Includes megajobs search engine. Free to jobseekers.

- **Intern Jobs (www.internjobs.com)** — a national database of internships for students and recent grads. Job-seekers can search the internship database by keywords or locations and can post a resume online. Free. Part of the AboutJobs.com network.

- **Internweb.com (www.internweb.com)** — where college students seeking internships in a variety of career fields across the U.S. can search for internship listings, as well as find many useful resources, including internship-related articles and career tools. Registration required to search for internships. Free.

- **Black Collegian (www.blackcollegian.com)** — the internship site for students of color.

- **The College Graduate (www.collegegrad.com)** — a database of jobs and internships searchable by industry, profession, and region.

- **Congressional Hispanic Caucus (www.chci.org)** — has a national directory of internships, fellowships, and scholarships, as well as a number of opportunities to work in the public service sector.

- **USA Jobs (www.usajobs.gov/studentjobs)** — the Federal Government's job site.

- **Get That Gig (www.getthatgig.com)** — creative, "cool" jobs and internships; also, links to other sites plus a wide variety of business and corporate internships.

- **Inroads (http://www.inroads.org)** — a site whose mission is to develop and place talented minority students in business and industry and prepare them for corporate and community leadership.

Journal Assignment

1. After browsing through the above sites, find an internship that would benefit you in your chosen major. Then, write a sample formal letter to your prospective employer requesting an internship with his or her company. Be sure to include: what job you are interested in; what your qualifications for the position are; why you want the job, how it would benefit you, and how you would benefit the company; and, finally, why you would make the best choice above all other candidates. Add your contact info at the end of the letter.

2. Apply for a job! Write a resume and cover letter for a specific job that you desire, according to the guidelines outlined in this chapter. However, visualize that you are applying for your ideal job after you graduate with your four-year or graduate degree; include the internships and any other experience you will have collected by that time, and create a cover letter and resume that would show you as the ideal candidate, highlighting all of your qualifications, and get you an interview. The purpose of this visualization activity is to reverse-plan your career path: when you are done, you will have a resume and cover letter that details everything you need to do in order to get to where you want to be.

Student Success Profile:

Chanel Jackson

Describe yourself briefly in a short biography (hometown, birthplace, high school experience, family, education).
I was born on May 15, 1992, in Watts, California. I was the youngest of four children. We moved pretty often so I lived in a few cities in Los Angeles County. In middle school, we moved to Hawthorne, California, which is where I also attended high school. I went to Hawthorne High School, which in my opinion was not a really good public school. I started 9th grade in honors classes, but by the time I reached my 11th grade year, I had chosen to take regular level classes. I did this merely because I had made poor decisions to have classes with my friends. By the time I was about to graduate, I had my eyes set to attend the California State University of Northridge.

What was your background before coming to community college?
Before community college, I always wanted to attend college. My father attended college but did not graduate. My mother graduated from an HBCU. My parents never forced college down my siblings' and my throat. They believed in letting us find our own way in life. But they did value education and wanted us to at least go to college and decide whether it was for us or not. But deep down, I knew I wanted to go.

What, if anything, prompted your decision to attend community college? What were your goals upon entering community college (why did you go)? Did they change after you started college? If so, how?
I graduated from Hawthorne High School in the spring of 2009, but could not enter college because my parents failed to turn in the financial aid paperwork in the time required, and neither did they have the money to pay the minimal amount for me to begin. I drove all the way to Northridge, California, to attempt to enter CSUN (California State University at Northridge), hoping to find a solution. That failed also. After having no more options, I went to LASC (Los Angeles Southwest College) with attempts to enroll there. Because I was only 17 years old, they needed to see my proof of graduation. I could not put my hands on my diploma, and the Hawthorne High School office was closed for another week. I was not able to attend that fall semester, which caused me to have to wait until the next term. Finally, I felt my time had come. I enrolled in LASC in the spring of 2010. All the while, I had made up in my mind that my goal there was solely to transfer to a university. I kept this vision the whole time I attended the school.

Describe your experience as a community college student. What were the highlights? Were there any special programs or extracurricular experiences that were memorable or inspiring?
Being a community college student was a good experience for me. I was initially saddened about even having to attend a community college because my plan had always been to attend a four-year school. However, once I enrolled, I began to enjoy it. I was able to decide what I wanted to major in by taking a variety of classes. I was also happy that each year brought me closer to my goal: transferring to a university. On the downside, I did not get the experience of living on campus. I must add, campus life and the atmosphere or moral there at LASC was completely different as opposed to the schools all my friends attended. It made it very difficult for me to get involved socially on campus.

How much time went by between high school and community college for you? What were the biggest challenges that you faced when you began attending community college?
I had to take a semester off school even before I was able to begin community college. I attended LASC for three years before I transferred to a university. Once I learned the system, my biggest issue was mental. I needed to let go of the fact that my journey would be different from either of my friends' journeys. I had to

push myself harder, commit myself to being driven more to continue my own story. All the while, it seemed so much easier and much more tempting for me to miss classes because I didn't live nearby.

Did you work while attending community college? If so, how did you balance your time between work and school? Do you have any kids or other family responsibilities? If so, how did you balance your time between home and school? Did you have all three? How did you handle that?
I sought employment and found work at a charter school as an Afterschool Program Director. I had to learn how to balance homework and work while still enjoying life. It taught me important time management skills. I also volunteered as an event planner for a youth group I had mentored in since high school. This made me put a lot of time and energy into my classes at school, my job, and working with the youth group. It literally taught me and caused me to learn how to prioritize and use my time wisely.

Community colleges generally have a high attrition rate, meaning a large percentage of students drop out. Why do you think this happens? What motivated you to persevere through college and transfer to a university?
I would say from my experience that there are different types of people who attend community colleges. Community colleges hold the highest numbers of non-traditional students. Also, parent-students also often attend community colleges. These groups of people seem to have more pressing challenges and stronger demands in life that they are not always able to act on the on-going demand for an education. On the other hand, there are people there who know they can receive a stipend for attending school, and to them this is the only reason they attend. The students who initially graduate high school and immediately attend community college sometimes get lost in the cracks because they are not in an environment that challenges them to transfer.

Of all the reading assignments you completed in college, which one had the greatest impact on you? What's your favorite book and why?
I enjoyed lots of readings from my English classes with Professors Cifarelli and Villesid. I even kept some of them after I completed the course.

Of all the writing assignments you had in college, which are you most proud of and why?
This is a hard decision. I would have to say it would be between my Sociology final and my Biology paper. My sociology professor was hardcore! She reminded us that she structured her class on a university level. That class was tough! She gave a minimum ten-page final that had all of us sweating bullets and nervous. When I received an "A" on my paper, I was in shock. Now, my Biology professor, one of my favorite professors at the school, assigned a twenty-page biology research paper. I am not good at science, so I immediately freaked out. I liked that he walked us through the paper and made sure we had the tools needed

to complete his assignment, and any other assignment we would one day have to complete.

Attending a college or university can be extremely stressful for many students. Does any particular thing stand out as being the most stressful aspect of going to school? What was it and why was it stressful? What coping skills did you use to overcome stress in order to succeed?
I cannot speak for students that are financially supported by their parents or are able to do well at financially supporting themselves. For me, and some friends that I have spoken with, it takes a huge toll on students when we have to juggle studies, assignments, classes, work, and relationships with professors and other faculty and students while having to stress about financial issues. Financial issues always remain in the back of your mind and leave you concerned with questions of how, where, who, when, and leave constant question marks of whether you will be able to continue as a student.

Many community college students give up when faced with adversity or challenges or barriers. You, however, didn't. What was the biggest challenge you faced and how did you overcome it? What advice would you give to a student who feels like he or she just can't do it, has too much going on in his or her life, or is just struggling academically and feels like maybe college isn't the right place?
My biggest challenge was merely being able to *continue*. I would often question whether I should continue my journey because I was missing out on the university student lifestyle. I also had a big issue getting over the age factor. My friends were graduating and completing college, while I, on the other hand, was beginning to apply for transfer. I felt like my time had expired. I would tell anyone who feels like school is too big of a challenge to look back at things in their past that they achieved and the struggles they overcame. The victory is so much sweeter when you look back at all it took to get there.

Were there any memorable faculty, counselors, other students, administrators or staff (at your community college or university) with whom you established a rapport and who made a difference? Is establishing relationships with people on campus important? Tell a brief story about someone with whom you became close and who was supportive.
Even though I did not feel this way while I attended, it is definitely important to establish relationships with people at your campus. I was able to meet a counselor, Daniel Ortega, and the head professor of the English Department, Darren Cifarelli, who ran the Puente Program. The two were extremely helpful to me with my transferring process. It went from allowing me to visit other campuses, answering questions, helping with my personal statement, and more. I think the Puente Program sort of became a form of accountability for me because when I entered there at LASC, I entered with the sole purpose to transfer.

130

Courage to Learn **discusses building social capital, meaning developing relationships and skills that are like an investment in your own future. What social capital have you gained since entering community college?**
I built relationships with a few of my professors. I am still in touch with them even today. However, I think I could have done a better job networking with other students at the community college. I have made sure to do a better job at my university by establishing relationships with my professors and GSIs, as well as other faculty members and students.

Deciding what university to transfer to is difficult. What factors did you consider when deciding where to apply and where to attend?
The location of the school was a big factor also for me. I knew I did not want to be too far from home. Also, with my personality, I did not want to be in the middle of nowhere or in the countryside. This would definitely make me more homesick. I also paid attention to the rank and status of the school. After I got acceptance letters, a huge decision was left to my financial offers because money was definitely a factor.

Universities are expensive. Many magazine and newspaper articles highlight the fact that attending a university is an investment that frequently doesn't pay off or isn't worth it. Perhaps you've seen stories about students graduating from various universities under mountains of debt and unable to find jobs. How did you handle the financial burden of attending college and a university? Is it worth it? Are you buried under mountains of debt?
There is good debt and bad debt. I feel that I am incurring good debt. Yes, I know that with this economy, a degree is not too promising. I have friends and family members who are still struggling to gain employment. However, the way I see it, I do not always want to have financial troubles. I am not good at other avenues (talents and acquired skills) that can land me jobs that will ensure financial stability. With that being said, my best option to increase my chances is definitely an education.

If you are working (while still a student or after having graduated), what is that experience like?
It can be overwhelming at times, but in today's economy I feel both are needed. It is often hard to establish a social life in-between work and school. Time already has to be balanced between classes, studies, and work. In addition, clubs and organizations meet at certain times and professors and GSIs have specific office hours. It can get crazy trying to find time for all of the above.

How did you manage the transition from a community college to a university? Did you feel prepared or underprepared? What were the biggest challenges that you faced during the transition?
I felt very underprepared when I made the transition. A university is a whole different world, opposite a community college. I just had to adapt to the new

system I was in. The class structure, homework, and social life are different. But, after I learned the system, I felt I was able to perform and succeed.

What plans for the future do you have (educationally, socially, and professionally)? When and how did those goals emerge?
I plan to attend graduate school at some point. I am still undecided at what school I want to attend. I also want to work in international relations with companies and work in underdeveloped countries to help better communities. I am not too sure what that looks like yet. I think the two coincide no matter what order. Working in these underdeveloped countries will help my research for graduate school. If I attend graduate school before I work in these underdeveloped countries, I will have more education, which will increase my opportunity and resources for work abroad. Most importantly, my number one plan is to be happy. My happiness comes before any title or position.

Looking back, what advice would you give to first year community college students today (i.e. if you could go back in time and talk to yourself on your first day of college, what would you say)?
This journey may have had many twists, turns, and obstacles. But, when it is time for you to transfer, your options increase and you will really understand why you stuck it through. After that, time pretty much hurdles you to your degree.

Chapter Eight

Networking to Build Social Capital

Student Learning Outcome:
Students will implement strategies to be civically and socially well-prepared by developing a combination of practical knowledge, interpersonal skills, social values and personal motivation to live enriched lives and benefit society by diagraming and prioritizing opportunities for building social capital and networking.

"Advocating an educational revolution, we recognize that our bullets are our books and our victories are an increase in Chicana/Chicano graduates committed to our people's progress."
—Philosophy de M.E.Ch.A
(http://public.csusm.edu/student_orgs/mecha/pages/plan_aztlan_mecha.htm.)

The term *social capital* refers to the process of building networks across a wide range of settings. This is intended to strengthen the ties which may produce human and financial capital, as well as to bring people together in a harmonious social interaction. The term *capital* refers to the amount of resources available for investment in a business venture. This can be money, buildings, cars, or even airplanes. The most successful businesses have had large amounts of capital available for their projects and expansion.

What Is Social Capital?

All the great business empires that have been established were able to flourish and prosper because their founders had the ability to build social capital. In order to understand this concept even more clearly, break the words down individually. *Social*, obviously, refers to a group of people joining together in some type of collective. *Capital* refers to goods available for investment in an enterprise. Therefore, social capital refers to the social networks which eventually become the "goods" available for an investment.

Building Social Capital

In order to develop social capital, you need to keep several things in mind. First, we are living in a time when people are relying more and more on technological devices in order to communicate with each other. This has had some positive and negative outcomes. The technology that we have now has allowed us to be able to communicate with other people around the globe at an amazingly high rate of speed and with pinpoint accuracy. A person in Ohio can communicate with somebody in Cairo via satellite phone. An e-mail can be sent instantly from one terminal to another halfway around the world and be responded to just as quickly. This has no doubt helped businesses and professionals across the globe. However, one of the costs, that is, a human cost, of this rise in telecommunications has been a steady decline in younger people to have the social skills necessary to be successful in today's world. In order to be able to communicate with others confidently and with assuredness, people must hone their social skills. If a college graduate goes out into the world without the ability to speak and communicate clearly and assertively, his or her chances of finding success are greatly diminished.

Observation Skills

Building social capital requires one to be a keen social observer as well as socially adept. If one is a keen social observer, one can witness the kinds of qualities that have allowed other people to become tremendously successful. One has to *be* an observer in order to understand *what it takes* to be observer. No army or navy in human history has been successful in ruling a battlefield or an ocean without at least a working knowledge of what the enemy has at his disposal. Without a strong knowledge of what others are doing, one cannot know whether certain results are worth attaining. That is to say, don't reinvent the wheel. If you observe that a certain type of product or business is not selling well, you would do well to take note of this, and avoid marketing the same type of product or business. Likewise, when you observe that which has not worked well for others, you can change or modify your product or service so that it can be marketed as more attractive than the competition.

Being Socially Adept

Next comes the importance of being socially adept. In order to understand this concept, I want you to think of an historical example of social capital. In 1969, Neil Armstrong walked on the moon. Most people think in terms of one man walking on the moon and perhaps not much else. In order to get Neil Armstrong to the moon, it took a presidential mandate followed by the development of the Space Task Group at NASA, whose sole function was to think of a way to send a man to the moon. By the time Armstrong finally set foot upon the moon, there were roughly 300,000 employees working at NASA and all sorts of subcontractors. A very large collection of people came together for the sole purpose of sending a man to the moon. The group of engineers, computer programmers, builders, and countless others working for the Apollo program were all vital to the success of the mission. It would not have been possible if even one of them had not been a part of that effort. This is a prime example of social capital. The employees at NASA designed a very large team, and this team broke off into numerous splinter groups, and these groups were connected to other people in other groups, and so on. They all had one goal in mind: sending an astronaut to the moon. They were all specialists in their own right, yet each had a role to play in that mission, and each contributed something valuable. The important part for you to remember is that these people were not working in a vacuum. They had to know each other, even if through many degrees of separation. That is to say, perhaps an engineer in Virginia did not know the administrator of NASA personally, but he may have had a supervisor who was a friend-of-a-friend-of-a-friend who knew the administrator.

Perhaps you may not be aiming for a mission to the moon, but the illustration above can yield some important lessons. No one lives completely in a vacuum. All around us, every day, there are people with whom we interact. You might be tempted to respond that not everyone in our world has the resources we need in order to succeed. That notion is correct. Not everyone we meet may have the capital we need, yet everyone has capital in one form or another.

One of the main tenets of the concept of social capital is that all of us have a very valuable capability that we can render for the good of society.

Everyone has a talent, a gift, or some other valuable ability that may or not be given to society. One of the main tenets of the concept of social capital is that all of us have a very valuable capability that we can render for the good of society. Perhaps the people you know may not be able to give you a certain type of capital that you need in your studies or your career, but that does not mean that we should not interact with them nor appreciate the gifts which they do contribute. In the end, your ability to achieve success in life will very much depend on how you are able to tap into the resources that other people may have already developed. This is not to say that you should take advantage of people. All too often in our society, people seem to be alert to how they can take advantage of other people. They want to *use up* other people's resources, rather than *invest in* other people's resources. Likewise, these narcissists never allow others to invest in them. They never want to share their own gifts, talents, or resources with others. It is not surprising that these people rarely achieve success. These people, who know only how to take and never how to give, are bankrupt in social capital. It may appear that these people "have it together" when in reality they are the ones least able to "put it together." The reason for this is that they have tunnel vision. They are peering into a very narrow tunnel to achieve some end, and they take advantage of those around them in order to succeed in these ends. Take the following as an example. Imagine that there is a student in your history class. He merely wants to get a decent grade, not an "A" grade, in the class because he needs the class credit in order to graduate. He, therefore, does not study and does not participate in the class. When the exam for the class is announced, he hires another student to give him a cheat sheet for the exams. He plagiarizes on the term paper. He will do anything *but study* in order to get an "A" in the class. Furthermore, the other students in the class exist merely as instruments for his success. They exist merely to supply him with answers for the test, for cheat sheets, or for pre-written essays. That is not an example of building social capital. That is a narcissistic way of attaining a passing grade. The student could have chosen to form a study group, gone to the campus writing center or his instructor for assistance or help getting started, shared his research with other students, or simply studied. Instead, he chose to use other people to benefit himself rather than to work collectively or independently.

The narcissist, in his heart and soul, does not really care about other people. He does not view others as people with feelings. Nor does he view others as having rights or as people whose rights should be respected. There have been extreme cases of narcissists in history who were able to achieve perhaps some temporary gains, but destiny was finally able to strip them of their relative success, and expose them for the despots they really were: Oliver Cromwell, Napoleon, and Adolf Hitler, to name just a few. Their successes, if that term can be applied, were fleeting, and they never really achieved anything for others, but merely achieved to satisfy an immature egotistical need for power, or as an immature form of compensation for some inner inferiority complex. In the end, their actions betrayed some form of selfishness. It can be seen in some of the brazen and short-sighted military actions they took against the advice of their commanders. They wanted their world for themselves, and no one has been able to achieve this god-like goal for himself. Rather, the world became the arena where competing, and, I must admit this, mostly male egos have wrestled with each other in megalomaniacal struggles to outdo each other and become the next big dictator or despot. None of them seems to have learned much from history. Perhaps it was because they were too busy cheating on their history finals when they were in college!

Using Social Capital to Achieve Success

However, the leaders in geopolitics and business who have managed to achieve great success and managed to sustain valuable and ethical enterprises have been rewarded with much longer reigns than have the despots of old. Men like Bill Gates or illustrious families, like those that established the major banks and financial institutions in New York, have been able to sustain their wealth and capital because they knew the fine art of building and maintaining social capital. They were able to achieve their wealth and prestige by providing a set of goods and services that became valuable in American society. Although there have always been rumors and perhaps some truth to the stories of some famous American families that were able to contribute to the family fortune through questionable activities, these families nevertheless were able to build most, if not all, of their fortunes the right and proper way. They did this by building a network of people who could contribute contacts, offices, and all the necessary capital to start a business or a set of businesses. These were, largely, caring individuals who felt a real kinship and connection with their fellow man. They were individuals who wanted to give of themselves and who cared about the welfare of the country. If you look closely at the lives of these financial giants, they were people who voted and became very involved in causes, both political and non-political. Many had friends in Washington, D.C., who were also very influential. Nevertheless, they knew almost instinctively how to become connected to those with whom they could form mutually prosperous relationships. In the end, it can be stated that what building social capital boils down to is knowing how to kindle and maintain relationships.

What You Can Do to Build Social Capital Now

One of the simplest things you can begin doing is to become more aware of the people who populate your world. As mentioned at the outset of this chapter, we are living in such a fast-paced and technologically driven society that we scarcely know our own neighbors. Adding to this dilemma is the fact that the media has done a fine job of thrusting the most terrible news items they can find and reporting them at the top of the news hour. Day after day, people hear of nothing but rape, murder, war, brutality, and mayhem. It has gotten to the point that the primary reason that we are unaware of who our neighbors are is precisely that we are afraid to know. We are living in fear of those around us, even while driving on the freeways. Therefore, more and more people are living in their own "micro-environments." By this, I refer to merely traveling between home and work, the grocery store, and perhaps a church. However, all this must change if people are to develop social capital.

One of the concepts I strongly believe in which has helped many people to build social capital is the concept of partnerships. If one is able to develop a high capacity for built partnerships, one can go very far in life.

Everyone Is a Resource

In a sense, developing social capital means broadening your horizons. Do you know everyone at your job? Do you know their names or job responsibilities? How long have they been working at their jobs? Begin noticing the people who you don't normally acknowledge. If we look closely at the very fabric of our daily lives, there are many more people than we even knew existed in our world. They are the unseen force which allows our days to flow as they do. Yet, whether or not

137

we realize it, we depend on these people. More specifically, we depend on the capital that they are able to contribute to our society. Even the people who collect our garbage, the well-paid sanitation engineers, are contributing labor, time and effort—all of which are necessary capital. Street sweepers are likewise contributing capital in the form of driving skills, mechanical skills, time and effort.

You many not depend on a street sweeper in order to succeed in business, but you eventually will depend on a great many people in order to secure your future. One of the concepts I strongly believe in which has helped many people to build social capital is the concept of partnerships. If one is able to develop a high capacity for built partnerships, one can go very far in life. As the saying goes, "No man is an island," and therefore, you should not be an island either. Start with small steps, like finding study partners in each of your classes. By finding others with whom you can study, you will begin laying the foundation of the art of building social capital. This is especially true if one of your professors assigns you into groups, and there are four or five people in each group. If you should find yourself in this situation, which eventually you will, then keep the following things in mind. First, although you may not realize it, a random group of students thrown together by chance in a classroom are already bringing to the classroom their own unique backgrounds. These backgrounds include skills, insights, aptitudes, and abilities. Get to know everyone by introducing yourself to the group. Take turns and have your other team players introduce themselves to the group. Have each member of the group talk about their backgrounds, including their favorite class or activity in high school. No matter what the current group assignment is, you can be assured that your group of randomly chosen students will have the necessary skills to put together a dynamic presentation, report, or term paper. Each of you will have your own specialty which can be tapped into for maximum results. For instance, in every group there is a computer specialist. This person can be in charge of uploading all the documents into a PowerPoint presentation. Perhaps somebody else in the group is good at doing research and finding all the relevant facts and data in the library or on the Internet. Another person may be very skilled at public speaking. This could be the person who delivers the presentation to the class. Yet another person could have strong leadership skills. This could be the team captain.

Thus, in using this approach, everybody benefits individually, and the group as a whole benefits as well. This is a prime example of building social capital. Everyone gets to know everybody else, and a network is formed, based on

This is a prime example of building social capital. Everyone gets to know everybody else, and a network is formed, based on acquaintanceship and skill.

138

acquaintanceship and skill. Try to see this classroom example as a microcosm of the type of relationship-building that needs to take place in society. Furthermore, building social capital does not necessarily entail merely creating one network in your life, but it does entail creating a series of overlapping networks. We all play different roles every day. In this way, we move within different circles. Other people's circles will include us as well. Therefore, we have to be mindful of the important roles that we play in other people's lives. For instance, that student in the example above who chose to cheat his way through his class did not build any social capital. Had he chosen to network in that class, he may have had the opportunity to make contacts that would benefit him in the end. If he had approached his fellow students with openness and honesty, they might have bonded and be resources that he could look to for support in other classes, job references, or friendship—which he himself could have returned with the same.

Networking is the key to building social capital and maintaining relationships that will benefit as well as enrich you.

Thus, as you begin building social capital, keep in mind that you must also give of yourself by way of time and talent to others. Others will need you just as much as you need them. Social capital, in its truest sense, involves mutually beneficial and complementary relationships, all flowing harmoniously in and among each other. This is why the idea of partnerships is so powerful. It allows you and other people to form units of talent. These units can be discrete, or they can be part of a cluster of units. Again, think of the classroom presentations as examples. You and another student can form a unit. The class, also, can be divided into many two-person units. Your two-student unit can help another two-student unit by way of contributing materials, data, or time. This is exactly how society functions. We are part of units, and these units are, in turn, part of larger units.

As you progress throughout your college and university education, keep this lesson in mind: we are all connected to a larger social network, and each of us depends upon a large group of people for our very survival. Whatever goal, project, or plans you may have for your future, your success will be doubled if you invest in building the relationships and bonds with others who share your vision for a brighter tomorrow. Ultimately, it is only through building alliances and coalitions that we are able to secure the bedrock of progress upon which our great nation was built. Begin securing your future by building social capital now. Your success will feel more rewarding and will be more stable if you are part of a strong social network.

Networking is the key to building social capital and maintaining relationships that will benefit as well as enrich you. You have already read about joining campus organizations and participating in campus events, where you will meet like-minded people with similar interests. And, you have read about internships and mentors, where you extend your social network into the professional realm. However, you may already be a part of other social networks outside of work and school, like a church group, a circle of friends, a sports team, a book discussion group, a band, or an online social networking site. You can find such groups to participate in online by searching the internet for groups in your area. You can go to your local public library or check around your campus and read the message boards for announcements of reading groups, protests, teach-ins, film screenings, musical events, or civic activities you can attend. You can locate the websites of political groups or other social groups and subscribe to their newsletter or listserv. Or, you can talk to people, everywhere you go. I've found that going to events, like readings by authors you might be interested in, public "town hall" meetings, or political rallies to be especially helpful in this regard. As always, be open-minded, and always look for your chance to be a part of something that makes a difference!

Journal Assignment

Begin by listing every group, community, or category that you consider yourself to be a part of and noting what interest it serves for you. Make your list exhaustive. Don't merely consider formal groups or organizations; also, jot down things like "bicycle riders" or "people who like to read poetry." The idea is to generate a list of *all* interests that you might share with others. Then, identify any formal groups, mailing lists, social networking sites that you have already joined that meet the interests listed. Lastly, for those interests that you have listed which don't have a formal social network associated with them, use the Internet or other resources mentioned in this chapter to find one or more social groups to join or newsletters to subscribe to—and describe it. You might even want to sign up while you are there!

Chapter Nine

Mentors

Student Learning Outcome:
Students will analyze the value of a mentor-mentee relationship, comparing and contrasting both roles by listing potential mentors and assessing the best choices for their academic and career goals.

"You are never strong enough that you don't need help."
—Cesar Chavez, Labor Organizer and Activist

"Mentors provide professional networks, outlets for frustration, college and career counseling, general life advice, and most importantly, an extra voice telling a student they are smart enough and capable enough to cross the stage at graduation and land their first paycheck from a career pathway job."
—Gerald Chertavian, social entrepreneur

Loosely defined, mentors are people with specialized knowledge that they wish to pass on to the next generation of students or apprentices. A mentor will typically take on students or apprentices and attempt to show them "the ropes," or the knowledge base students should know about a particular area. A mentor is a teacher, someone who enjoys teaching, who has the patience to guide and instruct someone in the art of a particular field. Anyone can become a mentor, but not everyone can become a *great* mentor to someone else. In this chapter, I will show you the secrets to getting the most out of a mentoring relationship, as well as what is needed to be a great mentor to somebody else. Everyone deserves to be paired with a great mentor, and I know that the many successes that I have enjoyed have come from working under great mentors. Therefore, I want you to reap the benefits of working under a great mentor.

The Role of a Mentor
The role of a mentor is meant to be that of a teacher, first and last. A mentor, as mentioned above, is someone who, because of his or her years or decades of working in a particular field, has gained the requisite knowledge and insight to show someone new to the field what it takes to become great within that discipline. He or she may have learned the tricks to becoming a successful worker in a field that few people outside the discipline would know. Many times, when

students enter a field right out of college, all that they know is the information base that they accumulated from class lectures and from reading the textbooks. Maybe, if they are lucky, they were able to land themselves a halfway decent internship during the vacation of their junior-senior summer term. While gathering information at school is extremely valuable and important, the wisdom a mentor passes on can enhance a student's education by providing rote knowledge and experience-based knowledge, often not covered in textbooks and classrooms. Most importantly, a mentor is not someone whose

> *The role of a mentor is meant to be that of a teacher, first and last. A mentor, as mentioned above, is someone who, because of his or her years or decades of working in a particular field, has gained the requisite knowledge and insight to show someone new to the field what it takes to become great within that discipline.*

tutelage should be sought only when one is an undergraduate, but as part of a lifelong learning experience.

I have found that the most successful people in life are those who have sought the wisdom of a mentor continuously throughout their lives. The reason is that people should never stop growing or learning. As a close friend mentioned once in passing to me, "The moment we stop learning, we stop growing." Therefore, one can never be too old, too rich, or too powerful to have a mentor. Even the President of the United States has his "advisors," who are "mentors in disguise." These are the trusted souls who have been around the block a few times, and who therefore have the expertise with which to advise the President. During their meetings with the Cabinet, the Presidents of the United States have always relied heavily upon the expertise of their most trusted military advisors, Army Chiefs of Staff, Secretaries of Defense, Press Secretaries, and so on. It is not just one man out there in Washington, D.C., making all the tough decisions on his own. That would be too burdensome a task, and too heavy a load to heap upon the mind of one person. If that were the case, it would require super-human effort to be the President. No one would want the job. In fact, I believe that one of the most rewarding aspects for many Presidents of the United States has been to put their closest friends and mentors into key positions in the Cabinet and be able to see their mentors and friends every day, continuing to learn and grow from those relationships.

Fortunately, for the great majority of us, we do not carry the burden of caring for the safety and perpetuity of the Free World on our shoulders, but it does not mean that we cannot gain a great deal from learning from a wise and learned mentor. In the next few pages, I will describe the things you should look for in a mentor, as well as what to expect and what *not* to expect from a mentor/student relationship.

Two Types of Mentoring Relationships: Formal and Informal

According to Wikipedia, the on-line encyclopedia, there are two types of mentoring relationships, "…formal and informal. Informal relationships develop on their own between partners. Formal mentoring, on the other hand, refers to assigned relationships…In well-designed formal mentoring programs, there are program goals, schedules, [and] training…Mentors inspire their mentees to follow their dreams." This is a well-written definition of the typology of mentoring programs. Let us look at this more closely for illustration.

Formal Mentors

In college, you will most likely encounter the two types of mentoring relationships: formal and informal. An example of a formal mentoring relationship would be a summer internship program, arranged and organized through the Career Development Office of your college or university. In this case, you apply with all the required paperwork to gain entry into a specific internship, either paid or unpaid. Even if it is unpaid, you should still apply. The coordinator at the internship site will either be your mentor or will assign you to a mentor. There can be great value in this "pre-packaged" mentoring relationship. The college or university through which you apply is actually doing you a great service and saving you much time, energy, and effort in playing matchmaker between you and a prospective mentor. Of course, matching you effectively with the right mentor for you involves some "luck of the draw," and there is every possibility that you may not be paired with a great mentor. You may just have to take your chances and find out by applying. Additionally, you may well have to go through more than one internship in order to finally find the type of setting which is the best match for you, and in which you can find the best mentor for your needs and working style.

Of course, as in all areas of life, personality factors will always play a role in the mentor and mentee relationship. Some of the things that ultimately go into making a mentor/mentee relationship effective and dynamic go beyond resumes or curriculum vitae. Ultimately, it is that unseen and indescribable thing called chemistry. You were born with a certain temperament, and out of that temperament comes a certain learning style and later a working style. Therefore, you may not want to approach the search for a great mentor too cerebrally or too intellectually, as the ultimate factors which will dictate whether you are the right "fit" with your mentor cannot always be listed on a sheet of paper. Sometimes it's just a feeling. Nevertheless, you should make it a habit of meeting prospective mentors with a clear, and unbiased, mind. Furthermore, time will also make its own contribution to whether or not a particular mentoring relationship will work. In other words, to use the well-worn expression, "Only time will tell," do not pre-judge people whom you meet, and be conscious of those people you feel comfortable enough with to open up to, ask questions of, and express yourself freely. And notice when someone really takes the time to listen to you and responds carefully with well-considered advice or thoughts. Those feelings show that a bond is being formed and that you may want to take the time to maintain that relationship, get contact information, and stay in touch.

Informal Mentors

Some of the people whom you would never expect—indeed, sometimes the people you would put last on your list of effective mentors—become your greatest teachers or informal mentors. I believe that everyone has something to teach us; everyone we know can teach us *something* about life. You may not realize this, but everyone you know has taught you something. They themselves may not have intended or realized that they have taught you a valuable life lesson, but all people inevitably do. You must learn to keep your heart, as well as your mind, open during the entire journey of life. Only then will you be able to learn from everyone around you. There are many different types of mentors, as well as many different types of teachers and instructors. They are all equally vital to our growth and development, as well as to our ultimate potential.

In fact, some of the most valuable things that we can learn in life are not taught directly by people themselves, but taught to us merely by watching them and observing their behavior. Sometimes, it boils down not to what people tell us, but rather by their actions (which, as they say, speak louder than words) that we are able to absorb life's most valuable lessons. The most constructive insights into human behavior as well as the most useful knowledge about how to be successful in life can be gained merely through osmosis, or the process of being close to people whose learning you naturally absorb, merely by watching and observing them.

Your Mentoring Program

Nevertheless, the formal mentoring program will become one of the most valuable aspects of your university education. As mentioned above, in the formal and well-designed mentoring programs, there will be goals, schedules, and training. One of the ways in which you can make the most of your mentoring program, no matter what field you are studying, is to establish certain goals for yourself. In other words, ask yourself these questions: "What do I want to get out of this mentoring relationship?" or "What can this mentor teach me?" As you get deeper and more involved in your field of study, and as your vocational and career aspirations begin to crystallize, these questions will become easier for you to ask yourself. Value the time you spend with your mentor. Set the goal of getting something useful and positive out of every interaction with them. Plan questions to ask. Make the relationship meaningful.

Scheduling

Next are schedules. Not only should you ask yourself what you intend to learn under a specific mentor, but you may also begin to ask yourself *by when* you feel you should have learned the most important lessons from the mentorship. If you have been granted an internship, or if you are already working in the environment in which you would like to establish your career, be aware that the person who is your mentor is probably very busy and may not have a lot of time to devote to being your mentor. In addition, the person who is to be your mentor may not have ever signed up to be an "official" mentor, but may be devoting unpaid time to work with you to show you how to be effective within a certain industry. What may be ultimately in everyone's best interest in these situations is for you and your mentor to agree on a timeline for completing certain learning tasks. Your mentor may ask you to design the schedule and then present it for approval. Be creative and resourceful with the limited time you have to work with your mentor. You may want to work backwards and start with the most difficult aspects of working in a certain industry. Break these tasks down into manageable chunks of learning so you don't feel overwhelmed.

The Mentor-Mentee Relationship

It can be a very overwhelming task to have an internship and work under a mentor. At times, you may find yourself in awe of your mentor. This is a natural reaction in a young person. It is the college version of "hero worship" that younger adolescents feel at times for sports figures or movie stars. You may find yourself looking up to your mentor as a demigod, someone who has become the very type of professional you wish to become one day. It is important to keep this adulation in check. Yes, your mentor is (or will be) someone with very admirable traits and credentials. They do deserve quite a lot of admiration for their wisdom and their accomplishments. Yet, you must remember that they are also human and subject to fallibility and failures. One thing that most people forget when they work with mentors is that those mentors had to go through certain setbacks and failures in order to achieve the successes that they now enjoy. This will also help you prepare for possible setbacks within your own journey. Learning how your mentor was able to overcome setbacks and failures in order to achieve his or her successes will be one of the most valuable aspects of your mentorship.

Working with a mentor can be a stressful and worrisome period for you. This is why you must take the time to pace yourself while working under a mentor. Obviously, there is going to be pressure on you to create a favorable impression. After all, your mentor could become your future employer. Alternately, if not a future employer, your mentor may become a reference—or the very person on whom you depend for referrals to job interviews in the future. Keep in mind that your mentor can refer you to jobs in the field and/or serve as a reference to support your applications and write letters of reference; he or she will most likely be contacted by one of your employers, so you must keep your relationship with your mentor on the most amicable of terms.

Additionally, try to maintain a very professional demeanor with your mentor. As mentioned previously, your mentor is most likely taking time, unremunerated, to teach you what you need to know about a certain field or discipline. The very least you can do is to behave towards him or her in a polite, courteous, and professional manner. A strong handshake upon every meeting, a smile, and consistent eye contact can go a long way towards establishing a long-lasting and mutually prosperous relationship with a mentor. From the very first day you are to meet with your mentor, make every effort to dress in a professional manner. Even if this is an unpaid internship, or if you are meeting your mentor in a casual setting, dress as you would in an office. This creates a wonderful impression upon a mentor of someone who can meet all the expectations required of a young professional in a job setting. Although it may be a bit much to arrive in a full-on business suit, you can never go wrong with the "business casual" look. Definitely use dress shoes, and, if possible, dress slacks, and, for the women, a business-appropriate blouse, skirt, or a pair of slacks.

Training

The third aspect to keep in mind when designing the ideal mentor/mentee relationship is training. Both you and your mentor must meet, discuss, and agree upon the type of training that will be involved in the internship. Will you be out in the field often? Will you be working in a cubicle? Are you expected to take notes? Will you be required to turn in weekly reports to your mentor? Will you be rotated among several mentors? Of course, every field and discipline is going to have its own training program. Even within the same field, the training may be different from one university to the next. Finally, human personalities being what they are, one mentor will have a very different training approach to the next. You may be paired with a mentor who feels that a few hours of gentle advice every week is enough to give you all the tools you need to send

> *Your mentor is most likely taking time, unremunerated, to teach you what you need to know about a certain field or discipline. The very least you can do is to behave towards him or her in a polite, courteous, and professional manner.*

you off into the world of work. Another mentor may feel that in order to be a successful mentor, he or she must give you very rigorous assignments and work you until you are exhausted. Just like different instructors in college, different mentors have different approaches, so it helps to be adaptable to any potential learning situation or any management style.

Finally, you must ask yourself what type of mentor will suit you best. Do you believe in a *laissez-faire* approach to mentoring and believe that your mentor should do the absolute minimum so as to give you the most "breathing room?" Or, do you believe that your mind is like a dry sponge, just ready to absorb whatever wisdom and lessons your mentor can pour into it? Perhaps your optimum learning style may lie somewhere in the middle. In the end, that may be the best compromise: you give your mentor the opportunity to give you whatever wisdom and guidance he or she can, but then you are given the room to maneuver and test your own style and creativity on the job. Of course, some careers allow for very little creativity. Some are very straightforward. If this is the case with your career, then allow your mentor to teach you all the knowledge that he or she has accumulated over time.

Accoutrements: The Tools of the Trade

One of the best ways that you can prepare yourself to work effectively under a mentor is to come equipped with the proper accoutrements to all of your meetings with him or her. By accoutrements, I refer to the tools that can be used to enhance your learning of all that your mentor can teach you. First, you should invest a couple of dollars in an inexpensive notebook. This can be one of the best items in your possession while working with your mentor. Use this notebook to take copious notes. Jot down nearly everything that your mentor says you should either take note of or remember. Of course, human memory being as fallible as it is, you should take notes as often as possible. This may be more important in the beginning stages of your work with you mentor than it will be later. The reason for this is that your brain will be flooded with stress hormones, and it will be difficult for you to activate your memory as you normally would due to all this stress. Therefore, give your mind a rest by allowing yourself the luxury of committing the important information down on paper, which will always be there for future reference. You will have enough to keep you worried and distracted without the added stress of trying to remember all that you should while working with a mentor.

If your college or university program requires you to submit weekly or monthly reports on your progress, a good idea is to use your notes from your meetings with your mentor. These notes will be replete with information that you can then integrate into your progress reports. You may also want to check with your professors to see if they will require you to have your mentor sign any forms from the university. This way, your professor can see the incontrovertible proof that you are working diligently with a mentor at a legitimate internship. You may elect to give a class presentation on your work at an internship and speak about all that you learned under a mentor. If you are not required to do such an assignment, volunteer: you might be able to earn extra credit by doing so!

Another inexpensive gadget to take with you when you meet your mentor is a tape recorder or a digital recorder. Instead of getting a cramped wrist, you may want to invest a little money in a recorder which will save you the effort of writing and will allow you to focus completely on what your mentor is telling you. When you return home in the evening, you may want to listen to the recordings again in order to memorize all the pertinent information given to you by your mentor at your internship site.

Therefore, as you embark on your journey of studying under a mentor, remember to keep your mind, ears, and heart open to all the good advice and learning that your mentor can provide for you. Your mentor will be one of your most useful contacts throughout your college years and beyond. Always stay in close contact with your mentor even after you graduate, as your journey towards grown and self-realization at that point will have only just begun.

Lastly, having known the value of having a mentor, consider being a mentor as well. Less experienced people than you need advice that you can provide: just as someone helped you out, you can help out someone else. The same qualities that you would look for in a mentor are the same qualities that you yourself might embody as a mentor for someone else. Just be willing to talk to people who may not be as far along in their education or in their careers as you are. Be open-minded. If someone asks you a question, give it your full consideration and provide a thoughtful answer, or at least refer the person to someone or somewhere that he or she can get the answer. Each one, help one. Showing someone else the ropes also solidifies your own knowledge. When you teach someone else how to do something, you end up learning it more thoroughly yourself, so the benefits of mentoring are multiple.

> *Lastly, having known the value of having a mentor, consider being a mentor as well. Less experienced people than you need advice that you can provide: just as someone helped you out, you can help out someone else.*

Journal Assignments

1. Think of someone whom you might consider to be a mentor. What qualities did that person have? Why did you respect him or her? What wisdom did your mentor have? What did you learn from the relationship? Write a brief description of that person, or tell a story about him or her that shows how knowledgeable your mentor was even if you didn't realize it at the time.

2. Alternately, imagine that someone younger than you has approached you for advice. This person is unsure about whether college is the right choice, and uncertain about what career path to follow. What advice would you give him or her? How would you advise this person, who looks up to you, to make these important decisions?

Chapter Ten

Student Organizations

Student Learning Outcomes:
Students will refine leadership, planning, and organizational and relational skills by creating a business plan for a new start-up club.

"We cannot seek achievement for ourselves and forget about progress and prosperity for our community... Our ambitions must be broad enough to include the aspirations and needs of others, for their sakes and for our own."
—Luis J. Rodriguez, author

Your undergraduate education will be greatly enhanced if you allow yourself some time to become involved with student organizations. There are quite a few varieties of student organizations on every campus. Of course, each college and university will emphasize different types of student-led groups. No institution of higher education would be complete without these student groups. It was, after all, students who banded together to create student unions in the Middle Ages, which later gave rise to the universities. So, in a sense, colleges and universities were founded by student organizations, at least in part.

The Student Union and Office of Student Affairs

As you settle into your college environment, a worthwhile use of your time is to head to the student union of your campus and inquire about the different clubs on campus. You may have already received a primer on student clubs during your orientation. However, to refresh your memory you may want to reacquaint yourself with your school's student groups. If the student union is no more than a large and fancy lounging area, then head over to the Office of Student Affairs. This office is devoted to overseeing campus-wide student organizations. It may oversee the budgets connected with such groups as well as arrange the activity schedule for student groups. These offices also arrange the locations on campus where student groups can assemble. Throughout the year, there will be many campus festivities involving not only student groups but the campus community as a whole, and the Office of Student Affairs must organize and supervise the events. At some schools, the Office of Student Affairs is responsible for all printed media, especially any type of advertisement posted on student bulletin boards. No one can set foot on a college campus and either solicit money or place ads or hand out flyers without first getting the approval from the Student Affairs Office. As a college department, it has a dean who is the ultimate coordinator for all student-run organizational activities.

Student Organizations' Club Day

Instead of making a trip to the Office of Student Affairs, what you may want to do instead is to wait for a "Club Day" or open house when all the student organizations set up booths to recruit new members. A good idea is to check either online or in the *Schedule of Classes* to see which day is devoted to student clubs or organizations. Such days can be quite entertaining with all the booths set up on the university or college quad, with games, food, and drinks enjoyed by all. During this open house or club day, all the student organizations will distribute free materials to students describing their mission and purpose on campus. Pick up as much literature as you can to find an organization or club that fits your needs, interests, or philosophy.

Fraternities and Sororities

Fraternities have enjoyed a long and rich heritage on college campuses. Typically, a fraternity will consist of a group of young men who are members of a club with Greek letters as the club name. There are those who enjoy making humorous observations of Greek life. Aaron Karo, in his book *Ruminations on College Life* (2002) gives this whimsical view:

> "I think you can sum up Greek life this way: Sororities are a bunch of girls who had each other, organized to travel in herds and fight over frat boys. Fraternities are a bunch of guys who love each other, organized to get [drunk] faster and cheaper and hook up with sorority girls." (p.53)

There are social disadvantages and advantages to joining a fraternity or sorority. At most schools, the Greek "houses" will attempt to recruit members during one of the first few weeks of school. This is called Rush Week, and it is a big cultural event on campus. If you are interested in joining a fraternity or sorority, this is your chance. Once you are recruited into a fraternity or sorority, you are "pledged" to that club. You will normally be paired up with another older and more experienced upper-class student who has been in the club for a while and can become a kind of Big Brother or Big Sister to you. The next big event is the initiation ritual. This is what gives a lot of students pause in considering whether to join. Typically, the initiation ritual will involve large amounts of alcohol being consumed in a set number of minutes or seconds. Be careful about rushing into a decision during Pledge Week because once you are asked to join, for there may be harsh social repercussions if you decide that you do not want to after learning of these secret rituals. These rituals are all part of the code. They have been kept secret by generations after generations of pledges, and they are not divulged. Whether the initial rituals for the females in the sororities are just as physically brutal is questionable. Nevertheless, many men swear by these pledges, stating that the experience of being inducted into a fraternity was the most important experience of their college careers. Many relationships last well beyond college, and the opportunities to join a social network that extends across the country should not be downplayed. Once you are finally past the pledge ritual, you then are entitled to live in a Frat House.

Typically, a fraternity house is a large two-story house just off campus where only members of the fraternity live and socialize. These houses are frequently the scene of large and noisy parties. Most of the time, large quantities of alcohol are consumed. This is something you need to anticipate. Not everyone drinks, and perhaps you may be one of those who choose not to partake of alcoholic drinks. In fact, if you do not drink at all, you may want to consider whether you really want to join a Greek House at all. The presence of alcohol is central to most of their social activities. If you are strong enough to resist peer pressure and are not put off by the presence of cases of beer and vodka, then, by all means, pledge yourself to a house. Other houses are less wild. Recent, severe repercussions for illegal and dangerous activities have forced some fraternities and sororities to scale back their initiation rites and partying tendencies. Some houses are less social and more academic, prizing their members' intellect and academic achievement. Researching your choice before you make it by talking to people who are members of the fraternity or sorority is the best approach; that way, you can choose to pledge or not based on your knowledge of what the house stands for and how good a fit it is for you.

Despite the disadvantages and risks, one strong benefit of pledging to a fraternity or a sorority is that you will be invited to many different types of mixers and seasonal holiday parties. This could become a great way to meet other people and establish the opportunities to find someone to date. Although you may not be searching for a "soul mate" at a Halloween party, being able to attend these events will give you the practice and skills needed to be able to talk to, and be comfortable with, others in a social setting. Who knows, you may very well end up meeting your future spouse at a social mixer hosted by a fraternity or sorority.

Another social benefit of joining a fraternity or sorority is that the social bonding is a lot tighter than what you would ordinarily find in the regular friendships students develop as a matter of course in college. One person told me that he was still friends with the other men in his fraternity after twenty years. He described how he and the other men helped each other find jobs and gave each other advice on how to succeed in finding lucrative business opportunities. As a result of being members of a small but tightly knit social group at a rather prestigious university, the men felt they were truly "brothers" and would stick up for each other, come what may. Again, these social networks can last well beyond your college experience, so choosing wisely can benefit you for the rest of your life.

At a large public university, it might be somewhat favorable for you to become associated with a fraternity or sorority. The reason for this is that you might feel "lost in the shuffle" and not feel connected to anyone in particular. This is nobody's fault, but it is a natural consequence of being enrolled at a large university. The tightly knit bonding described above occurs as a matter of course when one joins a student organization that allows one to move in a circle within a circle. Truly, these student organizations enable students to feel that they live within a manageable social world, for when the size and scope of a big campus are such that one feels like no more than a number, a process of depersonalization begins to creep into one's consciousness. Therefore, fraternities and sororities play an important role within the campus community in their striving to provide a more personalized approach to the college experience.

Athletic Clubs

If you choose not to join a fraternity or sorority, there are many campus groups and organizations to which you can belong. If you are athletically inclined, you can join an athletic club. This has numerous benefits. If you join a sports club, you will be able to meet other students that share your interest in a particular sport. This can be a blessing, particularly with sports that cannot normally be enjoyed in a gym or even at most public parks. A good example of this would be an archery club. Typically, students can join an athletic club after enrolling in a sports class. Thus, in the previous example, the archery club members would most likely be enrolled in an archery class at a college. Another obvious benefit of belonging to a sports club is that one can spend more time practicing the sport and gaining proficiency with the practice. An example of this would be a golfing club. Heaven knows how important it is to practice one's golf swing! It may take years to actually master a sport like golf, so why not give yourself a chance to practice your game and socialize at the same time. Having others share your interests in a sport can give you the opportunity to have something in common with them and be able to talk about it.

The variety of student organizations is part of what makes each campus unique. As you research universities that you will consider attending, in addition to looking at the academic offerings, you might also consider investigating the student groups on each campus to determine if there are similar-minded students that you might eventually become involved with.

The variety of student organizations is part of what makes each campus unique. As you research universities that you will consider attending, in addition to looking at the academic offerings, you might also consider investigating the student groups on each campus to determine if there are similar-minded students that you might eventually become involved with. Many campuses have student groups that are specialized, like the Hip Hop Congress, environmental organizations, student writing clubs, or political activist organizations. Student political groups, like MEChA and the African American Student Union, have different chapters at many institutions also, and some students have reported that they feel less out-of-place when they have opportunities to socialize or organize events with students who share similar political views or who are similar in race.

The Associated Student Body
If you are not athletic, musical, or political, another great way to become involved with a student organization is to join the Associated Student Body or Associated Student Organization, with the goal of eventually running for office and filling in an empty slot on the student council. By running for student body president or some other leadership position, you will begin to learn about the key personality characteristics of great leaders. You will come to know what distinguishes a great leader from a mediocre one, and your creativity and patience will also be put to the test. Your ability to remain calm while under pressure will set you apart from your peers and eventually give you the edge you need to become successful in life. These things become especially important if you are majoring in Political Science, as you will get to see in person many of the same principles you are learning about in class. This is when your education can "come to life" as you begin to practice the skills which will later define and shape your future political career. You may even see your time spent in the student council as an internship of sorts: you will be speaking at important forums on campus, as well as representing and speaking on behalf of the student body. This last point is very important if you plan to pursue *any* career which involves leadership capabilities. The ability to represent an entire group of people and to be able to speak on their behalf—and do both effectively—is the mark of a great leader.

The Associated Student Union is also the place where clubs can be chartered, so if there is no group on your campus that you feel like affiliating with, you can always start your own club. As different campuses have different guidelines and requirements to charter a club, check with your school's ASU for the specific guidelines—and start your own club.

Campus Ministries
If you are a person of strong religious faith or spiritual inclinations, then involvement with campus ministries may be a good option for you. Most community colleges as well as the large four-year universities maintain active ministries within their purview. These groups can run the gamut from Buddhists to Muslims, Catholics and Protestants. Although most, if not all, of the junior colleges are public, and therefore dependent on state money, they nevertheless welcome students to maintain their own activities on campus. The only critical distinction is that a state-run school cannot sponsor any type of religious activities on its campus; however, students are free to engage in their own student-run religious activities. You may find these students holding Bible studies in the

student union or holding hands and praying around the flagpole. As mentioned previously, a college experience can become more intimate simply by associating with other students who share the same pursuits and interests. Thus, if your spiritual sensibilities are strong, you may wish to seek others who share these sensibilities. These religious activities on campus might be great adjunct to any classes on religion you might be taking or plan to take in the future.

Unfortunately, you will not find any chapels or churches on a public college campus. This, as mentioned above, has to do with the constitutional separation between church and state. However, if attending a religious university would make all the difference in the world for you, then perhaps you may wish to transfer to a private university after completing your freshman and sophomore year at a community college. Naturally enough, private universities often sponsor religious activities on campus. In addition, private universities often have a specific religion represented on campus. Thus, if you are a Catholic, a school such as Notre Dame might appeal to you. If you are a Fundamentalist, or Evangelical Christian, Biola University might be more to your liking. It is on these campuses that you will find a church or at least a chapel, and out-and-out religious ceremonies, such as Mass.

The Campus Newspaper

Other student organizations may appeal to your future aspirations. For instance, if you enjoy creative writing and plan to form a career with this ability, you may wish to start an internship of sorts by writing for the college newspaper. By merely contributing essays to the editorial section of your college newspaper, you will be gaining invaluable experience in the fine art of writing. Of course, if you can land a position as a regular staff columnist for the school newspaper, so much the better. Good writing, like any other skill, requires regular practice in order to maintain effectiveness and creativity. Additionally, by writing about different events on campus, you will practice describing unfamiliar subjects in different ways. For instance, a professional newspaper writer must be just as skilled at writing about conflict in the Middle East as he would about a football game between two colleges. In the same vein, writing for a college newspaper will increase the size and scope of your vocabulary. Nothing will help you more in your writing career than to have a strong and solid grasp of the English language. Additionally, the other great benefit of writing for a college newspaper is that you get to socialize with other aspiring writers. As mentioned in regards to the other fields, your college experience will be made much richer as a result of forming these friendships with other students who share your interests and vocational aspirations.

Student Ambassador Programs

Another great opportunity to become involved is to join a student ambassador program. These organizations train young student leaders to become official representatives of their school during cross-campus functions. As with professional organizations such as the United Nations, student ambassadorships carry a certain amount of prestige and visibility during official campus visits.

Normally, these groups are composed of a handful of undergraduates who represent their schools to any faculty or students from other universities, or as ambassadors, they make "official" visits to other campuses and present their schools in the best possible light. These ambassadors may also participate in other campus activities, such as campus tours or open-house festivals. Whatever the exact nature of the functions of student ambassadors, which by their very nature will have different roles and responsibilities from school to school, it is still a good idea for you to become a student ambassador if you wish to hold any type of leadership position in your later career.

Although the process of becoming a student ambassador might be somewhat arduous and competitive, the results are well worth it. First, you will be able to hone your public speaking skills. This is an incredibly valuable skill to have in today's marketplace. It is well know that public speaking is a fear shared by many, and by many accounts, the most difficult to overcome. Once you can master the art of public speaking, many doors will open for you. Secondly, you will gain strong leadership skills. The ability of leaders to move their people or cause forward in a creative manner is what separates great leaders from ordinary individuals. By virtue of the fact that student ambassadors represent an entire university, any time spent serving in that capacity begins to lay the groundwork for future career opportunities where one is called upon to represent an entire organization. Furthermore, due to the

Therefore, as you embark upon the hands-on experiences of your college education, keep in mind all the benefits that you will accrue as a result of participation in student organizations. Often, lifelong friendships result from students' association with campus groups. And, getting involved with the organizations on your campus can help you feel more connected to the campus and students who attend the school.

nature and prestige of their capacities, student ambassadors learn early on about the importance of having to dress, act, and speak in a professional manner. These are all qualities that will become valuable to you in your future career. Lastly, student ambassadors learn the gentle art of negotiation and the skill of diplomacy. In any business environment, there will inevitably be political scenarios which must be handled with care and sensitivity. Student ambassadors learn early on how to be diplomatic. Politics exists everywhere. The earlier you learn this, the better. Knowing how to work with people in order to transact a favorable and mutually agreeable set of conditions is a skill you can take into any career, and it will set you apart as someone with superior social capabilities.

Therefore, as you embark upon the hands-on experiences of your college education, keep in mind all the benefits that you will accrue as a result of participation in student organizations. Often, lifelong friendships result from students' association with campus groups. And, getting involved with the organizations on your campus can help you feel more connected to the campus and students who attend the school. In some cases, you might even find that there are real world applications for what you study in the classroom, simply by being a part of an event that a student group hosts on campus. Lastly, participation in student organizations provides you with experience that you can list on your resume when applying for a job or on a transfer or graduate school admission application. Given the job market today and the competition to gain admission into the top universities, employers and admissions personnel will most likely be overwhelmed with qualified applicants. The fact that you wrote an article on gentrification for the school newspaper, or helped organize an Earth Day celebration, or assisted with a panel discussion following a film screening of a documentary about the plight of workers in Sudan or juveniles in Sri Lanka, just might make you look like the best candidate!

Journal Assignment

Imagine that you are a student on a university campus, but there is no student club or organization that interests you. Then, plan to start your own club or organization and write a brief description of it. What would the name of your club or organization be? What would be its purpose? Its mission? Who would be interested? What shared common interest does it serve? How would you recruit others to join? What sorts of activities would you plan? How would you advertise them?

Chapter Eleven

Social Life in College

Student Learning Outcome:
Students will anticipate challenging social situations and invent a series of recommendations to address those challenges by composing a dialogue in which they advise an imaginary student experiencing social discomfort.

"If you can show me how I can cling to that which is real to me, while teaching me a way into the larger society; then and only then will I drop my defenses and my hostility, and I will sing your praises and help you to make the desert bear fruit."
—Ralph Ellison, author

By far, the most universally appealing aspect of college and university experience is the social life on campus. When you first enroll in college, you likely felt a little nervous, and perhaps lost and confused. This is a normal and natural reaction. However, what made the difference, I am sure, is the fact that you met other students who were equally confused and unsure of their status as well! Once you were able to get your bearings by meeting people, even if they were only the administrative staff telling you which building your classes were in, then you were able to relax a little. If you have not already transferred to a four-year college or university, then you will most likely experience that jolt once again. The transfer from a community, or junior, college to a four-year college or university will be the last major hurtle you will experience on your journey towards a college degree.

Nevertheless, as you settle into your new environment at a community college, try to make friends with as many other students as you can. These may very well be the friendships you maintain for many years. I am still friends with people that I met back when I was a student at my community college. The people you reach out to in the next few semesters may very well be the people you end up knowing for the rest of your life!

160

The Value of Solidarity:
Discovering Your Common Bond with Other Students

There is a tendency in human nature to gravitate towards people sharing a common challenge or struggle, and one challenge is being a little nervous or unsure of a situation. I believe this is why one sees such close camaraderie among soldiers, especially in a combat situation. They are facing a common enemy and are faced with a life-and-death struggle that only their comrades-in-arms can understand. As quoted by Studs Terkel in *"The Good War": An Oral History of World War Two*, a folksinger from the 62nd Artillery explains: "You had fifteen guys who for the first time in their lives were not living in a competitive society. We were in a tribal sort of situation, where we could help each other without fear. I realized it was the absence of phony standards that created the thing I loved about the army." No one else in the outside world can quite grasp what it was like for them to be out there, on the frontline, and face death every day. This only tightens the bond between soldiers. This is why they cry when they lose a friend in battle. The person had become like a brother to him or her. Like soldiers, you too might unite against a common enemy in college, whether it is your difficult instructor, fear of the unknown, or a rival frat house. And, you might unite behind a common goal as well, whether to graduate on the honor roll, or pass the next Geology exam, or survive English 101.

> *We were in college, and we had a common, and singular, goal: to educate ourselves. Therefore, as you continue to enroll and sit in classes, remember that you are part of the student body and have one common goal that practically everyone at the college shares: to get a degree and move on to get well-paying jobs.*

Handling Diversity

While the comparison between a college campus and a theater of war might be a little on the exaggerated side, it does highlight one of the main needs that we humans possess: the need to bond with others who are like us, and with whom we feel a certain connection, regardless of race, creed, religion or national origin. The aim of achieving a college degree and of educating oneself has a universal appeal. In addition, this is why in college one sees students from all types of backgrounds becoming very good friends. When I was in college, I made friends with people from nearly every ethnic group: Middle Eastern, Asian, African American, Anglo-Saxon, Filipina/o and Chicana/o/Latina/o. It did not

161

matter from which country our forebears had emigrated. We were in college, and we had a common and singular goal: to educate ourselves. Therefore, as you continue to enroll and sit in classes, remember that you are part of the student body and have one common goal that practically everyone at the college shares: to get a degree and move on to get well-paying jobs. *This may help to solidify in your mind the commonality which breaks down barriers and unites people in a common and shared vision.* Note similarities as you note differences in others. In the workplace just like in school, you will meet people from all different cultures and countries, of different ethnicities and economic statuses, with different sexual preferences, religious beliefs, musical interests, hobbies, grooming habits, languages spoken, and so on. College is the place to explore, and when you do you will certainly see that while these sorts of differences are exterior and superficial ones, any one person might also share many similarities. Seek out those who are different from you. Understanding how other people think and why they think differently from you can expand your way of thinking—or strengthen your resolve to continue to think the way you think. However, if you only hang out with people who think like you do, act like you do, and so on, then you will be greatly limited in your ability to think because you will never have been challenged, face-to-face, to confront someone who does differ from you. While you may not change your mind, it can be very enlightening to see what other people believe and how they think—and respecting diversity or working with diverse populations are favorite topics for job applications and college application essays. Your experiences with people who are substantially different from you can help you build a solid resume or be a well-rounded applicant in addition to being fun and enriching.

Dealing with the Challenge of Feeling Out-of-Place or Overwhelmed

This is not to say that loneliness and alienation are not a very real part of college life. College can be a time of much loneliness and depression for many students, which may be because they transfer straight from high school to a major four-year college or university without knowing anyone there and feel lonely, vulnerable, and lost. According to the National Institute of Mental Health, common stressors in college life include:

- Greater academic demands
- Being on your own in a new environment
- Changes in family relations
- Financial responsibilities
- Changes in your social life
- Exposure to new people, ideas, and temptations
- Awareness of your sexual identity and orientation
- Preparing for life after graduation

(http://www.nimh.nih.gov/publicat/students.cfm, NIH Publication No. 97-4266)

Academic Demands

Let us examine each of these very real stressors to see how to mitigate them. First, you will undoubtedly have a greater academic course load than the one you were used to in high school. Simply stated, college material and coursework is more difficult. You will have to study more hours and put in more effort than you did in your more carefree days in high school. You will have to write more papers, go on to higher mathematics, and be required to demonstrate strong skills in the English language on your essays. Obviously, you will need to maintain a certain grade point average; otherwise, you will not be allowed to graduate. What all this amounts to is pressure: academic pressure. This can heighten your sense of anxiety and worry during your first few semesters in college. The best way to control this feeling is to pace yourself by not signing up for too many classes in one semester, or putting a limit on the number of hours you are willing to work every semester. As previously mentioned, most college and universities have student tutoring centers, including math labs, reading centers, and tutorials for writing effective term papers. Avail yourself of these free services on campus, as they will mitigate any chances that your time in college will be too stressful or depressing.

Adjusting to a New Environment

The next stressor identified as being of particular relevance to college students is the feeling of being in a new environment. When you first arrived on your campus, you most likely felt, lost, alone, and vulnerable. This is completely understandable. If you continually feel this way, the best way to combat it is to enroll in a college orientation class. Most community colleges offer this course. It consists of an overview of college, the unit and credit system, and an explanation of all the services offered by the college to its students. This class is normally offered by the Counseling department at community colleges. This is a bonus, as you can get to know at least one counselor who works at the college while taking the class.

Getting to know and working with the counselors at your college can go a long way towards allaying anxieties that may arise from being in a new and foreign environment. An invaluable investment of your time will be to make many visits to the counselors at your college. Preferably, however, you should narrow your list down to perhaps two counselors you really favor. This way, if one is out of the office, you can see the other. The feeling of being in a new environment will begin to dissipate as you begin to work more and more with your counselor in figuring out an Educational Plan, or "Ed. Plan," with him or her. Your counselor will be the person who can help keep you focused and free from the normal confusion that students experience the first year or two of college. This is the person who can help you decide whether to pursue an Associate of Arts degree, or an Associate of Science degree, or perhaps whether all you really need in your chosen profession is a career certificate. Of course, many students elect to transfer to four-year colleges and universities, and the Educational Plans are most indispensable in figuring out which classes to take to transfer effectively to your choice of school.

In the event that you do feel alienated, lost, depressed, or upset, talking to instructors or even librarians—anyone from the school who seems approachable—might also help. Counselors are trained in psychology, but some students feel as though seeing a counselor or a health professional for personal or emotional reasons is embarrassing, inappropriate, or stigmatizing. This is not true; however, it is important to seek out help when

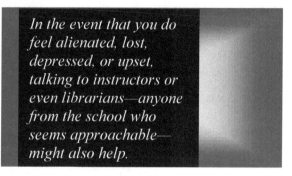

In the event that you do feel alienated, lost, depressed, or upset, talking to instructors or even librarians—anyone from the school who seems approachable—might also help.

you need it. Just like when you need help writing an essay, you might go to the college writing center for help, if you need help with a personal problem, you have a variety of places to turn. Go where you are most comfortable since discussing personal matters is often uncomfortable by itself. If there is someone that you feel you can open up to, that is the person to see. Most instructors and campus employees have been given information on how to handle a crisis and what resources are available on campus and off campus to help students, so you will at least get some sympathy, possibly some tips on how to handle your problems, and a referral to someone who may be able to help you better—most likely from your counseling office. No one likes to see another human being suffering emotionally or in pain over some personal issue. Talking about what is bothering you is the first step toward removing that barrier toward your success.

Family Disruptions

The next stressor named as being a contributor to student stress is a disruption in family relations. While you were in grade school and high school, there was a normal balance in your life between school and home. You spent between six and eight hours at school and came home. There was no doubt a certain comfort to the routine. Now, however, you are an adult. Most likely, you are driving to school. Even if you are using public transportation, such as the bus, which I did, you are nevertheless slowly forming an adult identity. This means that you are slowly becoming more independent from your family. The change in your lifestyle is even more dramatic if you end up living on campus at whatever four-year college or university you decide to attend. This is indeed a disruption.

Although there are undoubtedly many types of disruption and many variegated types of stressors that can occur within a family, the transition to college can represent a very real disruption to, and a dislodging from, a home environment to which you had become attached and from which you had found much comfort. This can be particularly salient for students from ethnic backgrounds where there is a strong emphasis on the family, such as Latino and Asian families. Many parents are also anxious when their son or daughter is ready to leave for college, and many of these parents unconsciously transmit this anxiety to their son or daughter. They may have always been worrisome parents and now have to process this particularly dramatic breaking away from the home, which can then bring on the dreaded "Empty Nest Syndrome." This is no small matter, as this syndrome, in which both the mother and father experience an inner emptiness as a result of their offspring heading off to college, can put a marriage to the test. Many a marriage has weakened at this stage, as both parents realized that they were staying together for the sake of

Therefore, if you feel that you have a need to talk or vent with someone who has the intelligence and education to understand your plight, by all means make an appointment with your counselor and ease your mind by unloading your thoughts with him or her.

the children. If you find yourself able to relate to these family situations, you might want to talk to your counselor. Remember, the counselors at both the community college and at the four-year universities are trained in clinical psychology. Therefore, if you feel that you have a need to talk or vent with someone who has the intelligence and education to understand your plight, by all means make an appointment with your counselor and ease your mind by unloading your thoughts with him or her. One of the big advantages of transferring to a four-year college or university is that those schools have counseling centers. Students can go and have a real one-to-one therapy session with a clinical psychologist. They sometimes also have workshops for students, focusing on such diverse issues as self-esteem, and body-image issues, and so on. Therefore, if you plan to transfer to a four-year school, you may want to avail yourself of those free or low-cost services.

Financial Stress

Your financial responsibilities may also put and undue burden upon your state of mind during your semesters in college. Many students work in addition to taking classes. It is a matter of practical reality for some students. Nevertheless, it may leave its mark upon a student's life, such as leaving him or her with less time to study or to socialize. The reason that this can be a particularly thorny issue is that, as mentioned above, your time in college affords you the best chance to make friends, meet really interesting people of all backgrounds and ages, and have the chance to broaden your horizons simply by meeting other college students. Therefore, if you must work, you may wish to arrange your work schedule so that you are at work more in the afternoons or early evenings, and therefore spend more time on campus during the day, which is when, proportionally, more students attend classes.

Also, look into financial aid. Many eligible students do not apply for the financial aid that would make their lives so much more economically easy. If work is really getting in the way of your educational goals and causing you stress, then clearly that is a problem. While not everyone is eligible for financial aid, many students are, and if you are facing a choice between working more hours at the expense of your grades, perhaps you should consider other options. Far too many students drop out of school due to work, and far too many students feel the necessity to work to provide immediate income to their families without considering the value of their education to their family's future financial well-being. Working excessive hours is often not the best or only solution to financial problems, and your counselor or the Financial Aid Office can help you find out what financial aid is available to you, which can save you a lot of stress.

Exposure to New People and New Ideas

On another front, when you begin college, your ability to spend time with your friends may not change. This will most likely be the case if you are taking classes at a local community college not far from your home. However, if you decide to go to a university which is located very far away from your family and friends, then your social world may be looking very different from what you had become accustomed to during those first few tense semesters. This change is even more dramatic if you are dorming with a roommate on campus. If you do find yourself in this latter category, you may want to telephone your friends whenever time permits as well as sending them e-mails and text messages. They will be very happy to hear from you, their long-lost friend! Additionally, you will feel better if you visit with them on the weekends or over the holidays. Not being able to spend time with friends and loved ones can be a very real source of sadness for college students. You are not alone if you feel this way. However, this is why it is so important that you reach out to your comrades-in-arms at your community college or university. They can never substitute for the friends you left behind at home, but they can certainly become part of a new social world that you can create for yourself. By making new friends as well as staying in touch with your old friends, you will be able to balance your life a little better in college.

A very exciting, but, for some, very intimidating part of going to college is that it will change the way you think. You have grown up with very basic and perhaps very meaningful ideas of right and wrong. We are all raised to believe in certain ideas and certain principles. This is important. They are the very guideposts that allow us to understand the consequences of our actions and that the world does not revolve around us. Below our level of awareness is the underlying belief that our ideas are correct or above challenge. We hold on to our treasured principles all throughout our childhood and into our adolescence. In basic psychology, you will learn more about *schemas*. They are the basic views about life and world that we inhabit which allow us to make sense out of the many mysteries that surround us. However, when you go to college, you will find that you have arrived at a certain point in your life when you will begin to question some of the values on which you were raised. During the course of your studies, you will hear lectures by professors with very different views about life than yours. This is all part of the experience of going to a college or a university. However, it is very important that you not make a habit of arguing with your professors. It is important, as stated several times previously, that you keep an open mind and an open heart when you attend your lectures. If find yourself believing that the professor has missed an important point or has made an uninformed remark, politely raise your hand and when called upon by the professor, respectfully state your views on the matter at hand.

College professors are only human, and it is important that you not expect them always to have the correct answer for every question. Nevertheless, there may be times when the professor will be right, and you will be wrong. This is one of the most humbling of all experiences while in college. The process of checks and balances that takes place within your mind is very subtle. You will arrive on campus, convinced that your worldview is correct and infallible. Your professors, as well as your peers, will challenge your views with their own. You should make the effort to defend your viewpoints by employing the most critical means of creating logical rebuttals and counterarguments to theirs. The other "check and balance" to your budding intellectual prowess is that you need

> *We all create and construct our own "reality" based upon our beliefs, our values, and our sense of certainty. Yet, keep in mind that to different people, depending on who you meet or who you interview, "reality" may take on very different forms and interpretations.*

to really learn to listen to others, especially in a university forum or debate, and attempt to see the world through their eyes. Keep your mind open to different realities. We all create and construct our own "reality" based upon our beliefs, our values, and our sense of certainty. Yet, keep in mind that to different people, depending on whom you meet or whom you interview, "reality" may take on very different forms and interpretations. It may very well be the case that you will approach your commencement day with your views intact or even *more* staunchly cemented in your mind. If so, more power to you. But, the ones who should really be applauded are the ones who arrived on campus with their beliefs, took them off so as to critically examine them and "try on" other beliefs, which were likewise examined critically, and then, after realizing that they did not find the new beliefs to their liking, returned to their original ideals or changed. *My friends, that is the heart and soul of getting a true college education.*

You do not have to abandon your views or your principles. They are guarded by the Constitution of the United States of America. Yet, the only way we grow is to look at all that we were raised to believe, not only about the world, but also about ourselves. You might find that you want to keep some of your beliefs and discard others. This highlights the importance that peers will play in your college education. In the end, our peers challenge us the most, even more than our professors or our textbooks. Make the most of this exciting time of your life by embracing, literally and figuratively, your friends in college. In the end, they will end up teaching you just as much about life and how the universe works as your physics professor does! It will make you a much more well-rounded person if you embrace people of other religions, creeds, and political views.

Relationships

The remaining source of social stress and joy while attending college is, of course, relationships and sex. This will be a time in your life when you will discover a lot about yourself, including your sexuality, and how you relate to the opposite (or same) sex. Some people end up meeting their soul mate. Be happy for them, but do not enter into a competition with them to try accomplishing the same thing. All of us have different experiences when it comes to dating while in college. Therefore, as with your studies, keep an open mind to meeting all kinds of people. You never know what wonderfully romantic entanglements may occur! However, if you do experience a break-up while in college, remember to avail yourself of the free counseling and to surround yourself with your college friends. Most importantly, stay focused on your classes.

Life after College

Lastly, many students worry about life after college. They wonder if they should pursue an advanced degree, or whether they should accumulate some work experience first. Only time will tell. It is a mistake to plan your life too narrowly while in college. Keep an open mind. You may end up changing majors or pursuing a double major! If you are destined to get a master's degree, then the right time will eventually come for you to decide on the best graduate school or the right type of work experience. Do not become too worried about that phase at this point in your education. Enjoy the moment.

However, if you are so inclined, in order to alleviate the stress or discomfort that worrying about advanced degrees might bring you, you can talk to a counselor or do some research into graduate degrees or possible career paths in your major. Often, there are events on campus, like job fairs or college recruitment days, where employers and college representatives come to your campus and have information to distribute about their programs or jobs. These are great ways both to meet people and to get useful information for planning your future. You may not find the perfect school or perfect degree immediately, but just as you carefully planned transferring to a four-year college, you should plan your career path and / or graduate school equally carefully. Some campuses also have a career center, where you can get help and advice researching the job market, or a transfer center, where you can find out about potential schools to transfer to. One of my co-workers, Darren Cifarelli, said, "That moment was really scary. With an English degree, it was Law School, teaching, journalism, or a writing job—but once I figured out what the options were, what each of them required, and what jobs or graduate study paths there were to follow, it became much easier to handle." Taking some of that anxiety and using it to map out possible post-graduate paths and visiting a career center on campus for help, as well as meeting mentors or guest speakers in one's field of interest, can make the future less anxiety-provoking.

Journal Assignments

1. What does diversity mean to you? How would you define diversity? Do you believe diversity contributes to the enrichment of your social and academic experience? Please describe how.

2. Briefly describe an experience you had where you were placed into a situation where you felt you didn't quite fit in and felt out-of-place. Where was it? How did you feel? Why did you feel out-of-place? How were you different from those who did fit it? What skills did you use to cope with the situation? Tell what happened. Then, reflect on either what you did to handle the situation; or reflect on what you would do differently today if you had to go back and relive that same experience, but knowing what you do now. What advice would you give someone who knows that he or she will soon be in an uncomfortable situation, based on your knowledge and experience?

Student Success Profile:

Ayumi Ikemoto

Describe yourself briefly in a short biography (hometown, birthplace, high school experience, family, education).
I was born in Kobe and grew up in Ehime, Japan. My father is a medical doctor, my mother is nurse and counselor, my younger sister is construction monitor, and my youngest sister is a music mixer. I attended a middle and high school combined special program for six years. I had all As, except in Physical Education and Art. My parents used to try to force me to become a medical doctor, but I needed to find my own desire to live my life without their control. It made me want to study in the United States where students can change their majors and minors throughout their college life.

What was your background before coming to community college?
My first community college life at Fulton-Montgomery Community College in New York was all ups and downs due to cultural differences. In Japan, I had never had any chance to express my feelings directly to others. During the first year of

171

my life in the U.S., I needed to challenge myself to open up my mind and speak out in my second language.

What, if anything, prompted your decision to attend community college? What were your goals upon entering community college (why did you go)? Did they change after you started college? If so, how?
The first community college in New York had a connection with a contractor in Japan. I did not know anything about the application process for community colleges in the U.S., and the contractor helped me to start my education globally. I remember that art was only the way that I could express myself more in detail. At that time, I was also interested in Psychology, and my educational goal was to become an art therapist. The word of therapy was still new for people in Japan, and I decided to move to San Francisco and work for a design store to see more possible uses of art. I loved working for the design store, but my deep desire was to help people and improve their quality of life. It made me want to study Nursing. I searched for RN Nursing schools which accept foreign students to apply for the program. Los Angeles Harbor College was my first choice, and I took several required classes to apply for the program. The classes I was taking were beyond my control, and I found out that the quality of instruction in each class is vital for me to understand the medical basics in English. One of my classmates from Harbor College mentioned a really good instructor who taught Anatomy and Physiology at Los Angeles Southwest College. I decided to transfer from Harbor College to Southwest College for better understanding and to make my dream comes true. My college life at LASC was all about studying all day long to become an RN.

Describe your experience as a community college student. What were the highlights? Were there any special programs or extracurricular experiences that were memorable or inspiring?
In New York, people used to see me as a Chinese girl. In San Francisco, they loved joking about my Japanese accent. At LASC, I was the only Asian girl in every classroom. Learning about Black History naturally in English class was a vivid experience for me. I did not know anything about civilization in the 1960s, and reading a book about a man's experiences in West LA and visiting the Southern California Library for Social Studies and Research was the most memorable experience throughout my entire educational life. Black History became more vivid and relevant as I realized the many similarities with history in Japan. I lost myself as I did not know if I was in Hawaii or in Hiroshima. My tears fell on my cheeks and my mind became a mixture of stories of World War II and the real life of people in ethnic minority groups.

How much time went by between high school and community college for you? What were the biggest challenges that you faced when you began attending community college?
I spent two years at community college in New York and three years in Los Angeles. It took me seven years total from high school to transfer to a university.

172

For me as foreign student, trying not to translate in my mind was the biggest challenge when I started to attend the community college.

Did you work while attending community college? If so, how did you balance your time between work and school? Do you have any kids or other family responsibilities? If so, how did you balance your time between home and school? Did you have all three? How did you handle that?
I did not have a working Visa at that time, and I could not work for any companies in the U.S. During my college life in LA, I worked as babysitter for a boy with autism and caregiver for a lady with tumors. I am not good at handling many things at the same time, and I only worked during the summer and the winter time. I wish I could work and study at the same time to reduce my stress by just focusing on studying, but keeping my GPA high enough to apply for the program was my priority. I studied really hard during the regular semesters, and I worked really hard during the summer and the winter.

Community colleges generally have a high attrition rate, meaning a large percentage of students drop out. Why do you think this happens? What motivated you to persevere through college and transfer to a university?
My interests moved in many other directions throughout my community college life. I think it is a good thing, but the process to find out the purpose of education became sometimes clear, but sometimes not clear. If students can find their interests clearly in the courses they attend, they can move forward to make it their life time work. On the other hand, if they do not enjoy any classes and their work means more to them, they tend to drop out. I was accepted to two nursing schools, but my experience in the clinical course was not what I had thought of as nursing. My choice, then, was to go back to Japan or transfer to a university. I did not want to regret my last two years studying at LASC, so I decided to transfer to California State University, Northridge and study Kinesiology. I was not clear on what the major is, but the therapeutic focus was what I was interested in.

Of all the reading assignments you completed in college, which one had the greatest impact on you? What's your favorite book and why?
My most memorable reading assignment was *A Child Called It*. That severely-abused child's experience filled my empty heart; I found similarities in my childhood. Yes, it was stressful to finish reading, but it helped me to understand my past experience and helped me to move forward.

Of all the writing assignments you had in college, which are you most proud of and why?
I think I was proud of writing about the person I am in Public Speech class. Writing a basic sentence was not difficult, but the whole process to make the writing like a story of my life was the biggest challenge for me. I tried to find a way to break things down to explain them clearly.

Attending a college or university can be extremely stressful for many students. Does any particular thing stand out as being the most stressful aspect of going to school? What was it and why was it stressful? What coping skills did you use to overcome stress in order to succeed?
The most stressful thing about going to school was managing all the courses I was taking. When I was taking Anatomy, Physiology, Microbiology and Developmental Psychology in one semester, I could not focus on all the courses. Understanding all the course materials was beyond my memory capacity. My school counselor advised me to drop out of one of them, and after I did, I finally felt comfortable enough to finish the semester. Yes, I was overwhelmed by trying to move too fast.

Many community college students give up when faced with adversity or challenges or barriers. You, however, didn't. What was the biggest challenge you faced and how did you overcome it? What advice would you give to a student who feels like he or she just can't do it, has too much going on in his or her life, or is just struggling academically and feels like maybe college isn't the right place?
In every classroom, I was the only Asian student at LASC. Personally, I do not care about the color of our skin, but some people do. I accepted all the opinions and tried to be open-minded. By not putting up a barrier towards others all the time, I overcame being a minority in college. Many people found similarities in me and became good friends with me. I would say, "Don't be judged, be open-minded and outgoing."

Were there any memorable faculty, counselors, other students, administrators or staff (at your community college or university) with whom you established a rapport and who made a difference? Is establishing relationships with people on campus important? Tell a brief story about someone with whom you became close and who was supportive.
My Kinesiology major instructors at California State University, Northridge were really tight with students. My biggest support in my university life was Dr. Loy Steven. He addressed my need to study Kinesiology at the beginning, and he introduced me to other instructors who were focusing on therapeutic exercise for people with physical disabilities. They are also from Japan, and I could naturally learn life lessons from their courses. I learned how to physically support people with physical disabilities on the land and in water, and how to be a big friend to keep motivating them to move forward. I was student staff at the Center of Achievement. My internship involved supporting water exercise for people with arthritis and was vital hands-on work. I also joined a community program called 100 Citizens to help reduce the rates of child obesity. Throughout my university life, I made connections with my instructors, classmates, clients and many more to enrich my understanding of what I can do to make my life happy.

Courage to Learn **discusses building social capital, meaning developing relationships and skills that are like an investment in your own future. What social capital have you gained since entering community college?**
I learned to open up my mind and express myself in English while I was attending community college. I gained the skill to listen to others and to make them understand who I am. I was always lucky to be surrounded by good people.

What was your social life like in college? How important was it to you personally and educationally?
I gave myself a task to enjoy the classes I was taking. To keep my GPA high enough to apply for Nursing schools, my college life was filled with time to study and for laughs with my friends. Many tutors helped me to find ways to do well in classes, and I also found my way to do my best.

Deciding what university to transfer to is difficult. What factors did you consider when deciding where to apply and where to attend?
It was hard to quit nursing school and transfer to a university. I looked for educational and instructional quality in clinical experience at the university, and CSUN had the best facilities. Nothing, however, was clear until I actually experienced it. I studied hard to be able to support my clients' lives. Their smiles were what motivated me to do the best. Making a good relationship with them and getting much support from instructors and classmates *was* my university life. It was not always easy, but getting the experience was vital to who I am today.

Universities are expensive. Many magazine and newspaper articles highlight the fact that attending a university is an investment that frequently doesn't pay off or isn't worth it. Perhaps you've seen stories about students graduating from various universities under mountains of debt and unable to find jobs. How did you handle the financial burden of attending college and a university? Is it worth it? Are you buried under mountains of debt?
International students need to pay high educational fees. In my country, most parents pay the fee for their children. When their children become their own parent, it is their turn to pay the fee. I think I will be able to pay the fee when it is my turn for my family. It was worth it for me to study abroad by making connections with so many people on the other side of the world. If I had stayed in my country, I do not think that I would have offers from several companies to work with.

If you are working (while still a student or after having graduated), what is that experience like?
When I was working as student internship staff at the Center of Achievement, I really enjoyed working for my clients. I wish it would be my lifetime job. Now, after graduation, I am working for a global company in the field of clinical trials in Japan. It is not easy to say that I enjoy the tasks I do every day. I think I am having an identity crisis due to the cultural difference. Still, I would not have

found out my deep desire to work to improve the quality of our lives if I had not had my university life.

How did you manage the transition from a community college to a university? Did you feel prepared or underprepared? What were the biggest challenges that you faced during the transition?
I was well prepared to transfer to any university. I had not done anything but study all day long at LASC. I really did not know what Kinesiology was before I applied to transfer to CSUN. I simply kept seeing the bright future while transferring. I do appreciate all of the instructors, tutors, and friends at LASC who helped me and motivated me to move forward by supporting me. If I did not spend two years at LASC, my life would be completely different.

What plans for the future do you have (educationally, socially, and professionally)? When and how did those goals emerge?
I am thinking about learning how clinical trials are managed in Japan within five years. After that, I would like to learn how global study is managed in the world.

Looking back, what advice would you give to first year community college students today (i.e. if you could go back in time and talk to yourself on your first day of college, what would you say)?
I would say, "Don't label yourself and make friends to find out what you really like to do."

Chapter Twelve

Reading College Level Textbooks

Student Learning Outcome:
Students will extract and construct meaning from written texts by applying college-level reading strategies to reading samples and reflecting metacognitively on their own awareness and deliberateness as readers must control in order to work effectively through a variety of texts.

"Today a reader, tomorrow a leader"
—Margaret Fuller, Journalist & Women's Rights Activist

Once you reach college, one of things you will discover is that the textbooks you are assigned are thicker, more ponderous, and more difficult to read than the ones you read in high school. College textbooks tend to be quite voluminous. Whereas you might have been able to get away with reading a chapter once and doing well on an exam in high school, in college things are a little different. The books have more chapters, and each chapter will most likely be longer in length. Therefore, you need good study strategies in order to be efficient when you read your books.

Buying Your Books
When you go to your college bookstore to buy the books you will need for your classes, check to see if you can purchase used copies. There is no sense in paying the full and exorbitant price for a college textbook when there are usually good used copies that you can buy for a deep discount. When I was in college, I used a method to obtain the best possible textbook: I would thumb through the pages of all the used copies and obtain the book with the least amount of highlighting in it. This way, I would not get distracted by the highlighting which somebody else had done. We all have different study skills and techniques, and it is up to each one of us to find out what suits us best. However, in your pursuit to find out which study skills work for you, the college textbook which you obtain will need to be as free from notations, highlights and underlining as possible. You will need a "blank slate" textbook in order not to be distracted by somebody else's

style of study. However, you also deserve a textbook which is affordable, and for that reason, I recommend finding a textbook which is as free from markings as possible. These notations from other students can only serve to distract you. Upon encountering these heavily-notated books, you may be tempted to surmise that the student before you had found all the important information in the textbook. You might therefore be tempted to further conclude that you will not need to study that much if you just use somebody else's notations in the margins. However, there are two problems with this approach. First, you may not have the same study techniques or reading techniques that other students prefer. Thus, if the student before you wrote copious notes in the margins, that technique may have worked well for him or her, but it may not be your preferred method of making notations. Perhaps you prefer to use a highlighter. Or, you may prefer to use a notebook. The second problem with this approach is that the chances are remote that you personally know the person who used the book before you. Therefore, how do you know that this person was highlighting or underlining the correct passages in the text? For all you know, this person was barely able to pass the course! You certainly would not want to use the notes made by an unknown student. Besides, you need to demonstrate to yourself that you can read these textbooks without resorting to trickery in order to pass your classes.

Once you find the textbooks you need, check to see if your instructor requires a workbook or supplemental reading material. Don't wait until the first day of class to see if your professor will require the textbook. Even if he or she does not require the textbook, it may still be a good idea to purchase it. The workbook may be a very handy tool to use when preparing for the exam. The other material you may need are other books, which may not be textbooks in the classic sense, but may be required reading nevertheless. Do not resist the idea of buying the supplemental books if they are required. They will ultimately contribute to your overall education. As a matter of fact, these books are sometimes the most enjoyable to read, as they are oftentimes written in a more fluid prose than the regular textbooks.

What to Do with Your Textbooks before the Semester Begins

One you return from your foray to the bookstore to purchase your textbooks, sit down and take a look at them. Try and imagine these books as your friends for the next semester or quarter. First, organize them into several stacks. If you have a desk with sufficient space on top, or a book shelf in your room, or somewhere at home where they will be safe, arrange your textbooks according to your classes. Thus, arrange your Calculus textbook and workbook and graphing calculator into one neat little stack. Next, put your English literature book and any related novels you had to purchase into another stack. Thus, you can begin to organize your books so that you will feel less overwhelmed. It is natural to feel stressed over the amount of reading that you must do in order to pass your classes. However, if you break down the reading assignments into little manageable units, and maintain your materials in an organized way, you will feel less pressure. The students who feel the most stressed are the ones who leave things until the very last minute and are forced to cram. These are also the same ones who are never organized.

As you start to read the first chapter of a textbook, keep in mind two things. First, no authors write in the same manner. Each one will have a different personality, and this will show in the work. I have read textbooks which were written by very witty authors and professors and, believe it or not, I was able to enjoy a good belly laugh now and then. Then again, there were other textbook authors who seemed to have no sense of humor at all. Of course, it also depends on the material. It is a challenge to be funny when describing the mesentery tissue which lies between the small intestines. Nevertheless, if you are fortunate enough to encounter an author with a good sense of humor, consider yourself lucky. The other thing to keep in mind when reading a textbook is that no two subjects are alike. Thus, if you taking Political Science together with Social Psychology, your textbooks will obviously bear little resemblance to each other. Therefore, as you study your texts, one after the other, your mind will have to adjust quickly from one sphere to another. In a sense, this is very good because it keeps your mind flexible as well as stimulated. These are perhaps the two fundamental qualities which your mind should acquire as you progress through college. You need to be able to have the intellectual flexibility to read about diverse topics, and you need to be able to adapt your mind comfortably to each. The other quality about college classes is that they stimulate your mind and cause you to think critically. At the very

Therefore, as you study your texts, one after the other, your mind will have to quickly adjust from one sphere to another. In a sense, this is very good, as it keeps your mind flexible, as well as stimulated.

least, this is what a good college education should give you. However, as with any relationship, it is a two-way street and will require considerable effort on your part as well.

Organize Your Reading: Make a Schedule

Another good way to begin organizing your reading of college textbooks is to break down the reading. Look at your class syllabus. When do you have your first test? Does the first exam cover the first four chapters? Will your professor want you to skip the third chapter for the exam? For this reason, I recommend that you not begin reading your texts until after you have attended the first class and received the class syllabus. Even after you receive the syllabus, the professor will often state that there are corrections to be made on it. Thus, you have to be clear on what it is, exactly, that you must read for the exams. After you return home, go to your textbooks and look at the chapters which will be covered on the exam.

Take note of how many pages each chapter contains. Then, on a blank sheet of paper, break down how long it will take you to read each chapter. For example, if your first exam in Political Science will comprise the first four chapters of the text, and each chapter is roughly thirty pages long, then you have roughly 120 pages worth of reading to do! This is no easy task to accomplish. For this reason, you have to know your own study preferences as well as speed. Some students can read a little faster than others. Others might need a little more time. There is no right or wrong when it comes to reading speed and study skills. Your only concern is to be able to do well on the exams. If you have a month before the exam, then it means you have four weeks to prepare. You can read a chapter a week. If each chapter is thirty pages long, and you have a week to read each one, then give yourself five days a week to read six pages a day. That is quite reasonable. Below is an illustration.

Political Science 101

Week One – Chapter One (Pages 1-30 of textbook)
- Monday –Read pages 1-6
- Tuesday – Read pages 7-12
- Wednesday –Read pages 13-18
- Thursday – Read pages 19-24
- Friday – Read 25-30
- **Saturday – Review pages 1-15**
- **Sunday – Review pages 16-30**

Week Two – Chapter Two   (Pages 31-60 of textbook)
- Monday –Read pages 31-36
- Tuesday – Read pages 37-42
- Wednesday –Read pages 43-48
- Thursday – Read pages 49-54
- Friday – Read 55-60
- **Saturday – Review pages 31-45**
- **Sunday – Review pages 46-60**

Week Three – Chapter Three   (Pages 61-90 of textbook)
- Monday –Read pages 61-66
- Tuesday – Read pages 67-72
- Wednesday –Read pages 73-78
- Thursday – Read pages 79-84
- Friday – Read 85-90
- **Saturday – Review pages 61-75**
- **Sunday – Review pages 76-90**

Week Four – Chapter Four   (Pages 91-120 of textbook)
- Monday –Read pages 91-96
- Tuesday – Read pages 97-102

- Wednesday –Read pages 103-108
- Thursday – Read pages 109-114
- Friday – Read 115-120
- **Saturday – Review pages 91-105**
- **Sunday – Review pages 106-120**

Using this method, you will be less anxious over the amount of reading you have to do. Break the assignments and reading lists down for every class. By avoiding cramming, which is the dreaded and commonly used method of study, you will be able to keep the information longer in your memory. When you cram, you have to stuff a lot of information down into your short-term memory and then regurgitate it on the exam. First if all, that is a very stressful way to study. Life can be stressful enough as it is; why would you want to add more of it to your life? Of

> *Break the assignments and reading lists down for every class. By avoiding cramming, which is the dreaded and commonly used method of study, you will be able to keep the information longer in your memory. When you cram, you have to stuff a lot of information down into your short-term memory and then regurgitate it on the exam.*

course, the excuse that students probably use is that some unforeseen circumstances got in the way of studying properly for the exam. If you have special circumstances which prevent you from studying according to schedule, do not stress over it. Simply make a new schedule in pencil, thereby allowing you to make further corrections if need be. We are all victims of circumstances. Life, as they say, gets in the way. There will be times when your car or your bicycle will break down or develop a flat tire. Do not despair. What was mentioned earlier about mental and intellectual flexibility should be applied to these circumstances as well. You need to have the adaptability to attend to these circumstances gracefully. The only thing that I recommend you do later is to modify your study schedule. By doing this, you keep yourself organized. Of course, this will mean that your reading load per day will increase. Merely forgo some of your usually pastimes, such as spending time on the Internet, if you find yourself in this situation.

Study Breaks & Index Cards
There are other techniques which I recommend that you use. After you have read your allotment of pages per day, get up and do something physical. Go

181

outside and get some fresh air. Then, come back inside and look over the pages again. Find words that are in bold. Either highlight these words or write them down in a notebook. Do not delude yourself into thinking that merely by memorizing the highlighted words that you will be able to do well on the exam. The words which are in bold are merely intended to introduce a topic or a concept, nothing more. Another good idea is to purchase a supply of blank 3 x 5 inch index cards which you can use as flash cards. Take one of the cards and label it with the chapter or subject heading. Then, as you read and re-read the chapters, write down the words that are in bold on your blank cards. In this way, when you are done reading the chapter, you will already have a handy set of flash cards ready to use for your review and preparation for the exam.

Highlighting

One of the trickiest study skills to master is the art of highlighting. As mentioned earlier, your task of studying will be made much easier if you have purchased a book which is relatively free of highlights. As you read the chapters, keep a keen eye on information which may be on the exam. This also underscores the need to pay close attention to the lectures in class. Many professors will be very explicit in telling their students what to expect on the exam. Others are a little more cryptic in their disclosures of potential text questions. Therefore, keep your "radar" on while you are in class, and listen for the hints that are often dropped by professors. Later, when you read your textbook, you will need to read on two levels. The first level involves reading for the sake of learning and gaining knowledge as well as questioning the text or engaging in a dialogue with it. That is very important. The second level will involve reading for potential test questions. The ability to read on these two levels simultaneously is a skill that definitely takes time to master.

Critical Reading Strategies: SQ3R

A well-worn technique used by many students is the famous SQ3R. In case you were not taught this either in elementary school or high school, I shall illustrate it here. This combination of a number and letters is short for: Survey, Question, Read, Recite, and Review. The number 3 represents the three "R" s (Read, Recite, Review) in the technique. The first letter, S, represents surveying. Look over the material in the chapter or assignment. Skim over it, and notice the key concepts and any illustrations or graphs. As mentioned previously, keep an eye for words or concepts which are in bold. Many textbooks are well organized and place the important concepts and vocabulary in the margins. Survey the chapter by reading through it rather lightly, as if you were reading a pamphlet or the morning newspaper.

Next, question the material (Q). Formulate questions in your mind. Pretend that you are the professor and that you will have to answer your own questions. They say that the best way to learn is by teaching. If this is true, and I believe it is, then you should write down your question, either in your class notebook or in the margins of your textbook. Ask the questions you might be asking in class. Think of as many questions as you can regarding the material, both before as well as during the time you are reading it.

After you have questioned the material, then read (R) it—closely. As you read the information, keep in mind the questions you formulated during your questioning phase of study. Try to answer all of these questions. Although writing your questions in the margins of the textbook is a good idea, you may want to rewrite the questions on a separate piece of paper. Therefore, when you read the book and find the answers to your own questions, you can write the answers directly below the questions. No one can explain a concept better to you than you can, so write your answers to your questions in a way that makes sense.

The next technique, recite (R), involves reciting the material in your mind. Find the most relevant or important information from each chapter and jot it down. Make flashcards, lists, or whatever notation you find most comfortable. Then, practice memorizing the words or equations as often as you can. Say a word ten times aloud, consecutively, until it sticks in your memory. Find any technique for memorization and recitation which suits you. You may find that in order to memorize a word, concept, or math formula, you may need to recite over several days. Tape the flashcards to your bathroom mirror, especially as the exam draws near.

As with music, some students love to have a cup of coffee by their side while they study, and others avoid all caffeinated beverages as it makes them too jittery. All of this underscores the process of self-discovery which occurs in college. Enjoy the journey of getting to understand yourself.

The final tool, review (R), involves going over again and again the material which you have read. Look it over and try to see if there are any loose ends in your comprehension level of the concepts. You may find that in any given chapter, there will some key portions which are more difficult to understand than the others. If your textbooks have chapter subheadings, look at these and review only the portions of the chapters which were difficult for you to understand. There may be times when you do not need to re-read every chapter but only certain challenging sections. Most textbooks have review sections at the back of each chapter. Use these tools as part of your review process. Try not to write the answers to the end-of-chapter review sections in your book since it is a good idea to test your knowledge several times over the semester with those questions. If you see the answers that you have written down in the textbook every time you review, then your memory is not getting the workout it needs to properly store and retrieve the data. Use a blank notebook and write your answers in it; then check your answers in the back of the book, if given. If you managed to answer most the questions correctly, then it means that you have a good grasp of the material. If your answers were very different from the correct responses, then it means that you will probably have to review the material more thoroughly.

Finally, do not rush through reading your chapters. It may be a beautiful day outside, but there will be plenty of other sunny days in the future. Also, keep in mind that students are different in the way their brains absorb information. There are some students whose minds are able to integrate information while they blast AC/DC on their iPods. Others require sheer silence in order to concentrate. You may want to experiment and find which modality suits your needs. However, I would recommend that you avoid studying in front of the television. Set aside a part of your home or dorm room and designate it for nothing but study. As for caffeine, you may want to likewise test your own preference and body chemistry to see if you respond to it. As with music, some students love to have a cup of coffee by their side while they study, and others avoid all caffeinated beverages as it makes them too jittery. All of this underscores the process of self-discovery which occurs in college. Enjoy the journey of getting to understand yourself.

Journal Assignment

Make a list of five books, articles, poems, or song lyrics that have impacted you the most in your reading. They can be on your list because they inspired you, made you feel excited or depressed, were easy to relate to, or just seemed so true, deep, and insightful that you couldn't forget them. Then, pick one that you want to write about and describe: 1) What it was about. 2) What about it had a great impact on you. 3) Why you think it had such a great impact on you. 4) How you managed to remember it (i.e. Why did it stick with you?).

Chapter Thirteen

Writing College Level Papers

Student Learning Outcome:
Students will apply a writing process that incorporates college-level writing strategies to demonstrate fluency with different modes of writing by revising a journal entry into a formal essay and reflecting metacognitively on the impact of the revisions.

"...some writers live and write in isolation. [Author] Maya [Angelou] may go off to a hotel, or to some room and write, but her connection with the world does not stop. She's always writing from that perspective. The self in relationship to others. The self in relationship to self. Also, in relationship to other people and other views, other philosophies, other ways of seeing...There is something about humanity at large that Maya reflects in her vision of the world and others."
—Dolly A. McPherson, Professor of English Studies

One of the most important skills that you will need to have upon entering college is the ability to write effectively. The ability to write strong and concise term papers is one of the fundamental abilities required of a college student. Ideally, your years of writing term papers in high school will have prepared you for the rigors of writing papers in college. When you compose a term paper, its very heart and soul will begin with its basic premise. Most papers will fall into two rough categories: persuasive, or argumentative papers; and expository, or informative papers. In the first category, students will typically try to persuade the reader of a particular notion or opinion. In the second category, the term paper is written to give a broad overview of a person, event, or other subject.

Thesis Statements
Central to the effectiveness of your paper will be your thesis. The thesis is the basic argumentative position that you will take in the formulation of your position. The key to an effective thesis is to be as specific as possible.

Step one in developing your thesis—the main idea of your argument, or your position—will be to narrow your term paper subject to a particular topic. Hopefully, your professors will give you some latitude on the type of topics available to you, from which you can formulate your stance. Of course, part of the process of developing your critical thinking faculties in college will be to develop the ability to take a position that you would not normally take in real life.

> *The thesis is the basic argumentative position that you will take in the formulation of your position. The key to an effective thesis is to be as specific as possible.*

Therefore, if anything, you should welcome the opportunity to write a persuasive essay on a topic which may run contrary to your own personal views of life or your own values. An example of this might be to take a position on a "hot topic" such as abortion, gay marriage, or capital punishment. As often as possible, try to see the world from a different perspective in your term papers; in other words, research all sides of the issue. This is not a call for you to abandon your principles, but rather for you to develop the capacity for mental flexibility.

The second point to keep in mind when formulating your thesis is that your argument will not or cannot be based upon personal evaluative opinion. Thus, for example, you should not state that "Communism is better than Fascism." Rather, your position must come from your research into the topic; therefore, instead of the above example, you might very well write, "The economic viability of Mainland China has shown greater internal and external stability than the temporary and slighter economic growth of Fascist states in the early twentieth century." Be careful, however, as your thesis should avoid being a mere regurgitation of what your researchers highlighted. Rather, your statement must be an original line of thought which is substantiated by the research. A strong argumentative thesis asserts a point—rather than merely stating a fact—which requires an essay to back it up. The rest of the essay, then, serves that purpose: to support the assertion made in the thesis statement.

A third point to remember is that you need to be absolutely clear about your position. It is probably a safe bet to say that most student papers fall on the side of being too general or too nebulous, and therefore leave little room to make a strong and persuasive argument, so avoid being too broad. If we take the above examples into consideration, we can narrow them down even more. For instance, an even more precise thesis might be, "The strict measures of control exerted by the Chinese government on the importation and exportation of goods and services as well as upon wages and prices has demonstrated a more effective economic viability than that shown by the Fascist governments of Italy or Germany in the 1930s."

Also, keep in mind how much room you will have to maneuver. This refers to the length of your paper. If your instructor assigns you a paper that is only five pages long, then you do not have to exert any unnecessary mental effort in concocting a super-duper thesis requiring ten books to substantiate as well as countless hours of research. But, if your professor assigns you a ten page paper, then you may very well need to formulate a thesis like the one in the above example. Another point to remember is that your thesis should be structured in such a way that it can be properly refuted. You will be marked down if your paper set out to prove a point with which most people agree. There is no argument there: seek out controversy, a position with which two reasonable people might disagree. So, to continue with our example, most people would agree with the statement "China has developed very strong economic policies in the preceding decade." Therefore, there is very little room to maneuver if one wishes to develop an effective counterargument. If there is no disagreement possible because this example is a statement of a fairly straightforward and obvious fact, then the essay that backs it up will be similarly obvious and boring. However, since in the penultimate example we contrasted the superpower China with a historical superpower, Nazi Germany, there we have more latitude for counter arguments. Additionally, contrasting Communistic economic policies with economics of Nazism stirs a controversy as it involves politics as well. This is what will make your assignment more enjoyable and interesting, as it will most likely stimulate discussion in the classroom and with your professor.

A final point to remember is that your thesis should contain within it the general framework of your argument. Look at the example: "The strict measures of control exerted by the Chinese government on the importation and exportation of goods and services as well as upon wages and prices have demonstrated a more effective economic viability than that shown by the Fascist governments of Italy or Germany in the 1930s." Note that the subcomponents of our economic argument entail positions on imports and exports, and wage and price controls, all of which have created economic and political controversy. Use this breakdown of your argument to help create a structured outline for the rest of your essay.

> *A final point to remember is that your thesis should contain within it the general framework of your argument.*

Introduction Paragraphs

Once you have developed your thesis, your next phase will be to develop a strong introduction. With your introduction, you will be accomplishing two purposes. Firstly, the introduction will serve as a good lead-in. This will capture the attention of the reader. Much like a catchy song or television commercial, your introduction will serve to promote a bit of salesmanship. Try to be as creative and imaginative as possible in designing and creating your introduction. Secondly, the introduction will contain within it your goal in writing this paper. In other words, what are you setting out to say or to prove? The reasoning behind your thesis should be made evident in your first paragraph. Do not concern yourself with the eventual "proof" of your thesis in your introduction paragraph. Many writers have used any one of these three categories of openings for their introductory paragraphs: an opening question, an anecdote, or a quotation.

An opening question, commonly known as a "poser," challenges readers to ponder a topic of interest, or even disinterest, by stimulating their thought patterns through a simple query. For instance, if you are writing a paper on environmental degradation, or the destruction of the rainforest, you might ask an opening question such as, "What would our world be like without any paper?" In this instance, the purpose of your opening question is to get readers to imagine themselves living in a world without one of our most basic commodities, paper and paper goods. Some environmentalists have suggested that we may indeed be heading in that direction, and that some basic items such as books and magazines may one day disappear. Therefore, a good opening question will quickly capture the reader's attention, set the mood or tone for the rest of the essay, and stimulate thought and discussion about the topic.

The second type of opening that has been used often is the anecdote. The anecdote in this case is merely some small historical incident or a brief story, which is presented at the very top of the paper and is itself the lead-in. This could be something that happened to you or someone you know, or perhaps something you read about or heard about which caught your attention. There should some sort of a tie-in to the rest of the paper. In keeping with the above example, you could open up the paper with a brief incident which relates to the environment such as an interesting moment on a beach clean-up day, or perhaps a story you read about the Brazilian rainforest. Avoid making the anecdote too long, lest you begin writing excessively about the topic upon which the anecdote is based. The anecdote should only be a brief opener, no more than a paragraph in length.

The third tool with which to open an essay is the quotation. This can be a very powerful and beautifully simple method of capturing your readers' attention. Thus in keeping with our example, you may want to find a quote from the Minister of the Interior of Brazil or perhaps a world famous environmentalist. It is a good idea to document in your References section, or on your Works Cited page, the person or source from which you borrowed the quote. This allows the reader to reference this source if he or she wishes to read more about the topic. For instance, if your term paper opens with a quote from Ralph Nader and it can be found in one of his books, then by all means, list the book in the References page(s) so that the reader can later read more about Ralph Nader and his work.

Following your opening device, fill your introduction paragraph with needed definitions of terms that may be unfamiliar to your readers, any necessary background information, a brief overview of your argument, and your thesis. Think of your opening paragraph like the preview to an upcoming film. In a short period of time, you want to get your readers' attention, make them want to read the essay, provide them with enough information to have a sense of what the essay will be about, and have an adequate context to understand the rest of the essay. This first paragraph, just like a film preview, is what your readers will most likely use to decide whether or not your essay is worthwhile: your instructor's judgment is strongly impacted by this first paragraph, so make sure it's great.

Topic Sentences

As you know, most papers will have three main sections: The introduction, the body, and the conclusion. In the first part of the paper, as mentioned above, you outline your thesis or central argument and weave it into the introductory paragraph. The next portion of the term paper, the body, is where the bulk of the material will be presented. As you construct the body of your paper, there will be several points to remember. First, it is a good idea to open each paragraph with a topic sentence. The topic sentence will introduce the subject of the paragraph and relate it back to your thesis statement. Each of these topic sentences can be a subcomponent of your thesis. Yet, if you must write a very long paper, each paragraph might be opened by topic sentences that relate to only one aspect of your thesis. Each topic sentence should contain an original line of thought; in other words, try to avoid statements based on fact in your opening arguments. So the body of your paper on deforestation might have a topic sentence such as "The Brazilian government's efforts to contain deforestation have not been as strong as they should have during the past three decades." Notice that we are not stating the obvious, such as, "The Brazilian government has taken certain steps to contain deforestation." That is too obvious; there is nothing to argue. We are not told anything evaluative with that remark. However, by writing "The Brazilian government's efforts to contain deforestation have not been as strong as they should have during the past three decades," you are stating your opinion that the efforts of the Brazilian government have been weak, or at least not as responsive as they should have been in stemming the tide of deforestation. Each topic sentence should be one of the "legs" upon which your thesis rests. In other words, each topic sentence, in the body of the term paper, should do an effective job of making the case for your thesis and providing *non-repetitive* points, which will provide for a solid argument.

Locating Support: Close Reading

As you fish for material to use in formulating your thesis along with its requisite supportive components, you may want to keep several of the following techniques in mind. First, as you read the sources you will be using, or are considering using, practice the technique of close reading. Close reading is a very effective technique in evaluating a potential source of material. You are reading closely. By closely, I mean *very carefully*. If you have found a book on deforestation, you may want to read it through cursorily in order to get the gist of its meaning. This should take you no more than several days. Do not get bogged down by reading every single word. Then, when you begin your close reading, you can go back and read it a second time, only this time you will be searching closely for very specific points of information. You may want to use color-coded page markers, like Post-It notes, and colored markers to highlight points which you feel you will need in your paper. As you do a close reading, continually ask questions of the book or the article you are reading. Do you disagree with the author, if so, why? Do you find yourself in agreement with some points and not with others? Why? Reading should be a dialogue between you, the reader, and the author, the writer.

Constructing Support: Synthesizing Information

After you have completed your close readings, you will want to begin synthesizing the information in such a way that you can begin to construct the paragraphs for the body of the text, each of which will be spearheaded by effective topic sentences. Most likely, you will write your paper in sequence, especially if the length is not very burdensome. Therefore, as you write each topic sentence, you may want to have the following rule of thumb in mind: for each sentence that contains basic facts, you should provide three sentences of your own personal analysis. In other words, maintain a ratio of 3 to 1. However, always keep in mind that you should be as clear as possible with each and every sentence, so that you do not lose your reader and make him or her become confused. One good way to provide each of the three analytical sentences for every one sentence based on fact is to go back to your notes that you made in your close readings. That is, go back to those original questions and ask yourself, again, why you did not agree with the author, or why you felt his argument was weak. Then, go back and integrate these points into your supporting sentences beneath each opening topic sentence in the paragraphs of the paper's body. The more carefully and thoughtfully that you have read, the more material you will have available to build and develop your paragraphs.

Structuring the Body of Your Essay

Yet another tip for you to have a dynamic paper is for you to structure the ideas within the paragraph so that they form a coherent idea rather than merely following the list of books you are using as resources. Think: What idea is my reader supposed to walk away with at the end of this paragraph? At the end of this essay? Ask yourself this question continuously as you develop your paper. Each sentence in every paragraph and each paragraph on every page should be part of the formation, defense, and conclusion of an effective essay. In keeping with this framework, ensure that there is a smooth flow to how you present information. Each new paragraph should reveal additional information that allows the central idea of the paper to become ever more specific and convincing to the reader.

One good way to ensure a strong directional flow in the presentation of ideas in the paper is to use transitional expressions to open up each new paragraph. Examples of this would be: "A useful illustration of this is ..."; or, "A prime example of this type of situation is ..."; or, "This has been manifest in the following ways..."; so keep these types of phrases in mind to ensure an adequate flow and to make these expressions into the mortar between the paragraphs which are, in the end, the "bricks" of your "edifice." And, choose the transitional phrases you use in topic sentences (as well as in sentences throughout your essay) that help show the relationship between ideas from one sentence or paragraph to the next. For instance, the phrase *for instance* introduces an example. The word *therefore* signals that a conclusion follows. *As a result* indicates that an outcome will follow. Using a variety of transitional phrases, long and short, will greatly improve the flow of your writing and guide your reader through the logic of your argument, so that each idea you introduce is clearly connected to the ones that precede it and those that follow.

Sentence Variety

As often as you can, maintain variety in your methods of expression. Try to avoid a litany of plain-sounding, dull sentences so as not to bore your readers to tears. Furthermore, as you complete a rough draft of your paper, test the stylistic cadence of the work by reading it to a friend. If you feel too self-conscious to read it to somebody, then do the opposite and have someone read it aloud to you. Nothing can be as effective as hearing your own composition being read out loud. This will give you the opportunity to listen to your sentence

> *As often as you can, maintain variety in your methods of expression. Try to avoid a litany of plain-sounding, dull sentences so as not to bore your readers to tears.*

structures as well as your chosen vocabulary, and it will ultimately help you decide if your paper needs revision. Your rough draft is merely that, a draft or prototype, and will most likely be undergoing a series of modifications with additions and deletions. As you go through the process of fine tuning your paper, it may help to allow a day to pass and for you to focus on other subjects so that when you return to revise your rough draft, you will see it with a fresh pair of eyes. Nothing can assist the creative process as much as time away from a project to be able to return to it with new ideas for its development.

The following four specific tips will dramatically improve your writing:

1. Use a variety of sentence structures. Varying sentence style and structure can reduce repetition and add emphasis. Long sentences work well for incorporating a lot of information, and short sentences can often maximize crucial points and enable effective emphasis.

2. Vary sentence openings. If too many sentences start with the same word, especially "The," "It," "This," or "I," reading can become tedious for readers, so changing opening words and phrases can be refreshing. Here are two examples:

- **Example 1:** I went to the beach on my day off from work. I saw that there were some huge waves. I feared that a storm was going to hit the beach. The clouds parted after awhile. I ate lunch. I swam. I got nauseous, though, and I had to leave sooner than I wanted to. I had a good time, but I wish that I had been able to stay longer.

- **Example 2:** On my day off from work, I went to the beach. Seeing the huge waves, I feared that a storm was going to hit the beach. Shortly after I ate lunch, the clouds parted, so I swam. However, I got nauseous and had to leave sooner than I wanted to. Overall, I had a good time, but I wish that I had been able to stay longer.

Example 2, while not great, is better than Example 1 because it is less repetitious and has a better variety of sentence openings; thus, it flows better.

- **Tip:** Especially avoid sentences that begin "There is...", "There are...", "There was...", and "There were...". Those are weak constructions. Instead of "There was no school last Thursday," try "The college president closed the school because it was raining so hard last Thursday." The second example avoids use of the weak construction "There was" and provides a more detailed description of the action taking place. It describes an agent—someone doing something.

3. Use action verbs rather than linking verbs. Linking verbs are the forms of the verb *to be* (am, is, are, was, were, be, been, being). They don't add much meaning to a sentence but just link the subject to the rest of the sentence. Action verbs describe something happening—an action taking place—so they add drama and excitement to sentences. For example, "He is tall" contains a linking verb (*is*) that adds nothing to the sentence. "He towers over me" contains an action verb (*towers*) which describes something happening. Action verbs have a greater impact on your reader because they provide a description of something happening that your reader can imagine.

4. Use transitions. Transitional phrases—like *for example, later on in the day, more importantly, therefore, as a result, subsequently, in addition*, and *above the skyscraper*—each help to establish a relationship in writing to the words that come before and after them. So, well-placed transitions help organize ideas by signaling to your reader that: an example follows, time has passed, an even more important point follows, a conclusion follows, a result follows, that you've moved on to a new point, that your adding a new point to the previous one, or that you are describing a slightly different location.

A Note on Style

There may be times when you might need longer sentences in order to create the right and proper flow to a train of thought. This may be the case more with term papers assigned in English or a Literature course, where a certain lyricism is needed to complete a train of thought. However, the trend in the social sciences, such as Psychology, tends to be more in the opposite direction: less is more. Within these disciplines, you may be expected to produce equally long papers, yet with shorter sentences. The reason for this is that you will be training to think more like a scientist by presenting only the facts that are relevant to your paper and keeping personal narrative to its absolute minimum. This is made even more complex by the fact that you will come to use different manuals for writing term papers in varied fields. For example, Psychology majors eventually must abide by the APA guidelines set forth by

In any case, the staff at your campus's writing center are experts in writing essays in all disciplines, and they can be of great assistance for you at all stages of the writing process.

the American Psychological Association in its manual for publication of written works. Those who are majoring in English or Literature most likely will have to become familiar with the MLA style and publication requirements of the Modern Language Association. It is a good idea to go to the library and to look up the latest editions of these manuals so as to become familiar with the rules and guidelines which they have established for certain aspects of writing a term paper, such as citations and references. It is best to buy one good style manual that has both APA and MLA styles in it; most, but not all, writing manuals sold in your college's bookstore will, but check for these important sections before you make an investment.

Furthermore, these manuals change every year, but these stylistic guidelines can also be found on the Internet (and sites like www.citationmachine.net can help generate the citations). However, the websites containing these grammar and stylistic guidelines are a poor substitute for the actual manual itself, either APA or MLA, as these books are as thorough as anyone could possibly need for the completion and even publication of a paper. Website listings are frequently short, with too much information left out. Almost every college website has a page on documentation, usually accessible from the campus library's home page; however, there are many, many variations in each type of citation, so consulting a manual that lists every single variation is the most effective way to ensure that your Works Cited or References page is 100% accurate.

Finally, most colleges and universities have writing labs or writing centers set up by the English department and staffed by tutors or English faculty. In any case, the staff at your campus's writing center are experts in writing essays in all disciplines, and they can be of great assistance for you at all stages of the writing process. While time is always in short supply, a single visit to a writing lab—possibly 30 minutes of your time—per essay can often improve your grade from a B to an A. Writing center staff can help at any stage in the writing process, even before you have started writing. You can bring your assignment to the lab, and the staff will help you brainstorm possible ideas for your topic. Or, they can read your essay and make suggestions on how you can improve it with additional examples or counterarguments, or a more effective conclusion, or better style for a stronger impact to your readers. Most writing center staff won't proofread your essay line-by-line, so don't expect that, but they will make good suggestions on how you can strengthen it. The help that you receive there is free, and you will

Be patient with yourself as you begin your journey of writing a paper in college. Writing effective papers is both, a science, and an art.

get some useful information to improve your writing, so it is well worth the time to go to the writing center and get the extra suggestions to boost your grade.

Be patient with yourself as you begin your journey of writing a paper in college. Writing effective papers is both a science and an art. Use the red ink marks, hopefully not applied in great quantities, on your paper as guideposts from which you can learn valuable ideas. All of the feedback and even low grades that you receive on your papers will become invaluable advice that you can use throughout your college and professional career.

Journal Assignment

Practice writing and revision. Take one of your previous journal entries (or compose a new one for this assignment, like "Describe the biggest challenge you face in writing") and go back over it, using the tips and suggestions from this chapter on improving your writing style. It might be fun or interesting to look back at your earliest writing from this class, like the journal entries from the Introduction or Chapter 1. Then, revise your writing so that it contains a strong thesis (or topic sentence for a paragraph), plenty of relevant support, stylistic variety (varied sentence structures and sentence openings, action verbs, and transitions), and a strong final point. Compare the two versions of your writing and note what changes made the most difference in creating a strong impact on your reader.

Chapter Fourteen

Overcoming Math Anxiety

Student Learning Outcome:
Students will reflect metacognitively on strengths and weaknesses in mathematics by writing a narrative which identifies and targets strategic areas for growth and improvement while maintaining areas of strength.

"And do you not know also that although they [mathematicians] make use of the visible forms and reason about them, they are thinking not of these, but of the ideals which they resemble...they are really seeking to behold the things themselves, which can be seen only with the eye of the mind?"
—Plato, philosopher

    Math, more than any other discipline, is responsible for students' failure to succeed in community college. Countless students are successful in all their other classes but get stuck in the math course sequence and are unable to graduate or transfer, so math requires special attention. Math requires a different mode of thinking than many other disciplines. It is less about your opinion than it is about using formulas and patterns and applying them in appropriate situations.

    This mode of thinking is used not only in math but also in criminal profiling, law, civics, and most of the sciences. Problem-solving, by itself, is a key aspect of virtually every discipline and major. Math uses creative thinking in the sense that you have to creatively decide what formula or pattern fits a given situation or context. Many students who are successful in math are able to visualize problems and how to solve them. Imagining concepts simply means to create mental representations for mathematical expressions.

    Mathematics and cognition (or thinking) go hand in hand. Math uses a type of thinking called "dual coding"—thinking with numbers, imagery and language. Dual coding in math requires two aspects of this type of thinking: imagining symbols and numbers; and imagining concepts to see the relationships of the parts to the whole. Visualizing numbers and symbols simply means to see the numeral "2" as representing the concept of two.

    Furthermore, it also requires a lot of studying and time spent outside of the classroom beyond doing homework exercises to study and practice. Math is a

197

skill that needs to be developed and refined in order to be learned. Many students are not successful in math because they don't take the appropriate amount of time to study it and practice it; others, on the other hand, have had negative past experiences with math and experience anxiety when taking math courses in community college.

Tips for Success

Here are some tips on how to succeed in math:

- Choose an instructor whom you understand and feel comfortable with.
- Choose a section of math that meets at a time when you are alert and relaxed.
- Sit in or near the front row so as to optimize your attention.
- When choosing a math course, be sure that it is the one required for your major and/or that it will transfer.

There is a natural progression in the study of math: each course builds on the previous course; each lesson builds on previous lesson. You must master the foundational skills before moving on to the next course. You are doing yourself a disservice—wasting effort, time, and money—if you sign up for a course without having successfully met the prerequisites or mastering the earlier concepts. Similarly, missing a lesson or skipping a chapter in a math course does the same disservice within each individual class. There's nothing wrong with dropping a course in which you feel you may get a low grade or fail. It is better to retake the course later when there's a better chance to succeed. Some students have a natural talent for math but most don't. What you lack in talent, you can make up for with hard work and study. Self-discipline, motivation, and a sense of responsibility are essential for high achievement in math.

In a math course, set your level of ambition and expectations high: aim for 100%, not merely a passing grade. Also, try to stay *ahead* of the class instead of just keeping up. Once you get behind, your obstacles may become insurmountable. Avoid large time gaps between math courses, or at least brush up well on material from prerequisite courses that you need to know before signing up for a class. Keep the notes and textbooks from all your math courses until you are finished with the entire sequence. You may need to revisit them when taking a more advanced level course.

If you have been consistently failing the regular tests, it is very unlikely that you will offset this by acing the final. Over-optimism can be your worst enemy, but practice and study time is the crucial key to success. Many other disciplines are easier to catch up in if you fall behind or miss a class, but math does not lend itself well to sporadic study. Learn to take responsibility and not make excuses or blame others. The grade you get is the grade you earn.

How to Study for Math

Use the "rule of three": for each hour of class, you should plan to study *at least three solid hours per week by yourself,* the actual time required depending on your abilities. While this rule applies to all disciplines, it is vital in math. This means for a 5 unit math class that meets 5 hours per week, you should study 15 hours per week consistently. (This is *a lot* of study time, so you should plan to take your math courses during a semester where your other classes are not burdensome.)

The following sequential approach has proven effective:

1. **Get a head start:** read ahead in the textbook to the next topic to be covered in class to gain familiarity with the subject. Attend all lectures and take careful notes. Never miss class! If you must miss a class, get the notes and homework from one of your classmates. Study the notes and reread the corresponding section from the text. Rework examples done in class and in the text. Attempt to do the homework problems, applying the approach, steps and notation presented in class and in the text. Check your answers with the answers given in the back of the text or in the solutions manual.

2. **Make a list of the questions that you may still have.** It may often happen that in class you feel you have a clear understanding of what your instructor says and does. This does not mean that you know it, let alone that you have been able to master it. Only doing it on your own and diligent practice will result in profound and lasting learning.

3. **When doing problems, ask yourself:** Does your answer make sense? Is it reasonable? If so, what does it all mean in the context of this particular problem? What are its implications?

4. **Ask questions:** Ask questions of everyone, from your instructor (in class or during office hours), to your classmates, to your friends. When you visit your instructor during office hours, bring a list of specific questions. Don't ask for answers. Ask for the explanation that justifies the answer; ask for the logical arguments in the solution. You should leave the office convinced of the logic of the argument. Don't ask your instructor: "Is this going to be on the test?" It *is* going to be on the test. Answer questions that your classmates may have. Helping or explaining to others enables you to get a better understanding of math concepts.

5. **Form a study group and discuss the homework problems in this group.** You pay good money for the textbook. Use your book, read it, and re-read it, work on the exercises, write in the margins, and put question marks where you have questions. Use the supplements that come with the book. Solution manuals can be quite helpful. CD ROMs can be very effective learning tools, too. Take advantage of technology, like graphing calculators or computer software, to verify your results and

get new insights, both graphically and numerically. Use the phone; use email; use the web.

Tips for Taking Tests

Make up a plan to study and organize your time accordingly. Know the previous material well. Math is cumulative! Try to find links connecting seemingly different topics; get the big picture. Ask yourself: Why are we doing this? What makes this an important problem in math? Why does the answer matter? Practice makes perfect: what initially may seem difficult and alien becomes very natural after much practice. Do the examples! Do not miss the class meeting before the exam! Important review may take place. Some of the test material may have to be memorized.

Understanding math will surely make memorization easier. Moreover, math rules often lead to a domain where numerical experimentation is possible. When in doubt, you should acquire the habit of conducting the appropriate experiment, finding the right formula to use, or identifying the pattern which will help you solve the equation.

For example, in the problem:
$$2u + 3 = 7$$
To solve it, you would need to recognize that a two-step process is needed.

First, subtract 3 from both sides.
$$2u + 3 (-3) = 7 (-3)$$
That leaves you with:
$$2u = 4$$
Then, divide both sides by 2:
$$2u/2 = 4/2$$
Your solution would be:
$$u=2$$
Finally, before moving on, check your answer by plugging your solution into the original equation to make sure that the equation is still true:

$$2(2) + 3 = 7$$
$$4 + 3 = 7$$
True!

The correct answer to your problem is a main goal. However, the logical steps and thought processes that lead to the answer are equally important in math. Make the presentation of your solution as clear and comprehensible to your instructor as possible. Show all the steps in a natural and coherent progression. Show all your work! Justify your answer! This has the additional benefit of allowing you to get partial credit. Try to be neat and well-organized in writing your solutions. Use your math intuition and make an educated guess when all else fails. At some point in the test preparation process, you may be able to predict the kinds of questions to be found on the exam. Your instructor's practice test will help. So does the chapter test in the book. Make up your own exam and take it under exam conditions. This is also a great way of fighting the "mental block syndrome" of math anxiety. After having successfully met all prerequisites, careful and solid preparation of all topics is the best known antidote to overcoming math anxiety.

Math Exam Preparation Tips
When taking the exam:

- Arrive early. Come well-equipped: pen, pencil, razor, calculator, scratch paper, etc. Read the instructions and do exactly as directed.
- Read the problems carefully, maybe more than once, and relate them to other problems you know. Keep in mind that the order of the questions often corresponds to the order in which the topics were presented in the class and in the text.
- Do easy problems first; do not let yourself get bogged down with a single problem.
- Always show all your work and do the problems the way they were done in class.
- Use every minute of available time: check and recheck your answers.
- If a question seems confusing to you, ask your instructor for clarification.
- Cheating, in any form, is ultimately self-defeating.
- Go over the exam when it is returned to you. Examine the problems you made mistakes on and learn from them; do this immediately and systematically.
- Keep a folder with all your tests and quizzes: this will be invaluable when preparing for the final exam, which is often cumulative.
- The final will most likely have problems similar to those on regular exams from the semester. Know these problems!

Math has the potential for teaching you skills and the art of problem-solving; it may also allow you to develop analytical ability, for methodical approaches to problem-solving skills are essential in almost any other field and profession.

Math anxiety can best be overcome by being confident and well-prepared. Remember, no matter what experiences you have had with math in the past, community college is your opportunity to start over and have new, better experiences.

Journal Assignment

Write your "Math Autobiography." Tell the story of who you are as a math
student, recounting any significant, important moments and experiences that
shaped your mathematical development or impacted your feelings about math.
They can be experiences which were positive or negative—where you had success
or where you experienced failure. At the end of your "Math Autobiography," try
to state what you will continue to do and what you will change in order to succeed
in your math courses.

Chapter Fifteen

Critical Thinking

Student Learning Outcomes:

Critical Thinking:
Students will classify and synthesize conflicting, contrasting sources of information, explore and evaluate them, and draw conclusions by writing argumentatively or participating in a debate.

Creative Thinking:
Students will use extrapolation to hypothesize future results for current controversies by writing an original, innovative science fiction story that imaginatively projects outcomes and proposes solutions.

"Responsibility to yourself means refusing to let others do your thinking, talking, and naming for you; it means learning to respect and use your own brains and instincts; hence, grappling with hard work."
— Adrienne Rich

Critical thinking is an imperative skill in virtually every discipline in college: it applies problem-solving strategies to math equations; it extracts meaning from novels, works of art, films, and songs; it analyzes and interprets history; it critiques society and proposes solutions in sociology; it formulates experiments and analyzes the results in the natural sciences. And so on.

Critical thinking is also a process of thinking about *why* you do what you do. It is thinking with a purpose, creating a plan, and applying it to a particular problem or situation. In this class, your journals ask you to think critically about the concepts in this book and apply them to real life by, for instance: reflecting on your interests and deciding what you want to do and where you want to go; investigating and evaluating the various ways to achieve those goals; choosing the best pathway from among the alternatives; researching and determining the requirements to attain your goals; setting goals for yourself, applying your knowledge, and working toward your desired outcome; obtaining results; evaluating the results; and revising or reassessing your plans as needed to incorporate your observations, assess your progress, and reformulate your plan until you achieve your desired results.

In short, critical thinking is a systematic approach to thinking, and a crucial component of this type of thinking is the reflective part—being aware of what you are doing and why you are doing it at every stage, and assessing your progress. Not thinking about the process of thinking is like blindly following instructions without ever questioning the instructions or knowing why you follow them, so critical thinking is *independent thinking*. Critical thinking is how we apply the foundational skills we learn and how we use them. Having information is only as valuable as what we do with it, though as a student your goal

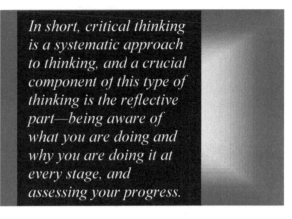

should be to make something meaningful with the knowledge that you have, and knowledge is built from concepts, principles, relationships, definitions, techniques, and ideas.

Analysis

Analyzing something is at the heart of almost all critical thinking skills. To analyze means to break down something complicated into its component parts, evaluate how they work together and why, and then show how each part contributes to the whole. Thus, as you begin to understand how something works, and what it purpose is, you can use it to structure your own knowledge and understanding. For instance, to understand how a car engine works, it is important to understand the unique purpose of each engine part and how each part contributes to making the car. The same thought process can be applied to the human body, a novel, a piece of music, the U.S. government, and so on.

Classification

Classification is a concept that you may have learned in science or writing, and it has two separate but common goals. On a broad level, it can help you to understand how the discipline, for instance in your major, organizes information or how information is categorized. This requires that you understand information as well as the principles used to organize that information, as opposed to simply being told what that organization is. In other words, you learn the system and how it works on a deep level rather than just memorizing an organizational chart, for example. In Criminal Justice, it is how we organize the different types of crimes. Felonies and misdemeanors are categorized separately based on the severity of the crime and the punishment allotted for each. There are subcategories for each type of crime and variations and exceptions within each category. Much public debate centers on whether certain crimes should be treated as misdemeanors or felonies or even be considered crimes at all. Critical thinking about crime and punishment would be to understand, for example, why certain drug possession charges are felonies while others are misdemeanors, and then to enter into the debate about whether the classification system is fair or discriminatory.

In the natural sciences, plant and animal species are organized in particular ways. Physiology is used as an organizing principle in zoology to classify mammals based on their characteristics. Art, literature, and music compositions can be organized according to time period or style. In political science, national governments might be organized based on their style of governance and placed on a continuum ranging from fascism to anarchy. How we organize information affects how we perceive it and what connections we make among the various parts because different methods of organization emphasize different aspects of the information. Using the criminal justice example above, if the laws of California were organized and presented to you as above—as either felonies or misdemeanors—then it would be quite different than if they were presented to you as laws that unfairly

> *However, being doubtful and having skepticism about other people's beliefs (and being willing to hear criticism of or question your own beliefs) is a good critical thinking practice.*

discriminate and laws that do not. The first method of organization emphasizes the severity of a crime and equates it with a particular punishment; in a sense, this serves to justify the reasoning behind prison sentences or fines. The second method of organizing *the exact same information* emphasizes the discriminatory nature of crimes and sentencing laws; this then undermines the justification provided by the first method of organization and suggests that some laws are oppressive and wrong because they unfairly discriminate. If you, as a thinker, were simply to accept the laws as they were first presented, you would be both less likely and less able to critique them. Therefore, it is important to be aware of *how* information is presented to you so that you are not deceived by it.

Independent Thinking

Having a healthy skepticism about information is also a form of critical thinking. This involves *questioning the truth* of what you were told, an important skill. A type of thinking that is called dialogic thinking enables you to question what you read and what you are told within an academic discourse. Dialogic thinking simply means to imagine as you read an article, textbook, or website that you're having a dialogue with the author. Similarly, in class, when a professor is lecturing or conducting a class discussion, it's healthy to raise your hand and ask a question about the material being presented. That's a dialogue or dialogic too.

Being introspective and asking yourself why you believe what you believe and why you doubt the things you doubt can help you be an objective critical thinker. Often, our experiences cause us to form beliefs. When enough people share a set of common beliefs, they become morals or rules, standards of behavior or standards of thought. Ethics are morals that have been adopted by a large group of people; for example, workers in the medical profession have all agreed to abide by a certain standard of ethical behavior.

However, being doubtful and having skepticism about other people's beliefs (and being willing to hear criticism of or to question your own beliefs) is a good critical thinking practice. Just because a large number of people believe in something does not necessarily mean that it is true. Many breakthroughs in knowledge have come from people who doubted accepted ideas of truth or right and wrong. Knowledge—that of society and that of you—will only stagnate if it is never questioned and simply accepted. Therefore, doubting and questioning is crucial to being a good critical thinker and student.

Critical Thinking Strategies

One strategy for reading a textbook can help build critical thinking skills. The strategy is to read everything you were assigned to read twice: once "with the grain" and again "against the grain." For longer readings and texts, this may not always be practical; however, at least do this for the critical portions and key parts of longer texts and definitely always do it for shorter, more manageable texts. Perhaps over time you can refine your reading skills to do both simultaneously, but the basic idea is this: as you read, read to understand, empathetically, so that you understand what the author is saying, what his or her perspective is, and what he or she values. You might take notes while reading this way to identify what the author's main argument is, what their key points are, and what the reasons are that support the author's viewpoint. Then as you read a second time, you might look for the weaknesses or flaws in what you're reading, taking notes by raising objections or resisting the author's argument by posing questions or noting where the author has assumed something that isn't necessarily true.

In this way, you are in essence having a dialogue with the author. And your reaction to the text can be anything from complete disagreement to complete agreement or anything in between, where you agree with some parts but disagree with others, like a compromise. Ideally, then, you would be able to argue any side of a controversial position, so if you were to write a response to the author's argument, you could explain both sides, the author's side *and* your side. This is true whether your intent in writing is to agree with the author's position, to strengthen it by adding additional supporting reasons, and to defend it against criticism by acknowledging its weaknesses or flaws and responding to them, or whether your intent is to disagree with the author's position and counterargue a different position by pointing out its flaws and offering reasons why you disagree, with counterexamples to disprove its validity. So understanding multiple points of view is important—even if you only understand another author's point of view in order to better state your own disagreement.

Another strategy involves connecting new knowledge to old knowledge. We as students all have pre-existing knowledge, beliefs, morals, and ethics, each of which contributes to whom we are as people and what we know as critical thinkers. But because none of us is stagnant, we all grow. This means that our knowledge evolves, so as we learn something new, we incorporate it into what we have already learned and emerge with new knowledge that is a synthesis of what we have just learned and what we already knew. It is sort of like arriving at a consensus in the above model, but is mostly internal. This technique can be applied when critically reading an article or textbook assignment, hearing a lecture from a professor, or watching a video or movie. A systematic approach requires that you think in five different modes for five different purposes: **to summarize, to make connections, to support, to criticize**, and **to synthesize**.

- **Summarizing:** When you are confronted with new knowledge, first you need to understand it. In order to demonstrate your understanding of new knowledge, it is helpful to be able to summarize it. Being able to write or verbalize a summary means that you understand something new. You explain from the author's point of view what it is that the author said or wrote.

- **Making Connections:** Next, connect the new information to the old information. In other words, relate to it by making connections between your previous, existing knowledge and/or to the outside world and society in general. Add what you just learned to what you already know. Ask yourself questions like: Does this remind me of anything else that I've read? Have I or anyone I know ever had a similar experience or had any experience with the subject? Does this remind me of anything that I have observed in the world?

- **Supporting:** As a reader, you seek a deeper understanding of something you've read and imagine that you are arguing the author's side on behalf of that author. Imagine you are both on the same team. Ask yourself questions like: What are the author's main arguments? What other reasons, not mentioned, could I possibly add to this argument to support it? Why would I or someone else agree with this author's position? Basically you are putting yourself in the author's shoes and imagining how the new information you have received fits into knowledge you and the author share.

- **Criticizing:** As a critic, you might identify the points of the new information with which you disagree or which you question. You might ask yourself questions like: What exactly do I disagree with? Which part of this argument seems suspicious? Where does this author's knowledge or new information conflict with what I already know? Are any statements by the author untrue, illogical, not the best way to look at the situation, or unhelpful? What are the alternatives to what the author is suggesting, proposing, or arguing? And, why are those alternatives not equally valid?

- **Synthesizing:** Finally, you have to synthesize the new information with the old information. There may very likely be conflicts between what you thought you knew and what you have just learned which need to be resolved. Sometimes new information just fills in gaps of knowledge that we never had in the first place, but other times we find out that we've read something that contradicts our previous beliefs, morals, ethics, or understanding. Often, we are left feeling uncertain about whether or not to trust new information that conflicts with what we think we know.

When approaching new knowledge, remember to evaluate it for credibility before simply accepting it as truth. Maintain your healthy skepticism. Note how forms of knowledge and information are organized and classified to detect inherent biases. When reading, whether it is a textbook or a website, *always* question the authority of the text. There are five basic criteria which you might use to do evaluate the reliability or credibility of a source:

- **Author:** What gives an author or speaker authority? Simply being published does not automatically mean the author is correct or even credible. Look for what credentials establish the author or speaker as an expert. This may require a bit of research. A well-recognized or famous expert in global warming with several books on the subject already published may be famous enough that his or her expertise is obvious, but a prisoner with no publications may be an expert on prison conditions or the legal system based on his or her personal experience.

- **Publisher:** Who supports and publishes the article or information? Many publications have an inherent bias; they actively choose what to publish and what not to publish based on whether or not it agrees with their values, morals or ethics rather than based on objectivity or scholarship. Certainly, a religiously-funded publication wouldn't publish articles criticizing religious practices that would undermine their own credibility as a moral institution, nor would the National Rifle Association publish articles endorsing strict gun control laws. Websites which profit from their advertisers have to cater to their advertisers' needs or risk losing the advertising revenue, so they may suppress or refuse to publish articles that don't serve their own commercial interests. Look for well-respected, professional peer-reviewed publications and websites. For websites, the more trustworthy ones generally have URL suffixes that end in .edu or .org, indicating that they are sponsored by educational institutions or non-profit organizations. URLs that end in .com are commercial, for-profit sites. For publications, look for professional journals that have editors who are experts in their field. As always, maintain a healthy skepticism.

- **Objectivity:** How scholarly and trustworthy is the information presented? Not only is the objectivity of the publisher worth questioning, so too is the objectivity of the individual author. Authors are subject to the same biases and commercial concerns that publishing institutions or sponsoring organizations are. The expectations in a scholarly publication by a professional and academic author are similar to those in a scholarly essay by a professional and academic student. Scholarly and objective writers will reveal their researched sources and document them with a References page, Works Cited page, or links to outside sources consulted. They will also recognize divergent opinions by anticipating and acknowledging opposing points of view and responding to them, rather than being one sided and presenting their own opinions as if there is no other way to think.

- **Currency:** When was the information developed and published? In most fields, the most recent scholarship is considered the most valuable and up-to-date. While this is not always the case, scholarship that is current builds on previous scholarship and incorporates the latest ideas. However, in literary and art analysis, currency is not necessarily an indicator of value since the conventions in those disciplines privilege original, insightful interpretations rather than modern ones.

Once you have convinced yourself that new information is valuable and credible enough for you to consider, then you have to decide what to do with it, and you have a range of options. This is why it's important to be introspective, to have an understanding of why you believe what you believe, and to know where your knowledge comes from. It is also why it's important to be willing to question your own beliefs as well as those of others. To be stubborn and to hold steadfast to old knowledge is to resist growth and learning, but to accept new knowledge without question is to risk being manipulated and misinformed. So the key is to figure out how to incorporate your newly-learned knowledge into your larger and broader knowledge base. If the new information is persuasive enough, you may simply change your mind and reestablish a new set of beliefs. If the new information is semi-convincing but not completely convincing, then you may add a bit of doubt to your current knowledge and plan to investigate further until you can resolve whether your old knowledge is correct or whether the new knowledge is correct.

Most likely what you will end up doing is synthesizing old and new knowledge together. New knowledge can confirm, modify, or enhance your pre-existing knowledge and beliefs, thus creating a new or revised understanding of what you thought you already knew. Most important in this process are the connections and relationships that you establish between your old knowledge and your new knowledge. If you have engaged with new material in depth, explored it, contemplated it, and evaluated it favorably, then this will almost happen automatically—but you will have to revise your understanding or resolve conflicts when it doesn't.

As a general principle, when you have two opinions or two sets of information which conflict with each other, you should resolve them using logic: make sure you understand the information. Evaluate the credibility of where you got that information. Look at how well-supported and how thoroughly-researched each position is. Where did the new information come from? And, where did you get your original information from in the first place? Which is the more credible source? Don't be fooled by writing or speaking that is rhetorically outstanding and persuasive because it appeals to you emotionally; instead, prefer information that is backed up by substantial research and expert opinion. Also, look for a general consensus among various people from different groups. If one particularly charismatic English professor told you that a novel had a specific meaning and message in it, it would be tempting to agree because the professor has a great personality or made a passionate argument about her interpretation. And if that particular interpretation is the only one you have ever heard or read, you might be inclined to believe that it is the only one that exists.

> *Don't be fooled by writing or speaking that is rhetorically outstanding and persuasive because it appeals to you emotionally; instead, prefer information that is backed up by substantial research and expert opinion.*

Similarly if a scientist showed his or her findings in a report, and that was the only report on the experiment that you were aware of, you might also be inclined to believe it without question. However, if you were to look up criticism of the English professor's novel or investigate other similar experiments that other scientists conducted, you may discover a different interpretation or another set of lab results. And this should be enlightening more than confusing. Although it is not always true, especially when interpreting a work of art, when there is consensus among experts in a particular field, then often those shared common opinions approach being morals or principles rather than individually held beliefs; conversely, when only one or a few select members of a larger group, like English professors or scientists, hold a set of beliefs that is at odds with the majority of people in that profession, then frequently those lesser held beliefs are not as well-substantiated and not accepted in the profession. However, it's important to note that minority opinion does not necessarily mean an opinion is wrong. Again, look for the effective use of logic, thorough scholarly research, and professional presentation of the material.

How to Interpret Meaning

Interpretation of a work of art or literature, a survey or other data, or even a set of lab results involves both creative and critical thinking. The primary question that interpretation responds to is: What does this (play, novel, short story, poem, painting, song, lab result, or survey data) mean?

Disciplines that interpret works of art, like music, art, or English literature, have their own special set of techniques for the analysis of each genre, which would be too detailed to go into here. The same holds true for the scientific disciplines which may analyze and interpret data sets. However, what they all have in common is that in analyzing and interpreting anything, we look for patterns. As mentioned above, analyzing means to break something down into its component parts and see how each one fits together and contributes to the whole. Remember the parts of the car engine? Well, imagine if you couldn't see the car at first but had to decide how the parts fit together and what their purpose was? Interpreting is a skill that involves looking only at the component parts (the data from a survey, the characters and setting of a novel, the technique of a painter, the structure of a jazz composition) without knowing what the whole is exactly. And interpretation would be your explanation of what the parts form when put together or assembled into a coherent whole: in other words, what does it all mean? Depending on how you assembled the parts of a car engine, or the elements of a work of art, it could end up being or meaning different things. This is the nature of interpretation. What matters most is your ability to explain why you created what you created from those parts. That may sound a little scary, but there are ways to find clues, like a detective investigating a crime, which might help you figure out how things all fit together.

Therefore, you might look for trends in the data or patterns in the novel in order to see what the most significant observations are. After an experiment or survey, you might ask yourself questions like: Are all the different groups surveyed responding the same way to each question, or are there noticeable differences? And furthermore, what might account for those differences? Why do they differ? What about the groups would explain their different responses? After reading a novel, you might classify characters into different categories as a form of interpretation; then, by observing which characters are successful and rewarded and what traits they have in common and comparing them to characters who are unsuccessful and punished and noticing what traits they have in common, you might arrive at an interpretation of what the novel is suggesting about proper human behavior or solutions to problems in society.

There are particular conventions and theories to use in each discipline, but the basic idea remains the same: look at the components, make observations about them, and come up with an explanation that accounts for the variation among those different parts in a group or set, note similarities, and come up with an explanation that takes into account as much of the data as possible. Generally, the best interpretation is the one that accounts for the most information and variation among the different component parts. The idea, then, is to be as *inclusive* as possible, to make your interpretation be an explanation of as much of the data that you have and can account for, leaving out as little as possible.

It should be noted that interpretation is not finite. In art and literature and history, for example, multiple interpretations can coexist. There are as many interpretations of meaning in Shakespeare's plays as there are critics who have written about Shakespeare's plays! The idea of a single universal truth is one which has fallen out of favor recently in academic disciplines such as Art and English and Music and even history. You might think that history contains a single truth, but many modern historians feel that the truth is dependent on the perspective of the person writing the history, so, for example, the history of America written by an indigenous Mexican writer who focused on the loss of land to Western European settlers and warmongers would not resemble that same history as written by an American Indian who took the perspective of those indigenous people, nor would it be the same if written from the perspective of a western European settler, or that of an African-American scholar and descendant of slaves. Those disciplines do not privilege a single truth above any other, but rather embrace the complexity of the different perspectives as components of a larger interrelated web of histories which intersect and form a truth.

> *There are particular conventions and theories to use in each discipline, but the basic idea remains the same: look at the components, make observations about them, and come up with an explanation that accounts for the variation among those different parts in a group or set, note similarities and come up with an explanation that takes into account as much of the data as possible.*

Creative Thinking

Creative thinking is also a form of critical thinking. It involves processing knowledge and information into a creative response, often to gain insight into a subject from an unconventional perspective. Creative writers are critical thinkers. For instance, to write a short story, novel, screenplay, or dramatic script about a social controversy such as the plight of homeless people, the writer has to decide what message he or she intends to send, and how best to illustrate and dramatize that issue with the use of storytelling conventions. In other words, creative writers make arguments through telling stories, which requires them to think critically about their subject in a slightly different way. Not only do they have to arrive at a final judgment or consensus or point, but they also have to figure out how best to put it into a storytelling format that would engage readers and dramatize the issue or message that they are trying to get across in a creative form.

However, creative thinking is not limited to creative writers. In business, many visionary thinkers were able to imagine new products or solve problems in unique ways which had never been tried before. Creative thinking, therefore, is generative rather than analytical: it seeks to find new ways to explore ideas, solve problems, and move knowledge forward.

There are five basic approaches to thinking creatively:

- **Synthesis:** This style of creative thinking is discussed above and involves combining previous or existing knowledge in new ways. Using knowledge from one discipline to solve a problem in another synthesizes old knowledge into something new. For example, you may have read a novel in an English class which addressed class inequality and have noticed that the main character tried to correct the imbalances of power in every interaction he had with others who had different degrees of power than he did by targeting key institutions and community leaders to bring them down and create equality; if you applied this solution to a real-life problem of inequality in a sociology class, then you would be using synthesis thinking.

- **Evolution:** Evolution is a form of creative thinking which suggests that new knowledge evolves from old knowledge, but at a very slow, almost incremental rate. Looking for new and improved solutions to old problems or making refinements to conventional procedures are examples of knowledge evolving. The basic idea is that nothing is ever perfect, and there is always room for improvement. For example, the ways in which cell phones are constantly updated with software upgrades and new models shows the use of evolutionary thinking.

- **Revolution:** As the name implies, revolutionary thinking involves a large-scale change or a complete paradigm shift. This involves rethinking issues or solutions altogether with a completely different approach. Rather than a teacher wondering how to engage students more effectively in a lecture, a revolutionary thinking teacher might decide to replace lecturing altogether with hand-on activities.

- **Extrapolation:** Extrapolation means to take what is known about a subject and use conjecture to imagine what it would be like in the future or what the result might be if something changed; it enables you to look at something old in a new way and imagine alternatives that may not exist yet. It is sort of like what science fiction writers do. They may look at a field like robotics and wonder what would happen if the robots attained some sort of independent consciousness? What if they took over the world after a world war between humans and machines? Then,

213

they might think, how can this potential future problem be avoided? They also might go back and revise history. The literary genre of steampunk often rewrites historical moments as if technology never evolved beyond the steam engine in order to explore alternatives and critique our dependence on modern technology. Posing "What if?" questions is using extrapolation.

- **Creative Insight.** Creative breakthroughs can occur when thinkers shift attention from one aspect of a problem to another, looking at the situation from a different angle. The term "path fixation" refers to stubbornly trying to fix a problem or continue down the same familiar pathway to knowledge that one has always been on. This can be problematic because it is limiting. As a goal, critical thinkers should want to solve problems and expand their knowledge with new ideas. On a college campus where administrators felt that too many students were loitering and smoking cigarettes all over campus, one solution might be to notify campus police to issue citations and monitor common areas with a heavier presence; however, a creative insight might be to recognize the need of those students to have a designated area to hang out where smoking was permitted and to create one. Thus, the goal of solving the problem, rather than intensifying conflict ineffectively, is attained.

A Final Note

Think of the television franchise *CSI*. Being a critical thinker is like being a CSI operative. When analyzing a crime scene, the CSI investigators find evidence, analyze it, come up with a few theories that explain the evidence, evaluate the various theories, reject those that don't account for all of the evidence available, and arrive at a theory or interpretation of the crime scene. Most importantly, however, as the CSI investigators continue their investigation, they often re-evaluate or reject evidence they have found which has been tampered with or is tainted, they often reinterpret old evidence after it has been analyzed closely in a lab, and they often discover new evidence that they have to incorporate into their old knowledge using synthesis. When they do this, they arrive at a new theory that re-interprets what the crime scene told them previously. In other words, as the evidence changes, the theory changes: knowledge evolves.

Journal Assignments

1. Create a system that classifies the information you have learned from reading this book so far. What are the categories? What is the classification principal? How can you sort out information into discrete categories without creating any overlap or excluding any information? Make a chart that has headings for the different types of information this book contains, and underneath each heading make a notation with as many examples of those types of information as you can.

2. Locate a controversial article about a hotly debated topic in your intended major; then apply the critical thinking process described in this chapter and write an argumentative essay about it. Be sure to include a thesis statement that takes clear position on your subject, a summary of the article, a statement of your position and the reasons or evidence that justify why you have taken that position, and either pros and cons or opposing arguments, and a refutation of them.

3. Alternatively, with the above controversial article, practice believing and doubting—or reading "with" and "against" the grain. Make a list of what you agree with and disagree with in the article.

4. Have a class debate. After a brief presentation on a topic or a case study, divide up into groups according to your position on the controversy. Discuss the various reasons that people in your group have for holding their opinions, and prepare a presentation to the opposite group which addresses why you and your group feel the way you feel, acknowledges potential disagreement, and then responds to this agreement with reasons.

5. Write a short story (even a science fiction story using extrapolation) that dramatizes a controversial issue related to this class or your major and imagines a solution to it.

Student Success Profile:

Kenneth Reyes

Describe yourself briefly in a short biography (hometown, birthplace, high school experience, family, education).
My birthplace is Sylmar, California in the San Fernando Valley; it's in the outskirts of downtown Los Angeles. I grew up in the San Fernando Valley, and for community college I went to school in South Central Los Angeles. I had a

unique high school experience because I was in sports but I wasn't a studious person.

What was your background before coming to community college?
In high school, I didn't care about school. All I wanted to do in school was to get good enough grades to play sports and have fun with my friends. I am the youngest of three brothers, and I had both parents in the household.

What, if anything, prompted your decision to attend community college? What were your goals upon entering community college (why did you go)? Did they change after you started college? If so, how?
Growing up, my parents motivated my brothers and me to get an education. My brothers and I didn't take education seriously until we came across our own empirical encounters of the value of an education. Before coming to community college, I did not have a studious attitude.

Describe your experience as a community college student. What were the highlights? Were there any special programs or extracurricular experiences that were memorable or inspiring?
The empirical encounters allowed me excel in community college. Going into community college, I was not a studious person; I looked for the easy route and short cuts to get me out of everything. I didn't get accepted to one college I applied to after getting out of high school, and while all my friends were talking about their colleges, I was worried about what I was going to do for rest of my life. I eventually knew doing below par for three years and doing well for one year was not going to get me into college; I needed to be consistent. Before going into a community college, I viewed it as another opportunity to go to college. I wanted another chance to prove to myself and to the people who told me I shouldn't attend college. I wanted to go to school because I wanted to provide certainty for myself. A college degree doesn't guarantee me a job, but by receiving a college degree I can put myself in a position to solidify a job. I didn't want to live in constant fear of not knowing where my next paycheck was going to come from. My experience as a community college student was one of the most inspirational moments in my life.

Were there any memorable faculty, counselors, other students, administrators or staff (at your community college or university) with whom you established a rapport and who made a difference? Is establishing relationships with people on campus important? Tell a brief story about someone with whom you became close and who was supportive.

Community college taught me life lessons I'll carry for the rest of my life. One of the many highlights I encountered in community college was meeting my academic advisors, Dr. Daniel Ortega and Dr. Angelita Salas. These two academic advisors taught me the importance of an education, both having an everlasting effect in my academic career. In my first semester, I was a part of the Puente program and Trio STEM Scholars. These two programs were designed to help minority students get into four-year universities. Being a part of the Puente program taught me to get involved with my community and to help other students achieve a common goal.

How much time went by between high school and community college for you? What were the biggest challenges that you faced when you began attending community college?
I took a matter of two weeks off before enrolling in a college course when I finished high school. I took a college course the semester after I finished high school. The biggest challenges I encountered in college were financial planning and time management. I couldn't afford to pay for textbooks because they were too expensive, so I made copies of the textbooks in the library and rented many of my books. Time management was an issue because of the time I spent commuting to different colleges to attend classes.

Did you work while attending community college? If so, how did you balance your time between work and school? Do you have any kids or other family responsibilities? If so, how did you balance your time between home and school? Did you have all three? How did you handle that?
When I was in community college, I worked seasonally. When I wasn't taking classes during the winter and summer semesters, I worked construction to help pay for the fees and materials for the upcoming semester. I wanted to help my parents financially because we were going through a financial calamity, making it difficult to pay for school materials.

Community colleges generally have a high attrition rate, meaning a large percentage of students drop out. Why do you think this happens? What motivated you to persevere through college and transfer to a university?
Students all have their own experiences while attending community college, and it leads them to dropping out. College can be one of the most stressful periods in people's lives, and it can be discouraging. I think there is a high attrition rate because of miscues students encounter with financial aid and lack of guidance. After a long period of time, students feel trapped when they are given the "run around" to solve their issues with school, in which leads them to dropping out. Another experience students encounter is the lack of guidance. Some students are

too intimidated to ask for information about what is offered on their campus, so the student eventually never knows about the resources offered on campus. When a student is confused about what to do and how to transfer to another university, they are afraid to ask for help. What motivated me to persevere through college was the support I had from my family and wanting to pursue a better life for my family and myself.

Attending a college or university can be extremely stressful for many students. Does any particular thing stand out as being the most stressful aspect of going to school? What was it and why was it stressful? What coping skills did you use to overcome stress in order to succeed?
Attending college can be stressful, but there is not one particular thing I can identify as the most stressful. Going through adversity in college is what makes the college degree worthwhile because of the amount of sacrifice and dedication someone puts in to reach a goal. The biggest challenge I faced in community college was paying for college materials and class availability. To cope with the struggle of class availability, I went to multiple community colleges to find the classes I needed. I didn't want to let class availability become something that discouraged me from transferring. The best advice for someone who is struggling with community college is to go see a counselor at your college to discuss what you are going through. The counselor will help you along the way in your educational career and give you the proper guidance through your community college journey.

Of all the writing assignments you had in college, which are you most proud of and why?
It's difficult to pinpoint the writing assignment that I'm most proud of, but I would choose the personal statement I wrote when applying to universities. My personal statement is one of the pieces of work I am most proud of because I put everything I had into this piece, and it was an opportunity for the universities to see another side of me besides academics.

Were there any memorable faculty, counselors, other students, administrators or staff (at your community college or university) with whom you established a rapport and who made a difference? Is establishing relationships with people on campus important? Tell a brief story about someone with whom you became close and who was supportive.
The three faculty members who made a difference in my life were Dr. Daniel Ortega, Dr. Angelita Salas, and Professor Darren Cifarelli. I believe in establishing a relationship with faculty because you are able to get their advice on

multiple aspects in your community college journey. I remember the first day I walked into Dr. Ortega's office. I walked in with my brother because he was the one who introduced me to Dr. Ortega. I sat down with him, and he told me, "What do you want to study and why?" I wanted to be a financial analyst to prevent people from going into financial hardship and help people who need financial help. Dr. Ortega told me, "Okay, I have enough people in the program, but you are in the Puente program, so you have to prove to me why I took a risk on you and on putting you in the program." After my first semester in community college, I talked to Dr. Ortega about my education plan and he mentioned to me, "Have you thought about UC Berkeley or UCLA?" Truly, I never thought about it much because I did poorly in high school and thought my chances were over to go into high caliber schools. Dr. Ortega told me, "You should think about it; you have the potential to go to those schools." Since that day, I knew Dr. Ortega would have an impact on my life.

Courage to Learn discusses building social capital, meaning developing relationships and skills that are like an investment in your own future. What social capital have you gained since entering community college?
Courage to Learn taught me several lessons I can apply in the future and help me with my community college journey. The social capital I gained was establishing a lasting relationship with my fellow classmates, faculty, and staff members. Other social capital I established since entering community college was having a positive attitude and being social. Socializing increases your network, and you are able to establish everlasting relationships.

What was your social life like in college? How important was it to you personally and educationally?
My social life in community college was not average. I decided not to have much of a social life because I wanted to focus all my energy and attention on school. Occasionally, I went out with friends, but I would mostly stay in and focus on my schoolwork.

Deciding what university to transfer to is difficult. What factors did you consider when deciding where to apply and where to attend?
Deciding which university to attend was difficult, and the factors I took into account were the financial aid being offered and the place I felt the most comfortable.

Universities are expensive. Many magazine and newspaper articles highlight the fact that attending a university is an investment that frequently doesn't pay off or isn't worth it. Perhaps you've seen stories about students

graduating from various universities under mountains of debt and unable to find jobs. How did you handle the financial burden of attending college and a university? Is it worth it? Are you buried under mountains of debt?

I was able to handle the financial burden by applying to multiple scholarships and spending minimally so I could pay for my education. I do believe it's worth investing in school because we are investing in something that will advance us and put us in the best position to succeed.

How did you manage the transition from a community college to a university? Did you feel prepared or underprepared? What were the biggest challenges that you faced during the transition?

I managed the transition from a community college to a university by continuing the habits I had in community college and staying connected with the people who led me to the university. The biggest transition in college was the independence the professors gave us, and the amount of preparation you have to do for school. It's something I'm still adjusting to but I am adapting slowly.

What plans for the future do you have (educationally, socially, and professionally)? When and how did those goals emerge?

The plans I have are to graduate with a double major in Economics and Business Administration, and to be a financial advisor and analyst for a financial institution. The social goal I have is to get involved in campus and take advantage of the opportunities the University of Southern California has to offer me.

Looking back, what advice would you give to first year community college students today (i.e. if you could go back in time and talk to yourself on your first day of college, what would you say)?

The advice I would give to a first year community college student is to take advantage of the counselors and programs offered on campus and not to worry about the difficult times you will face; it's part of the process and it will be worth it in the end. Remember community college is your second opportunity to renew yourself and attend any college you want, so take advantage of it. We have to make sacrifices to achieve the things we really want.

Chapter Sixteen

The Application of Theory In Higher Education

Student Learning Outcome:
Students will learn the importance of and processes for effectively connecting classroom theories to real-world experiences through practical application of theoretical knowledge in both writing and critical thinking; and accurately assess relevant knowledge and skills related to personal, professional and/or academic goals.

"Experience without theory is blind, but theory without experience is mere intellectual play"
—Immanuel Kant

The Role of Theory

Whether you're a doctor diagnosing a patient, and FBI agent profiling a serial killer, an English scholar applying Marxist theory to a novel, a corporate CEO using leadership skills, a mathematician deciding which formulas are needed to solve a problem, a psychologist recommending a behavioral change or coping skill to a patient, or a scientist testing a new medication, you are using a theory to help you interpret the information that you receive.

Academic theory is defined as a supposition or a system of ideas intended to explain something, especially one based on general principles independent of the thing to be explained. In other words, it is a plausible or generally accepted principle or body of principles offered to explain phenomena that we can observe.

During your collegiate career, meaning at the community college and at the university, you will be introduced to many academic theories and asked to understand and apply them to everyday life. You will be asked to dissect, analyze and explain theory in many of the assigned readings and written assignments across the curriculum. Thus, it is essential to understand the uses of theory while at the community college so you can be prepared for the university.

Theory is the outcome of the need people have to make sense out of life: it allows us to organize and interpret the enormous amount of information that exists in the world. Each and every one of us has a set of organizing principles, an "informal theory," that we use to make sense of our experiences. Parker (1977) defined informal theory as "the body of common knowledge that allows us to make implicit connections among events and persons in our environment and upon which we act in everyday life" (p. 420). As McEwen (1996) explained, informal theories are influenced by a person's own background, experiences, and value system. These factors serve as filters through which people examine and interpret the experiences of others.

Unfortunately, informal theory is not self-correcting (Parker, 1977). People have no basis on which to determine whether their examinations are accurate or not. Formal theories validated by research are needed to determine whether individuals' observations hold for the persons with whom they work and the situations in which they find themselves. Rodgers (1980) defined formal theory as "a set of propositions regarding the interrelationship of two or more conceptual variables relevant to some realm of phenomena. It provides a framework for explaining the relationship among variables and for empirical investigation" (p. 81). A theory is an abstract representation based on a "potentially infinite number of specific and concrete variations of a phenomenon" (Strange & King, 1990, p.17).

Theory has four influential uses: description, explanation, prediction and control (DiCaprio, 1974). At first level, *description*, theory provides a conceptualization of what is happening. At the second level, *explanation*, theory can be used to explain the causes of behavior. At third level, which very few theories achieve, *prediction* is the goal. The final level, which most theories have yet to accomplish, is *control*. For example, in nuclear physics, a radioactive isotope can be *described* as decaying. Scientists *explain* this by saying that it happens because the forces holding the nucleus together fail and it breaks apart. When they build nuclear reactors, they do so with knowledge that *predicts* how and at what rate this will happen, and they do so in a controlled environment specifically in order to collect the energy and *control* it.

Not all theories are of the same value to scholars. In order for theories to be useful, they must reveal certain qualities: comprehensiveness, clarity, and explicitness, consistency, simplicity, and practical usefulness (Walsh, 1973). Initially, a theory should make predictions that account for a broad range of behavior or observable phenomena. Concepts and relationships should be defined accurately. The theory should allow for inclusion of findings within a logical framework. Explanations should be simple and easy to follow. Lastly, the theory should create testable hypotheses leading to useful research (McEwen, 1996). You may be familiar with the term "conspiracy theory," a derogatory term for some theories which are not considered valid or are too far-fetched believable. For instance, there are a few people who believe the Apollo moon landings of 1969-1972 were faked. According to the theory, the landings were a hoax staged by NASA, filmed on a sound stage on earth in New Mexico with faked photos and stories planted in the media to help the US win the space race. This is a theory; however, it is disputed by a majority of people. Using Walsh's criteria, it is likely not comprehensive because there is a large amount of evidence to the contrary. Much of the conspiracy is unclear also, with the "theorists" disagreeing about how the landings were faked and what was fake about them. While it is explicit, it is also inconsistent, complicated and has little practical use. Most historians and scientists don't believe the conspiracies around the Apollo moon landings, so they have little value except to crackpots who are entertained by writing and discussing government cover-ups. The Apollo moon landing conspiracy is fairly obviously false and probably harmless and easy to dismiss, so you might wonder why it is necessary to evaluate theories based on criteria. Can't you just figure out what is believable and what is not? Well, sometimes. However, some extreme misuses or misapplications of very sound theories have yielded catastrophic results. Darwin's theory of evolution, Osborn's theory of eugenics, and Nietzsche's theory of the ubermensch ("superman") would fare well under Walsh's criteria, but Hitler used it as a basis to create the Nazi party's ideology and to justify the Holocaust, so not only is it important to identify whether or not a theory is valid, but it is also important to use theory in an ethical way.

Knefelkamp (1978) suggested a number of questions for evaluating the utility of theory:

1. *On what population is the theory based?* It is important to determine the population on which the theory was based and whether the theory has been tested with individuals who have different characteristics. Some aspects of the theory may be specific to the original population, while other concepts may apply for people more generally.

2. *How was the theory developed?* The assessment instruments or techniques that were used in the original study should be clearly described. Assessment tools should be available for further theoretical study and evaluation of developmental outcomes.

3. *Is the theory descriptive?* Does the theory provide a comprehensive view of individuals' development and specific aspects of the developmental process?

4. *Is the theory explanatory?* Does the theory outline how development occurs?

5. *Is the theory prescriptive?* Does the theory discuss ways in which specific outcomes can be produced and lead to the prediction of events or relationships that can be verified through observation or experimentation?

6. *Is the theory heuristic?* Theory should generate research ideas.

7. *Is the theory useful in practice?* Theory should help in understanding and evaluating the effectiveness of practice.

Most theories fall short on one or more of these criteria. McEwen (1996) also noted that it is important to remember that no theory is really objective. Each reflects from the viewpoint of its author. However, existing theories are sources of awareness that serve as a means of organizing one's thinking and guiding the choices that we make.

You may recall Chickering's theory of identity development from an earlier chapter. If you remember, Chickering theorized that our identities develop within what he called the seven vectors of development: developing competence, managing emotions, moving through autonomy toward independence, developing mature interpersonal relationships, establishing identity, developing purpose, and developing integrity. His theory was that we progress through these vectors at different rates, none of which are better than others, and that his theory describes the growth of our feelings, thoughts, behavior, and ability to relate to others. Ultimately, he described the ways in which we can progress toward greater maturity, intellectual complexity, and stability. This is a basic outline of his theory, which you have already read about and applied to yourself.

Chickering based his theory on research conducted on college students, compiled from data collected from 1959 to 1979; his theory describes a comprehensive view of development, predicts intellectual complexity and individual stability, and it forms the foundation of students services and identity theory to this day, so it is definitely useful in practice. Therefore, it satisfies all of the conditions Knefelkamp suggests above. Chickering, himself, applied his theory to learning and education: "Students do not learn much just sitting in classes listening to teachers, memorizing prepackaged assignments, and spitting out answers. They must talk about what they are learning, write reflectively about it, relate it to past experiences, and apply it to their daily lives. They must make what they learn a part of themselves." Thus, this theory has impacted how we teach in our classrooms. In applying Chickering's theory to yourself, you have already applied an abstract theory to a specific example. When you completed the Chickering journal assignment from Chapter 1, you went through the detailed explanations of Chickering's vectors and evaluated your own strengths and weaknesses in each one. Then, you drew conclusions about what areas that you need growth in.

Applying Theory in Writing

In writing, applying a theory to a specific instance or situation usually requires a bit more pre-writing or critical thinking than the average essay because before you can write, you have to analyze the topic you have been given and figure out how to apply the theoretical perspective to a given set of observations. While this may initially sound abstract and complicated, it is probably more familiar than you think.

For instance, medical theories state that certain diseases present specific symptoms; doctors' diagnoses are based on seeing whether their patients' symptoms match the description of the disease. Another example: serial killers often display certain characteristics or adhere to certain "types"; FBI profilers create a profile of the people they are hunting based on matching the evidence to the types. An English major might read the novel *Of Mice and Men* by John Steinbeck and notice that it addresses class conflict and the oppression of the working class; she might then choose to apply the critical lens of Marxism to illuminate the relationship between social institutions, the economy, and class structure in the novel. The CEO of a *Fortune 500* company might observe that morale in the office is low and that there seems to be an atmosphere of distrust; that CEO might take inventory of his management style and realize that he has been micromanaging people despite knowing that, according to the latest research on leadership, empowerment of employees is far more effective. And so on. These are examples of applying an abstract theory—in other words, a general rule about typical symptoms of a disease or patterns of criminal behavior—to a specific case.

This is using deductive reasoning: applying a theory to a specific case or example. It is very common in higher education, and the reasons why we study theorists are only to apply their knowledge and expertise to our own examples, but also to see how their theories hold up under scrutiny.

How to Apply Theory to Empirical Phenomena

Deductive reasoning, or deduction, is one form of valid reasoning or logic that begins from broad general statement or hypothesis and examines the possibilities to reach a logical conclusion. Empirical means: "based on, concerned with, or verifiable by observation or experience rather than theory or pure logic."

Assignments that ask you to apply an expert's theory to a specific case or example are basically asking you to look at empirical phenomena through the lens of that theory; in other words, what would the theorist say if he or she looked at a particular situation. What would the theory predict if certain conditions are present or there is a change?

The first step to do this is to make sure you understand the theory. This isn't as easy as it may sound; many theorists write in academic language, using jargon, technical terminology, and difficult vocabulary. Read it as many times as necessary so that you can summarize it in a couple of sentences. This may be causal relationship (x leads to y), a rule or law, or a set of observations that are usually true when certain conditions are present.

For example, Michel Foucault was a French theorist, historian, literary critic, and philosopher. One of his theories, in a work called "Panopticism," suggests that all of modern society and its institutions (schools, hospitals, the military, the workplace, and so on) are modeled after a prison. He establishes a set of conditions that exist in a particular type of prison called the Panopticon. Among them are: data collection and record-keeping of the inmates, centralized power structure for the guards, the illusion of inmates being under surveillance at all times without knowing whether or not it's true at any given time, and quarantining inmates.

To apply Foucault's theory to a specific example would mean to examine a particular school and note what features match the set of conditions that Foucault identifies as being prison-like. Schools collect data on students in the form of student records, discipline reports, demographic info, grades, and so on. The school administration has centralized power in the administrative hierarchy with a president or principal at the top and may also have patrols by campus police. There are also security cameras on campuses, which may or may not be monitored, maintaining the illusion of surveillance. Finally, students are restricted to classrooms and certain areas. While this isn't exactly a perfect match, through the lens of Foucault's theory, the prison-like aspects of the institution of school are more evident. A reasonable conclusion, therefore, based on the similarities, might be that Foucault is indeed correct as evidenced by your application of his ideas to one school or the school system. Alternately, to take it one step further, another conclusion might be that students are in fact socialized into tolerating prison-like conditions.

Theory application essays often involve, as exemplified above, making a claim and presenting an argument based on the theory and supported by empirical evidence—evidence you yourself gather—and then which you examine through a critical lens. There are a few common problems which students may encounter while writing these types of assignments: losing track of their own "voice" or failing to clearly attribute quotes and ideas to the nearest; unsubstantiated statements for generalizations; and insufficient analysis or excessive summarization.

- **Losing Your Voice:** Students often encounter a lack of clarity regarding their own voice being confused with the theorist's ideas they are using. This can cause confusion for readers about whether any particular statement represents the view of the theorist, the student, or someone else. What's important to do is to carefully and clearly identify whose views and ideas you are presenting. For example, you might write, "Conflict theory, according to Karl Marx, is a theory that claims society is in a state of perpetual conflict due to competition for limited resources." Alternately, you may write, "I believe that the social order creates conflict in order to perpetuate class difference." This way, it is clear whose ideas belong to whom.

- **Failing to Substantiate Claims:** Another in common problem in applying theory in writing is making a statement that has insufficient evidence or details for proof. When you make a statement in an essay of this type, ask yourself how you know what you know or stated. What can you provide that would support your claim? Then, put that evidence in your paper, remembering to cite your sources. Be careful not to make claims that are too strong or too general based on insufficient evidence. You wouldn't want to conclude that all Americans dislike our current president based solely on a survey of ten friends on Facebook.

- **Excessive Summarization:** Yet another common problem students often encounter is summarizing too much of a theory without adding anything original to it. The bulk of an essay that applies theory to empirical phenomena should not spend the majority of the paper simply summarizing the observation or the theory itself. One way to avoid this is to be aware that theory indicates which details or which variables are the most relevant. As in the above example with Foucault and Panopticism, Foucault set the focus for the observations about the school by providing the specific features of Panopticism to look for. The fictional observer of the school above then knew what aspects of his or her observations of the school were going to be relevant.

Much use of theory in higher education is related to research in the sense that we research theories and we apply them in experiments, fieldwork, or analysis of a text—quite often and across many disciplines. Many of your classes will ask you to conduct research, and many students are intimidated by the length of theoretical articles and the complexity of their language. However, a big part of learning involves learning the language of the subjects you study: the scientific jargon of physics, the terminology used in literary analysis, the language used to describe student behavior and learning theory. In a sense, you need to learn to speak the language of the discipline you are majoring in or interested in being a part of. The result of not "talking the talk" is that you will be excluded from the conversation. In higher education, much has been made of its cultural bias and exclusivity including accusations of racism and classism. In other words, being able to conduct research and apply theory is a gatekeeper; whether you agree with this or not, access to higher education can make a difference between you being a professional or an amateur. Therefore, it's essential to become adept at doing research and using theory. The most advanced concepts in higher education are contained in the theoretical literature of the discipline. One of the highest honors for an academic is to have his or her research published in an academic journal; similarly, one of the most important aspects of using your education in the workplace is the skill to apply abstract researched theory in a practical setting, putting your learning to good use. Master these skills and join the conversation.

> *In a sense, you need to learn to speak the language of the discipline you are majoring in or interested in being a part of.*

Journal Assignments

1. Write a journal entry in which you reflect on how theory can assist in career development. How can it guide and inform your career decision-making?

2. In your chosen field of study—your major—look up a popular theory by a prominent theorist. Evaluate it using the criteria established by Knefelkamp. Summarize it briefly, in a single paragraph, and then apply it to a specific example that you find on your own or as assigned by your instructor.

Chapter Seventeen

Stress and Health Management

Student Learning Outcome:
Students will self-assess perceptions, awareness of and ability to handle stress by generating and analyzing a nutrition chart and by creating a music playlist appropriate to their weekly activities.

"To keep the body in good health is a duty... otherwise we shall not be able to keep our mind strong and clear."

—Buddha

The demands of what is required of being a college student can bring about stress. Studying, meeting deadlines, worrying about passing grades—coupled with many other things going on in a student's life—will do that, and quite frankly that is the reality of going to school. The impact of stress, dropout, weight issues like the "freshman 15", eating disorders, unhealthy habits, or inappropriate immoral and anti-social behavior can be devastating. However, that does not mean that the stress cannot be controlled. There are strategies and tools that can be used to manage and control stress. Thus, this chapter will highlight some tips on how to keep your stress under control and how to relax when the stress seems overwhelming.

Exercise
Regular exercise plays an integral role in reducing or preventing stress. Taking 30 minutes out of your day due to some type of physical activity at least three times a week can be very beneficial to reducing stress, not to mention the physical benefits. You would have to determine what exercise is best for you based on what you enjoy doing. For instance, if you are a person that enjoys the outdoors, you might want to take up hiking, running, jogging, or walking outdoors; if you like the water, you can take up swimming and so on. Even going for walks regularly can help you clear your mind. The key is to find an exercise that you enjoy and will stick to consistently.

Time Management

Often times, time management can be one of the biggest challenges a student faces while in college, and not being able to manage time can induce unwanted stress. The main culprit of that stress is procrastination; the habit of putting tasks off to the last possible minute can be a major problem in both your academic career and your personal life. Side effects include missed opportunities, frantic study hours, stress, being overwhelmed, resentment, and guilt. Much of this can be avoided with better time management. Thus, in order to keep track of your time, you can use a daily planner, a digital device, or any tool that will help you manage your time accordingly. Whatever tool you decide to use, you must make sure that you organize your time and include the following:

- **Study time**
  In order to succeed in your coursework, you must allow time to study. This can be determined by the course rigor along with how many hours you are in the classroom or how many units you are taking. For instance, for every hour you are in class you must study 2-3 hours outside of the classroom. Thus, if you are taking 12 units, you must devote at least 24-36 hours a week outside of the classroom. This is why they call it being a full time student.

- **Quiet Time**
  With all the stressors of the college life, you want to definitely make time for quiet time to let yourself unwind and give time to yourself, whether it is just sitting down and reading a book, journaling, or simply sitting somewhere peaceful and relaxing. This can be at least a half hour to an hour a day if necessary.

- **Social Time**
  The demands of a student can create a lonely place at times, so you must also allow time for socializing, such as getting involved in a campus group like the Associate Student Organization, Cultural or Academic groups, etc. If that doesn't interest you, try to make time for make lunch or dinner plans with close friends: it is important to have support from your social group.

- **Fun Time**
  After a quiz, mid-term, completed assignment, final, or the end of the school session, it is important to allow yourself some fun time and reward yourself for your achievements. This can be a night on the town with close friends, dinner, a movie, or watching a play or ball game. Whatever you like to do, just do it and enjoy yourself.

Defeating and Overcoming Procrastination

Remember you are still a student, so study time should still take precedence over everything else, but you still want to allow yourself other activities to maintain a healthy mental and physical balance. Procrastination can be a major problem in both your career and your personal life. The behavior pattern of procrastination can be triggered in many different ways, so you won't always procrastinate for the same reason. Sometimes you'll procrastinate because you're overwhelmed with too much on your plate, and procrastination gives you an escape. Other times you'll feel tired and lazy, and you just can't get going.

So, what should you do? Be introspective: explore your feelings enough to know why you put off the things that you need to do and address the root causes. Manage your time effectively. Here are some tips and strategies to help you cope with the demands that life, school, and work may put on you:

Stress

Stress, worry, and anxiety often arise from a lack of balance: you feel you are spending too much time studying, so your family is neglected. You go out with friends to have some fun, and your studies suffer. Benjamin Franklin suggested that we divide our lives up into thirds: one third should be spent *working*; another third should be spent *resting*; and the final third should be spent *playing*. That, according to Franklin, was the optimal breakdown to maintain high productivity. None should occur at the expense of the others. Balance is the key.

> *Benjamin Franklin suggested that we divide our lives up into thirds: one third should be spent working; another third should be spent resting; and the final third should be spent playing. That, according to Franklin, was the optimal breakdown to maintain high productivity. None should occur at the expense of the others. Balance is the key.*

When I go to the gym, listen to music, or play baseball, I find that I have more energy to study and that I'm able to be more involved with my family. When I am well-rested, I am able to work at a rapid pace and be productive with my time. I have found that when these three elements in my life—work, rest, and play—are in harmony, I thrive. I'm happy, productive, and effective at everything I do. However, when my life is out of balance—and it frequently is—I find that everything suffers.

Also, I find that when I am in an environment that supports what I'm doing in that environment, then I am also more productive and effective. My office has healthy plants and some scented items. I have posters on the walls of some famous authors' quotes and pictures of my daughter on my desk. I have a CD player and keep some of my favorite CDs at work with me so that I can maintain a comfortable and relaxing work space. Since I find the environment peaceful and relaxing, I can go there to relieve stress, and I can be productive at my job.

Feeling Overwhelmed

Occasionally, you may have more stuff to do than you can reasonably accomplish, and this can certainly lead to feelings of being overwhelmed and wanting to give up on everything. Often, feeling overwhelmed can lead to additional procrastination because you feel like if you can't do everything, then there's no point in doing anything. If you feel this way, you should stop what you are doing, establish priorities, and reduce or simplify your overwhelming to-do list. Here are a couple suggestions for how to go about doing that:

- Review your "to-do" list, and eliminate anything unnecessary or unimportant. You need to focus on priorities, and you can't do everything. Delegate what you can delegate. At work or even in relationships, you may need to reconsider the value of that job or relationship if its demands on your time are overwhelming. Is it worth it?
- Make sure that you are well-rested: don't allow work, play, or studies to consume all of your energy. Find that balance. Maximize your effectiveness at the tasks that are crucial.

Laziness

Procrastination also often arises because we are out of balance and feel too tired from work or other obligations, or because we are too emotionally drained from our daily experiences, to do what we need to do. When this happens, a seemingly simple task feels like just way too much to deal with. This can become a pattern or bad habit, and we sometimes develop a "survival skill" that tells us that we need to conserve our energy because we are so drained, either emotionally or physically, which reduces our mental clarity. The best solution is to disrupt the pattern and eliminate the habit. Do a self-assessment and try to determine what is draining your energy. If possible, eliminate it in your life or minimize its impact on you. Exercise can help with the feeling of laziness. It may be counterintuitive, but exercising actually makes you feel more energetic.

Lacking Motivation

Temporary laziness can come from having low motivation. We all go through down times and experience moments of depression, but when these sorts of self-defeating feelings become chronic, then it's time to make a change. Discovering your passion, working toward clearly-defined goals, and having a purpose behind everything you do can all go a long way toward motivating yourself to achieve your full potential. I think we all know someone who hasn't lived up to his or her potential. Generally, people like that simply lacked the motivation to achieve their goals and to be who they could have been. It is sad when that happens, so don't let it happen to you. Find your inspiration. Set goals. Work toward achieving those goals. And keep your eyes on the prize.

At different times in your life—but *especially* in college—you may find that your initial motivation is just not that inspiring any more. It is normal and acceptable to realign your career goals in college to better match your feelings. In college, just like in life, we meet people and take classes that change us. They may inspire us to change majors, pursue a different career, or quit our jobs and seek employment in an entirely different field. Have you ever asked yourself, "What's the point of doing this?" Most likely, that was a moment of frustration or a moment in which you felt unmotivated to continue doing what you were doing. Ask yourself: what were you doing? And why? We find new passions as we are exposed to new things. Follow your heart and follow your dreams. There's nothing less rewarding than a life with no passion in it where you find yourself working at a job you can't stand and go home feeling unhappy, unfulfilled, and drained of energy every night. And there's no reason to go to college to pursue a life like that! Center your studies and choose your major and career path around an inspiring purpose. When you are inspired, when you have the motivation to go on, you will find that you won't want to procrastinate anymore. You'll have more energy because you'll want to do everything you have to do in order to achieve your goals. And finally, whenever you have moments where you feel down, you can review why you do what you do. You can remind yourself that you are studying hard for a test rather than playing video games all night because you want that nursing job or that accounting position. Then, the studying will assume its rightful importance and your energy level will increase correspondingly.

Lacking Discipline

It's hard to accept, but many of us are simply undisciplined. Not everything we do can be fun. Some things are chores. They have to be done, yet they provide no personal satisfaction. For me, these are things like vacuuming or doing laundry. We have to wash our clothes or we won't have any clean ones. I've found that chores like these are more manageable when my life is balanced and I am feeling healthy. One way to rationalize the importance of doing chores even when you don't want to is to contextualize them within the scope of everything you do—and to make sure that you are in balance. Doing the laundry isn't so bad when it doesn't dominate your life and when you have already had a ration of fun time and your school work is up to date.

Poor Time Management Habits

Many people, myself included, have bad habits that lead us to procrastinate. Sleeping in late is a common one. The solution is to change your habit: if you tend to oversleep and miss important events or deadlines or the entire day, then force yourself to change that habit. For example, oversleeping on the weekends is often caused be inadequate sleep on the weekdays. Reorganize your schedule to enable yourself to get adequate sleep consistently all week long. Then, set your alarm to wake up early on the weekend, and do something productive—ideally, something that you enjoy—on weekend mornings.

If you have trouble motivating yourself, you can set up a self-serving system of rewards. If you complete a task or overcome a challenge by waking up early or by doing the laundry, you can reward yourself by watching some TV show you like or by spending some fun time on social media sites or doing something else you enjoy. Make sure the reward matches the task. You can even plan out your day in 30 minute blocks: do a chore for 30 minutes and then enjoy a reward for 30 minutes.

Perfectionism

Perfectionism can also lead to procrastination. We can convince ourselves easily that if we don't do something right or perfectly, then there's no point in doing it at all. If this were the case, then education wouldn't work! We have to fail sometimes because the attempt is what is important; that's how we learn. Often we will put off doing something simply in order to convince ourselves that we have run out of time to do it right, and then—only then—will we accept a less than perfect execution of the task. In this way, we can feel that we aren't responsible for the imperfection. There just wasn't enough time. Believing that you must do something perfectly can lead to extreme stress and cause delays that are infinite. The solution is to allow yourself the room to fail. Allow yourself to be imperfect. Break down seemingly insurmountable tasks into stages or steps or parts. Not everything has to be done all at once. For instance, writer's block in essay writing often comes from the desire to write a perfect essay in one sitting in one draft. Usually, that's impossible. You can't conceptualize, write, revise and edit an essay all in your head before you write and then expect to write a single, perfect draft. Professional writers don't even do that. One step at a time!

Health and Nutrition

Maintaining a healthy diet has numerous benefits. Not only will it boost your energy level, it can also help you stay at a healthy weight, improve your physical ability, enhance concentration, delay the effects of aging, and help prevent sickness. However, most of us know what to eat and what not to eat, but we find ourselves in situations where we only have limited choices. Perhaps rushing home from school worried about a microbiology test the next day tempts you to just stop for some fast food at the drive-thru because you don't want to waste precious time shopping at the supermarket or cooking when you could be studying. Perhaps the easy availability of fast food and the low prices are tempting as well. Or, perhaps you like to go out to parties every weekend and there's always a cooler of beer nearby and way too much carne asada on the grill to just say no.

Obviously, we can't always avoid situations like those above all the time, nor do we want to be the one person at a party on a diet and refusing to eat any birthday cake! However, controlling your environment—where you hang out and who you hang out with—can make a big difference in your diet and health by not putting you in difficult situations like the scenarios above often enough to adversely impact your health. Plan ahead for the week. Go food shopping once a week and plan all of your meals, ideally around some of the guidelines below, in order to reduce the amount of time it takes to make meals or buy ingredients. Bring your breakfast, lunch, or dinner as well as snacks and drinks to school with you or on your outings so that you have an alternative to fast food. A great deal of food preparation can be done ahead of time and kept in the refrigerator until you leave. You can even make several meals at once to take with you to school or work. As long as the majority of the food you eat is healthy, a few weekend party indulgences won't harm you. The idea is to make the bulk of your diet healthy.

Reduce eating fast food and other unhealthy meals to the bare minimum. Many nutritionists recommend that we eliminate or minimize the amount of meat that we consume because our bodies require more energy to break down complex proteins, like meats and dairy products. Diets rich in raw fruits and vegetables provide the most energy. And, needless to say, drugs, alcohol, and smoking are all well-known to negatively impact the human body, accelerating all sorts of health risks, diseases, and even death. Avoid those at all costs!

Even if you don't drastically change your diet, since that by itself can be stressful, increase the amounts of raw fruits and vegetables that you eat and note the difference. Of course, I am not a medical doctor, so the advice below is meant only as a guideline; consult your physician for the best advice on how to maintain your health.

Some of the basic advice given by nutritionists is as follows:

- **Reduce Fat Intake:** Avoid fatty foods, saturated fat, fried foods, and dairy products (like milk, oils, cheese and butter). These items, especially foods high in saturated fat, can reduce heart health.

- **Reduce Salt Intake:** Salt is present in heavily-processed and fast foods in enormous quantities. It is used as a flavor-enhancer, but it also masks the flavor of food. Our bodies take a few weeks to adjust to a reduction is salt intake before we can taste the flavor of food in its more natural state. Look for reduced-sodium or no-sodium foods.

- **Hydrate:** Drink plenty of fluids; your kidneys depend on a minimum of eight glasses of water a day to function efficiently. Water is best: don't drink your daily calories.

- **Eat Lots of Fiber:** Eating fiber helps with digestion, reduces the risk of cancer, and can lower cholesterol. Foods rich in fiber are: oatmeal, brown rice, beans, most vegetables, and cereal.

- **Eat Reasonable Amounts of Starch:** Starchy foods like pasta, rice, bread, cereal and potatoes are rich in (good) carbohydrates. They contain several similar benefits that fiber-rich foods do.

- **Regularly Consume Antioxidants and Other Vitamins:** Vitamins and minerals are contained in foods such as fruits, vegetables, and grains. Antioxidants fight off free radicals that damage our cells, DNA, and membranes.

- **Eliminate Sugar and Sweets:** Aside from contributing to tooth decay, sugar turns to fat in the body. While it can often provide an energy boost, it really is just a lot of empty calories with no other nutritional value. And you crash after a sugar high anyways. Apples are a good substitute.

Nutritionists say that initially when you change your diet, you may feel worse because your body is adjusting to the change. This is why most weight loss diets are so difficult to maintain. Give yourself time. Exercise and slowly adjust your eating habits to include less meat and dairy products and more raw fruits and vegetables: you'll feel the difference!

Like a finely-tuned racing car or garden, your body needs the right fuel (food) and regular maintenance (exercise, lifestyle and mental attitude) to achieve its true health potential. Nothing is more important than healthy eating and living! Thus, you must attend to your diet properly by eating right and making sure you get all your proper nutrients and vitamins. This will allow you to deliver with your full power and performance. Without healthy eating, your body's engine will cough, splutter and eventually stall.

Music

Finally, I can't say enough about the power of music (and art) to reduce stress. Music has a positive effect on the body; in fact, there is a growing field called music therapy which, not surprisingly, uses music as therapy. Listening to music is probably second nature to you already, but it can be used more deliberately; it has a well-established link to our emotions. But you already know this: you probably have many songs in mind that affect you emotionally—that inspire you or drive you to tears. Listening on a portable device while

Like a finely-tuned racing car or garden, your body needs the right fuel (food) and regular maintenance (exercise, lifestyle and mental attitude) to achieve its true health potential. Nothing is more important than healthy eating and living!

you go about your daily life can keep you in a relaxed mood and reduce stress considerably. And, best of all, it doesn't require you to devote any extra time to it. You can play music while you exercise, cook, study, or drive to work or school. Listening to commercial radio is only second-best because the commercials can be stress-inducing, but it's a viable alternative if you are away from your iPod.

Believe it or not, although it's not my favorite, classical music has even been shown to slow elevated heart rates, lower blood pressure, and decrease the level of stress hormones we have in our bodies. Though classical is not to everyone's preference, it may be worth a try. All music has benefits: it can improve memory, aid in meditation, improve focus, and reduce feelings of stress. Note that music can be a distraction as well as help to create focus, so *deliberate* use of it in particular situations can reap the greatest rewards. When one of my friends used to study in college, he chose to listen primarily to instrumental jazz because music with lyrics required concentration to hear and distracted him from reading and studying—the words in the songs mixed with the words on the page; however, music without words slipped into the background and allowed him to concentrate on studying and reading without distraction. In fact, he said that he was able to concentrate better with the music than without it. When he wasn't studying, though, he listened to speedmetal and punk! Your musical preferences will vary of course, but finding the right soundtrack to your life, the right song for the right place, will keep your stress level manageable. Singing or even shouting (depending on your musical taste) can release tension, so even if you aren't at a karaoke bar, you can still benefit. Sing your own songs.

Finally, playing soothing music at night before you go to sleep can help your sleep be more peaceful and more relaxed. In college, if you learn nothing else, you will learn the value of a good night's sleep!

Journal Assignments

1.   What challenges (current or potential) do you face with effective time management at school that get in the way of completing your coursework? List them. Then, next to each one, identify strategies from this chapter that you can use to overcome each of those barriers.

2.   Keep a food log. Yes, list everything you eat and drink for an entire week. Everything. In a brief paragraph, evaluate your list at the end of the week in terms of the balanced nutritional guidelines above. Did you eat enough fiber, starch and antioxidants, etc.? Did you over-consume fast food, fat, oils, sugar, or salt? Where could you improve your diet? Were there any situations where you ate an unhealthy meal that could have been avoided? How can you avoid them next week? Write a brief plan for your meals next week: for each day of the week and for all three meals, list what foods and drinks you plan to have. Aim for a variety of foods that meet the nutritional guidelines above over the course of the whole week. Finally, make yourself a shopping list to purchase all the necessary ingredients for your week of meals.

3.   Either in real life or simply on paper, make a playlist or mixtape of music that can best accompany various activities in your life using your own hobbies and tasks as inspiration. For example, what would the best playlist be for the gym, on a date, while studying, while driving, when feeling discouraged, when you are celebrating, and so on. Use your playlists when the time comes. Alternately, think back to a crucial time in your life that you struggled to go through: if that time in your life were made into a movie, what songs would be on the soundtrack? What would the main title song be and why?

Chapter Eighteen

The Fear of Success and the Fear of Failure

Student Learning Outcome:
Students will use visualization and self-efficacy to extrapolate positive future outcomes from their current baseline in order to improve self-esteem, increase success, maximize growth mindset potential, and tolerate disappointments.

"I think the big mistake in schools is trying to teach children anything, and by using fear as the basic motivation. Fear of getting failing grades, fear of not staying with your class, etc. Interest can produce learning on a scale compared to fear as a nuclear explosion to a firecracker."
—Stanley Kubrick, film director

"I've missed more than 9000 shots in my career. I've lost almost 300 games. 26 times, I've been trusted to take the game winning shot and missed. I've failed over and over and over again in my life. And that is why I succeed."
—Michael Jordan, athlete

The Fear of Success

The fear of success or fear of failure often emerges from students who lack self-confidence or who have absorbed negative messages about education or themselves. In chapter 3, we discuss financing a college education, and I have spoken to so many students who are dead-set against taking out loans for college. To me, this indicates that they don't trust higher education to increase their future earning potential, or that they have somehow convinced themselves that they may have to drop out. However, this is really more often indicative of a student's lack of self-confidence, underpreparation, or negative thinking. Successful people build self-confidence, are well prepared, and think positively; this is not to say that they are unrealistic or that you should be unrealistic: it means that there are healthy and unhealthy levels of skepticism; it means that you can teach yourself to face situations where you may be uncomfortable; and it means that there are ways to overcome obstacles like negative thinking and make yourself into the person that you want to be.

240

First and foremost, decide who you want to be and how you are going to get there. This book should have taught you how to do that already. Make an informed decision based solely on who you want to be, and stick to it without compromising. Goal-setting like this should be based on carefully researched plans. Choose a profession and research it; select a major; research university programs and decide on the campus that best meets your needs and will get you to where you want to be. Hold that thought. In fact, hold that thought until you get there!

Far too many students at my college have come from high school into our community college, been successful, and then "settled" for attending a university that is located conveniently close to home or chosen their educational pathway based on which university offers the best financial aid package. In all these cases, that is basically letting someone else make decisions for you. Don't do that! Don't give up your power of self-determination. Decide what university to attend based on what is the best fit for you. Financial aid and the location are two of many other factors. What about you? What about the quality of the education, the reputation of the university, or the strength of the programs offered?

> *Far too many students at my college have come from high school into our community college, been successful, and then "settled" for attending a university that is located conveniently close to home or chosen their educational pathway based on which university offers the best financial aid package. In all these cases, that is basically letting someone else make decisions for you. Don't do that!*

Especially as it relates to college, keep this in mind: publicly-funded education is frequently under attack by taxpayers and lawmakers because of the expense it causes to state and federal budgets; however, there are many other state and federal expenses. In many countries which value education, public education is free. The workplace needs educated workers, and the country needs educated citizens, but often news broadcasts will demonize the cost of public education, making it sound as if it's not worth the expense to you, the state, or the country. Don't be fooled by this propaganda. Higher education is not and should never be the privilege of the upper class, nor should it be reserved only for those students who already have money and leisure time. A university education is your right: should you choose to exercise that right and attend, then you belong there. If you were to ask me, the country needs people

241

who value education to graduate from institutions of higher education and then go on to make laws and pass legislation that will keep the doors open to all people.

Focus on the greater rewards that higher education will provide you. Getting a degree from a university is hard work and may possibly open you up to criticism from friends and family members who think you are wasting your time. However, it will lead to you have a better life, higher average pay at work, an intellectually enriched mind, and a better job. If you have children, you will have set the bar for your kids at a higher level, so that when they are ready for college, they'll have a college-educated parent to guide them.

Self-Confidence

Take a moment to imagine yourself at the university you dream of attending, your long shot, the school you believe you only have a slim chance of going to but have always wished you could. Take your time. I'll wait.

Are you done yet?

When you are done, take a moment to reflect on what you imagined. Did you imagine yourself all stressed out and intimidated by all the other "smart" students? Did you imagine how you'd feel telling family and friends that you failed your first Biology test? Did you imagine being called on in math class to answer a question that you didn't know the answer to?

Did you imagine something else negative?

I hope not.

On the other hand, was your daydream a positive one, where you imagined yourself raising your hand in class and correctly answering a question? Did you imagine calling your family or friends to announce that you got the highest score on the Biology midterm? Did you imagine showing the rest of the class how to solve a math problem that had the whole class stumped? Did you imagine something else positive?

I hope so, but if not, you aren't alone. Try again, and this time force yourself to imagine a positive experience.

Not very easy, is it?

The above exercise, imagining yourself in the future, is called visualization. It's difficult to do at first and probably feels a bit weird, but it does show you your own level of self-confidence. If you had trouble imagining something positive, then you may not have thought hard enough about committing to higher education, you may have lingering doubts, or you may lack self-confidence.

It's hard to imagine success, especially when there are so many factors conspiring against us. Our past failures, mistakes, and discouragements may lead us to feel like we will continue to fail, to make mistakes, and to be discouraged. Other people, often our own friends and family, can be supportive, but can also be negative as well. Humans seem to be competitive by nature; more likely, we learn that competition is natural when it's not. This leads people to compare themselves to others. We do it ourselves, and other people compare themselves to us. Thus, when we are trying to better ourselves, it can be perceived as a threat, almost unconsciously, by other people, who respond to that perceived threat and implied competition, by doing and saying things that will keep you where you are and prevent you from achieving your full potential, so that they can continue to feel superior or at least equal. This can be extremely discouraging and damage self-esteem. It is hard for people to admit that someone else has done something that they themselves couldn't, unless of course that person is the exception. Or magical.

The media frequently promotes propaganda that suggests students of color or working class students can't succeed in college, except in rare circumstances. It is very infrequent that a news story or movie will be made to show that regular people can be successful. We see movies all the time about the rare exception, the gifted person, who somehow magically overcomes the odds against them to become recognized as the genius they truly are. But that person is always an exception, and that depiction is usually racist, sexist, or classist. It suggests that the average person of color, or average woman, or average working class person can't be a success; only those rare exceptions that Hollywood makes movies about can succeed. What about those of us who are not exceptions and not magical?

Confident people almost always imagine themselves succeeding at things that they plan to do. To make sure that they feel confident, they visualize in detail everything that they can about their future plans so that they are mentally prepared for whatever comes their way. Then, they make their imaginary future become something real.

243

Have you ever had to give a speech in front of a class or to another group of people? Few people like giving speeches; it's a fear that people often rank as more frightening than the fear of death! One of the best ways to get past the fear of giving speeches is to imagine yourself giving a great speech, to much applause, until any inkling of nervousness is gone. This can take some time, but it's well worth the investment.

Of course, this can be applied to any fear-provoking situation, not just speeches, and most relevantly, it can be applied to your own future potential in any situation, not just education.

Preparedness

The other technique for overcoming that fear is to be prepared. And you already are.

With regard to self-confidence, have some! Having explored higher education at a community college, you have already taken the steps necessary to find out if you can succeed at a university. You have explored the tutoring and counseling services available; you have worked out the financing; you know how to identify your own strengths and weaknesses and do something about them.

While some students may have attended community college because they were not accepted into any universities out of high school, most students attend community college because the price is a bargain or because they want to test what going to college feels like. There are other reasons, of course, but the point is that community college is in no way remedial: university-level transfer courses at a community college are equivalent to university courses, so, chances are, you have already demonstrated your ability to succeed at a university level. And, as previously stated, if you do end up at a university and struggle with it, you know the importance of seeking help from counselors or tutors or other students and can overcome those obstacles placed in your way.

Very few, if any, college students attend a university without having some sort of crisis of self-confidence. Having read this book, however, you probably know more about the university experience than most incoming students do. It's normal to be nervous and to question your own abilities as a student. Without going to the extreme of becoming a basket case, it would be unhealthy and unrealistic not to have some doubt and trepidation. But with this book, your community college experience, and your efforts so far, you already have the tools you need to be successful. That is the crucial preparation that you need to be successful and thrive at a university.

Keep practicing. Your community college experience will better prepare you for a university experience if you treat one like the other. While at community college, take your classes as seriously as you would at a university. Develop and refine your time management and study skills using the techniques discussed elsewhere in this book. Just because other students may act like they don't care or they aren't serious doesn't mean you have to act the same way.

My suggestion is to ignore other negative people. Don't worry about what they say or who they say it to. Just do you. Let them talk. You focus on your education and attaining your goals.

Furthermore, don't compete with other students. Cooperate: form study groups, network, make friends, socialize—that's all fine. However, many students become more insecure when they compare themselves to others. They constantly compare themselves to others who are already successful or who are graduates who are working in the field. I have counseled countless students who tell me that their friends have already graduated or already have jobs; these students that I counsel often seem to have lost some self-esteem because they are, in a sense, competing with those students who have progressed through higher education more quickly, even if these other people started first.

It's not a race. There's no such thing as "getting behind" or coming in last place when it comes to finishing your education. Do it *right*; don't do it fast. Doing well in your classes and getting the information you need to be successful at higher levels is infinitely more important than finishing your general education requirements in record-breaking time or "catching up" to your friends from high school.

Competition may be healthy in the workplace, but I doubt it is productive in the long run. With short term goals, like meeting a sales target at a retail establishment, getting employees to compete with each other for a prize can create a situation where everyone is trying to outsell the other employees; however, this doesn't translate well into long term goal setting. Even in this retail store example, employees constantly competing with each other will probably become selfish about winning the sales contest and less inclined to cooperate. Jealousy can creep in if one employee wins more frequently, and employees who don't win can become discouraged and stop trying because they feel they don't have a chance. That sort of thinking is microscopic: it looks at the little picture, the short term gains, and fails to recognize the value of a long term investment.

Look at the big picture. When it comes to your goals and your future, specifically as it relates to your education and subsequent career, you are making a long-term investment. Unlike many retail store employees who only work for a company for a short time, the big picture and far-reaching outlook matter when it comes to your future. In education, what you do today is an investment in your future. Your career (as opposed to your job) depends largely on your education; your quality of life for yourself and your future or current family depends largely on your career. So it's not about winning the little daily competitions we are faced with, and it's not about being better than someone else. *It's about bettering yourself.*

Instead of focusing your time and energy comparing yourself to others and competing with them, focus on making yourself better than you were yesterday. Focus on self-growth and compete with yourself.

And finally, set your own expectations for yourself. Other people are other people: I mean that your friends and family may have expressed expectations for you. One of my colleagues told me a story about how he took 7 1/2 years to get his B.A. degree, and his family constantly hounded him about when he was going to graduate—at every holiday every year for 7 1/2 years! However, when he did finally graduate and then go on to graduate school, he pointed out to me that when applying for jobs and for graduate school, no one ever questioned why it took him so long to graduate. Because it didn't matter! What mattered was that he *did* graduate and that he did well in the classes in his major.

Feeling shame for taking your time with your education is usually the self-imposed result of comparing yourself to others and of unhealthy competition. There are countless reasons why students might need more than two years to finish community college, from not being able to get needed classes, to working full time, to raising a family, to simply not wanting to rush. It's okay to take your time. Remember, the work you do and the classes you take when you first start college build the foundation of knowledge that you need to succeed at higher levels. If you rush through your lower division classes and end up not retaining the important information that they provide (both academic knowledge and other ancillary skills like test-taking, study habits, note taking and time management), how successful could you possibly be at the higher levels?

> *Feeling shame for taking your time with your education is usually the self-imposed result of comparing yourself to others and of unhealthy competition. There are countless reasons why students might need more than two years to finish community college, from not being able to get needed classes, to working full time, to raising a family, to simply not wanting to rush. It's okay to take your time.*

Take the time to do your education right.

Bitterness and Disillusionment

Often, students become pessimistic because they think they don't have a chance to transfer to a good university and that they can't possibly compete at "that level." Perhaps this feeling emerges as a result of having had bad experiences in education or of having heard about the experiences of others.

This ongoing cycle can continue from generation to generation. Family members may have shared their negative experiences with education; as they are people you might look up to, they may have told you that they couldn't succeed in higher education and you may have absorbed that message, thinking that if your relative couldn't make it, neither can you.

Everyone feels down and self-critical at times. It's normal to have occasional negative thoughts and unfortunately it's also normal to be exposed to the negative thoughts of others. Negativity can be healthy at times, but it can also become crippling and self-defeating. If you find yourself spending too much time doubting or worrying about your future, remember the visualization exercise earlier in this chapter: our thoughts make our future. Therefore, it helps to clear your mind of negative thoughts and scrutinize where these negative thoughts come from and what purpose they may have. They are often thoughts of unfavorable outcomes, things we fear to be true, but which are unlikely.

As yourself whether or not the negative thoughts you may have are really true. Or ask yourself whether the negative ideas someone else may have are really true. For example, is a university education really worth the investment and expense? Rather than letting that thought haunt you and bring you down, look it up. Online, check to see what the relative salaries are for those with college degrees compared to those without. Too general? Look up your specific field and the profession you intend to enter. How much does that pay? Is a degree required? You probably can't even get the job you want without a degree. So, what choices are left? The job market for jobs that don't require a college degree is dwindling. Food service, retail, and hotel/restaurant jobs don't require degrees for entry level positions, but many establishments require degrees for management positions! Where do you want to be in your future, still at entry level?

Do your research and have faith in yourself. Someone who is trying to discourage you may have an ulterior motive for being discouraging. They may not have gone to college themselves and by convincing you not to go, they justify what they did as being right. That way, they never have to see you succeed and face the fact that they were wrong. Also, be thorough in your research and look at the big picture, not one individual microscopic example that confirms your fears. Don't find one example of someone, for example, who went to college and couldn't find a job and had all sorts of loans to pay off. *Those* are the exceptions. *That* is the propaganda that maintains the status quo of privileged people only attending college. And apply this critical thinking skill, this healthy skepticism, to other negative thoughts besides those about attending college as well. That was just my example.

In addition (and this may sound obvious), choose to be happy and think positively. It is a conscious choice. You can choose to let negative thoughts overwhelm you, or you can choose to face them as obstacles to be overcome, each one strengthening you and building your self-confidence. It's easy at first to become "psyched out" about the unknown—a new class, a new relationship, a new teacher, a new school. So make the unknown *known.* Educate yourself about the class, the person, the teacher, or the campus, and be prepared, so that you have nothing to fear.

Allowing the negativity from others to overwhelm you or control you, and even allowing your own negativity to hinder you or cause you to set goals that are lower than what you truly want to achieve, allows other people to have power over you. You should make decisions based on what you want, not what other people tell you to do. Don't let negative thoughts or other people control you. That can become a self-fulfilling prophecy. When you set your mind to do something, when you set a serious goal for yourself and commit to it, you will pursue that goal with all your heart and all your energy. And as a result, you will be successful. When you do things because someone else told you that you should or because they thought it was a good idea, you are likely not to have fully bought into the idea, not to take it seriously, and not to be committed. That is undoubtedly a recipe for failure. When it comes to college, if you find yourself at a campus that doesn't inspire you or in a major that doesn't motivate you, you are highly unlikely to be successful.

Finally, have you ever heard the expression, "I want to go to college so I can be somebody"? I hate that statement. Remember: you *already are* somebody. No matter who you are or where you come from, you are somebody right now. College doesn't define you. It can help you grow or evolve, but it is not *all* of who you are.

Turn Discouragement into Encouragement

Remember that mistakes can help you succeed. Failure is a great motivator. It might sound backwards, but think of it this way: if, for example, you do poorly on an essay assignment in your English class, rather than cave in and feel ashamed or like giving up altogether, feel angry with yourself or feel disappointed. You should; no one likes to do poorly, but don't become discouraged; become empowered: let that anger or disappointment motivate you to prove that you are better than that and drive you to do better on the next essay assignment.

Learn from your mistakes. It's okay to make them. Everyone does. Correct your behavior: figure out what went wrong and resolve either to correct the problem or prevent it from happening again. Learn to teach yourself! In the English class essay scenario described above, perhaps you

> *Finally, have you ever heard the expression, "I want to go to college so I can be somebody"? Remember: you already are somebody. No matter who you are or where you come from, you are somebody right now.*

didn't do the reading carefully enough. Perhaps you waited until the night before the assignment was due to begin it. Perhaps you missed crucial aspects of the assignment from not reading the assignment prompt carefully enough. Perhaps you struggled to understand the reading assignment and didn't take the time to get help with it from your instructor or a tutor. If you aren't sure what went wrong, ask your instructor. Soliciting feedback from instructors and tutors is a good way to ensure you are on the right track and are grasping the material and applying it to your assignments.

Journal Assignments

1. Write a descriptive paragraph or essay in which you describe yourself as you want to be in 10 years. Imagine a scenario from a typical day in your daily life where you are there, and write a scene or story in which you are the main character. Include at least allusions to the following and be as detailed as possible: Where will you live? What degrees will you have? What will your job be? What is your living situation?

2. Do some research to answer the following question, which we all have as we embark on or journey into higher education: Is a university education really worth the investment and expense? Online, check to see what the relative salaries are for those with college degrees compared to those without. Look up your specific field and the profession you intend to enter. How much does that pay? Is a degree required? As indicated in the chapter, look for comprehensive data—like a study or statistics—as opposed to a single example of one person.

Student Success Profile:

Jane Hafoka

Describe yourself briefly in a short biography (hometown, birthplace, high school experience, family, education).

I was born at Harbor UCLA medical center in Torrance, CA. I grew up in in the greater Los Angeles area. My childhood was split in Watts and Hawthorne. I attended 3 different elementary schools, 3 middle schools and went to Leuzinger high school but dropped out during my junior year. I took home schooling instead and graduated before my peers by a few months. My family is a huge part of who I am. They have been my biggest supporters and are always encouraging me to never give up. I am the youngest of 8 kids. My parents came to America in the late 70s to look for a better life. They moved from the East Coast to California in the 80s and finally settled in LA around 1984.

What was your background before coming to community college?
I started working right after high school. First as a sales associate in Bakersfield at a fabric store and afterwards as a cashier at a supermarket in Compton. I always knew I wanted to finish school, so when the time came, I went to Southwest with my niece who was enrolling. While waiting with her in the financial aid line, I figured I might as well start my education again too, so I enrolled as well. I am more than glad I made that choice.

What, if anything, prompted your decision to attend community college? What were your goals upon entering community college (why did you go)? Did they change after you started college? If so, how?
I wanted a career and higher pay. I knew that could only be accomplished by earning a degree or, by some miracle, obtaining success in the entertainment world. I took the route of education and haven't looked back. I wanted my AA and to transfer to a UC where I would obtain my BA. I know I have grown since enrolling. Even though I was 23 when I started classes at Southwest, I was still very immature. I am a more educated woman now, still curious as ever and ready to take on any challenge.

Describe your experience as a community college student. What were the highlights? Were there any special programs or extracurricular experiences that were memorable or inspiring?
My experience was sometimes fun, tiring and interesting. I enjoyed being a part of Puente and taking trips to different UC campuses. That was a definite highlight. Being a part of EOPS has also certainly helped my transition from community college to a university. It is a great program that really helped me become a better student.

How much time went by between high school and community college for you? What were the biggest challenges that you faced when you began attending community college?
I went back to school after 5 years of graduating high school. As soon as I entered my first class, I felt like I was where I needed to be. The amount of time that passed wasn't so much that I forgot what school was like. There weren't many challenges that I faced, so being in close contact with my mentors helped me navigate the school system with some ease.

Did you work while attending community college? If so, how did you balance your time between work and school? Do you have any kids or other family responsibilities? If so, how did you balance your time between home and school? Did you have all three? How did you handle that?
I wasn't working when I started classes, but I got hired at a small Japanese restaurant not long after. It was hectic balancing both school and work. There isn't too much time for much else. You have to be able to prioritize in order to succeed,

and there were times where I slipped. However, I always managed to get back on track. I do not have any kids but I take care of my mom who has type 2 diabetes and high blood pressure. I make sure she eats right and gets some exercise every day.

Community colleges generally have a high attrition rate, meaning a large percentage of students drop out. Why do you think this happens? What motivated you to persevere through college and transfer to a university?
I think a lot of students do not have a good support system. I believe you need to have someone pushing you and encouraging you to keep going. I was motivated by the amount of time I have to get a good job, buy my own house and start a family. I also love learning, so that made going to school each day much more special. My mentors, Daniel Ortega and Darren Cifarelli, also kept me motivated to stay in school.

Of all the reading assignments you completed in college, which one had the greatest impact on you? What's your favorite book and why?
A book that I will not forget is actually a play that I was assigned to read for a theatre class. It was called *Fences*. The story was very powerful and it made me think a lot about society and what an enormous role it plays in our daily lives.

Of all the writing assignments you had in college, which are you most proud of and why?
During my first semester I wrote an essay about being Tongan in America for the "Say the Word" contest and it was recognized by my English teacher. I was so proud that it would be featured in the next book. It gave students a chance to learn more about my culture.

Attending a college or university can be extremely stressful for many students. Does any particular thing stand out as being the most stressful aspect of going to school? What was it and why was it stressful? What coping skills did you use to overcome stress in order to succeed?
The only part I do not like about school is waking up early. I am not a morning person. On the other hand, I love to learn and discover new things. If I wasn't motivated by that one aspect, I would've stopped going to school a while ago. I also dislike the long nights of studying and writing papers, but at the end of it all I feel accomplished and that feeling undeniably helps me to push forward.

Many community college students give up when faced with adversity or challenges or barriers. You, however, didn't. What was the biggest challenge you faced and how did you overcome it? What advice would you give to a student who feels like he or she just can't do it, has too much going on in his or her life, or is just struggling academically and feels like maybe college isn't the right place?
The biggest challenge was passing Math 125: Intermediate Algebra. I have always struggled with math and I failed it once. In that, I went to the tutoring lab and

spent more time focusing on math. My advice would be to expect difficulties, expect adversities, but never to let it overcome you. You have to be a fighter in this world we live in. I don't mean violence but to fight with your heart and mind. Believing in yourself is also pivotal; no one can get you to the top but you.

Were there any memorable faculty, counselors, other students, administrators or staff (at your community college or university) with whom you established a rapport and who made a difference? Is establishing relationships with people on campus important? Tell a brief story about someone with whom you became close and who was supportive.
My English professor and Puente counselor were two figures who really helped me succeed at Southwest. It is very important to establish relationships with your professors, counselors and mentors. These people will push you, encourage you and help in any way they can to make sure you achieve your goals. When at times I didn't believe in myself and I wanted to give up, my counselor always had my back. He believed in me when I didn't.

***Courage to Learn* discusses building social capital, meaning developing relationships and skills that are like an investment in your own future. What social capital have you gained since entering community college?**
My writing skills have improved greatly and receiving input from my English professor has helped with that immensely. I have also established friendships with Southwest students who are just as driven to succeed as I am.

What was your social life like in college? How important was it to you personally and educationally?
I made sure that I kept my social life and my academic life apart. School has always gained priority but there were times where I let myself enjoy a movie and just hang out with friends. You have to let yourself have a little bit of "me time" or else you might crash and burn.

Deciding what university to transfer to is difficult. What factors did you consider when deciding where to apply and where to attend?
I always knew I wanted to attend a UC. Berkeley and UCLA were my top choices but receiving acceptance from Santa Cruz and Santa Barbara instead had me thinking hard about which school to pick. I chose Santa Cruz because the campus is beautiful, diverse and different from what I am used to.

If you are working (while still a student or after having graduated), what is that experience like?
It can be stressful working and going to school at the same time, but it is a challenge that really molds you into being independent and being able to manage time wisely.

How did you manage the transition from a community college to a university? Did you feel prepared or underprepared? What were the biggest challenges that you faced during the transition?

While I am still in the middle of transitioning, the only challenge right now is getting all my things moved in to my dorm. There are also a few small grants that are being offered that I need to work on.

What plans for the future do you have (educationally, socially, and professionally)? When and how did those goals emerge?

I plan on becoming a lawyer and helping people, in particular the Tongan community. I want to reach out to people and let them know that success is everyone's own right. Becoming a lawyer has been a dream since childhood and my dad's face would light up when I would tell him my dreams. His smile always brings me to a better place and I know he would want me to do what my heart desires. He was extremely generous and I know he is proud of my accomplishments thus far.

Looking back, what advice would you give to first year community college students today (i.e. if you could go back in time and talk to yourself on your first day of college, what would you say)?

As mentioned before, I would tell him/her to never give up because there are times when you just want to drop everything and go out with your friends. You need to think about the future and the hard work you put in first. Time is precious so every moment should be used with the utmost consideration. If I could go back and talk to myself, I would say "It's about time! You're going to be great."

Chapter Nineteen

Choosing the Right College for You

Student Learning Outcome:
Students will apply research and assessment to make choices based on evaluation of potential colleges according to criteria derived from students' academic and professional goals.

"Education is our passport to the future, for tomorrow belongs to the people who prepare for it today."
— Malcolm X

Choosing the right college for your needs is no easy task. You will have to consider many things. For instance, some colleges are better than others are for different majors. That is to say, some colleges may have stronger faculty than others for certain fields. The quality of their research may be more respected at these schools. A good idea for where to begin your search is to invest in one of the *U.S. News and World Report* college rankings. They break schools down by categories of majors and explain the different criteria they use for these rankings.

Begin with Your Major

Your primary consideration in deciding which course of study suits you is your major. According to Dawn Papandrea on the Collegebound.net website, you will first have to decide upon a major. Then, once you have decided upon a major, you should research to see which colleges offer this major. It can be a very difficult experience to pour over promotional college materials, all of them purporting to be offering you the best college experience possible. It may very well be the case that more than one college is right for you. In the end, however, it is up to you to make the choice based upon all the considerations which will be discussed in this chapter.

Setting a Goal

Let us start with some basic issues in deciding upon the best college or university for your needs. First, as mentioned above, is your major. If you plan on getting an advanced degree, such as a master's degree, for your career, then you should not be overly concerned about the college or university which you will be choosing for your undergraduate degree. However, choosing a location for undergraduate work involves picking the right stepping-stone, and since going to a good undergraduate school helps you get into a good graduate school, you should consider your entire academic plan before making a final decision. Granted, you should be putting as much effort into choosing the best college for your undergraduate major since that will be your immediate need, but, in the end, it will be your master's degree which will open more doors for you. Nevertheless, let us examine the other factors involved in choosing a university for your undergraduate degree.

What Size School Suits You?

Large Universities: Benefits

Consider whether you want to attend the four years of your undergraduate life at a large or a small school. At a large university, you may feel invigorated by all the things one can do at such schools. These schools, many of them public state universities, offer a lot of attractions such as numerous clubs, carnivals, fraternities and sororities, on-campus faith organizations, and so on. These large universities end up becoming almost like little self-enclosed worlds. With medical assistance and psychological counseling offered on campus, one can come to feel that literally all of one's needs can be met while on the school grounds. A big campus can make you feel as though you are in another world. In a sense, it is very understandable why some students end up becoming career students: they recognize how wonderful such a large and comprehensive university can be and do not want to leave that environment.

Large Universities: Drawbacks

On the other hand, a large urban campus can cause some students to feel as if they are "just a number." The possible effect of a sprawling campus for some students is to make them feel as though the atmosphere of college is overwhelming. They may feel as though they are in a maze. For this reason, you need to be aware of your preferences when it comes to choosing the right college for yourself. Some students, aware of the acreage involved at some universities, invest in a sturdy bike so that they can cycle across campus. This may make the experience a little easier as they do not have to walk from one end of the campus to the other. If you do decide to attend a large urban university, you may want to make a list of all the things which will make the experience a little less stressful for yourself. These things might range from bicycling to weekly outings at your favorite haunts. It is important to get away once in a while from a stressful environment. The benefit of doing so is the fact that you will return to the environment refreshed and renewed. We all have a need to distance ourselves from a stressful environment and allow ourselves a chance to be nourished in whatever manner gives us pleasure and relaxation.

Large Universities: Other Considerations

While on the campus, you may want to visit the recreational areas, such as the Student Union. This is usually the area where students go to relax and unwind. There are usually places in the Student Union where you can buy some comfort foods, such as snacks or even a pizza. Additionally, there are usually billiards, ping-pong tables, and other diversions available for student use. Some universities even have small movie theaters where they show the latest movie releases. Most universities allow students to join the ASI, or the Associated Students, Inc. This is the backbone of student organizations and activities on campus. If you join the ASI, which at some schools is optional, you can then use some of the other recreational areas which are reserved only for members. At some schools, this may be the swimming pool at the Student Union, or perhaps other equally enjoyable amenities. Visit these places as often as you can, thereby making your stay at these large universities as stress-free as possible.

Looking into the Community

Look beyond the campus into the community as well. Just because you can get all of your needs met on campus doesn't necessarily mean that you will want to do that. Choosing a school that has accessible recreational amenities that you like is also important. If you like surfing, consider how far away the beach is from campus. If you like music or art, investigate how many clubs and galleries are in the local area. My co-worker, Darren Cifarelli, attended U.C. Santa Cruz for two years. He said that while it was a beautiful campus with a liberal political and creative atmosphere, he became bored easily after having grown up in Los Angeles, where there were many clubs to go see music, lots of bookstores to browse through, and tons of movie theaters, political events, and art shows to visit. "At Santa Cruz," he said, "though I'd love it now that I'm older, I just felt so isolated. There was one good used book and record store. One all ages club—and that was a long way away on the bus. One movie theater. I barely lasted two years there, and I still love that campus, but my age 18 hyperactive self just totally couldn't stand being away from all the big city stuff." It does matter where you live since you will be spending at least 2 years there.

Small Universities

On the other hand, you may end up preferring a small campus to a large one. In the end, the intimacy and coziness of a small school may be the right environment for you to learn. Usually the private universities establish these small havens of learning. You may feel that you need to be connected to other people in order to learn effectively. The advantage of small schools is that they are, indeed, more intimate. You get to know your professors more intimately than you would at a larger university.

Small Universities: Benefits

The environment of a small campus may also have other factors associated with some of your beliefs. For instance, your choice for an undergraduate institution may be based on religion. There are many fine private universities which are religious in their orientation. These schools were usually founded by some order, either Catholic or Protestant. The advantage of these schools is that their academic programs are normally quite rigorous. The chances are excellent that you will get a good education at a private religious school. Furthermore, if you are person of strong religious conviction, you will have the opportunity to attend services at least twice a week, once with the other students during the weekdays, and of course on Sundays. These schools encourage their students to pray and shed any self-consciousness about their religious convictions. If you have suffered any previous religious discrimination at either your high school or at a public college, then a private religious university might be the choice for you. Simply looking for a campus that enables the freedom to worship without any undue pressure to conform to a single religion—or which seems to be non-denominational or atheist—might help you to feel more comfortable. Some of these campuses have beautiful churches and chapels on the grounds. This can certainly make for a peaceful and meditative experience while studying and attending classes daily. Prayer can be a wonderful antidote to the stress of getting your college education. Even if you end up deciding upon a public (and, by default, non-religious) university, you may want to make your own "inner chapel" in your mind and find a nice quiet corner on the campus, perhaps under a tree, and recite a favorite prayer, such as the Serenity Prayer, and allow the stress of the day to slip out of your mind and body.

Small campuses are usually very appealing from the point of view of simple aesthetics. When I was at the beach one sunny day in 1998, I took out my copy of *Peterson's Guide to Graduate Schools*. Although not exactly the type of book one would normally take to the beach, I really needed to read this guide. The upcoming fall semester was going to be my last at California State University, Long Beach. One of my former professors informed me that the students who graduate with their bachelor's degree and decide to get valuable work experience usually never go back for their master's degree. Their paychecks are usually too addictive to give up, and they end up working for the rest of their lives, always promising that they will return to school, but never doing so. Therefore, I had resolved to find a good graduate school for myself. My major had been psychology as an undergraduate. I knew that I wanted to stay within the field of psychology or counseling. I also wanted to be able to do educational counseling work with students. Therefore, as I sat on the beach on that beautiful day, I began to pour over the listings. *Peterson's Guide* ranks schools in specific categories and cross-references the listings as well. One school caught my eye. At first, I thought I had misread it, but my eyes had not deceived me. The University of La Verne, a school I had never heard about previously, was listed among the countless other schools. It was a private school, but the cost seemed too inexpensive for a non-public school. They offered a Master of Science in Counseling, with a concentration in Higher Education. I decided to investigate it further. I called the school, and they invited me to attend one of the orientations for new graduate students, which was held in October of that year. The timing was perfect for my orientation. It was autumn, and although Southern California does not have the type of autumns which have made New England famous with tourists, there are enough deciduous trees in and around the campus of the University of La Verne to create an impressive effect. These trees were releasing their annual brown, orange and red leaves on the grounds of the school. When I arrived on campus, late in the afternoon, I was immediately taken by the small and cozy atmosphere. It looked like a setting in New England. The campus had an intimate feel to it; I felt like I had stepped into a postcard. At that moment I realized that this would be the place I would earn my master's degree. Three years later, I graduated from the University of La Verne with a master's degree.

Although I was quite happy attending my classes as an undergraduate at California State University, Long Beach, I knew that a change of scenery would be the right prescription for my master's degree program. Long Beach is a sprawling campus with 35,000 students attending classes. The head count was about 30,000 during my two years there. It is a very large school. I adored that campus and still do, but I wanted my graduate school to have a smaller, quieter, and more serene setting for my studies. La Verne fit the bill. It had, at that time, only 6,000 students, one-fifth the student population of Long Beach. It is a private school, which also appealed to me. The combined tuition total for the two years was going to be in the area of $15,000, which, to my mind, and the minds of most people with whom I consulted, was actually quite inexpensive, especially for a master's degree program. Additionally, the campus had other things which were new and very appealing to me. For instance, there was a non-denominational chapel on the grounds. Additionally, the school had a religious heritage. It was founded by the Church of the Brethren in the late nineteenth century. Although the campus now has a secular curriculum, it still maintains unofficial ties to its church. The Church of the Brethren still stands just several hundred yards off campus. With its high Gothic bell tower and pointed arches, it stands as a monument to the strong faith of its original founders. All of this was novel to me. I had been attending two public colleges, Long Beach City College, and California State University, Long Beach. Both were secular. There are no chapels on those campuses nor was either school founded by a religious order. The idea of attending a university with a chapel on the grounds and its big Gothic church just off campus was simply too attractive for me to decline. These are the kinds of choices you will have to make as you begin your search for both your undergraduate and graduate degrees. However, you should make an effort to attend two different schools for your bachelor's and master's degrees. This has been regularly recommended for students. It is almost axiomatic that one should not try to earn a graduate degree from the same institution from which one has received a bachelor's degree. A student's mind will be stimulated much more by the different faculty, a different setting, and perhaps also a different school philosophy. What is always the objective is maximum intellectual stimulation for a student, and this will include applying to a different school for a master's degree. This is not to say that a student could not successfully attend the same school for both the bachelor's and master's degrees. If this is what you intend to do, then, by all means, pursue both degrees at the same school.

Small Universities: Drawbacks

While smaller universities often have specializations and feel more personal, they can, as in the example above, often prove to be isolating, especially if they are in a smaller community than students are accustomed to. Also, larger schools have the advantage of being able to offer a wide array of courses and specializations, while smaller schools, due to their size, may not have the same range of programs, courses, or even degrees. If you are positive that you will not change your major and the campus has a solid degree program in your area, this won't be a problem; however, if you end up changing your mind and getting interested in pursuing a different degree from the one you originally intended to pursue, your options may be limited. Consider the school's reputation and explore the community before applying to make sure that you are comfortable there.

Other Tactical Considerations: Location

There are other tactical considerations for you to consider. For instance, do you want to attend a campus that is near or far from your home? Do you wish to enroll at a school that is perhaps far from home, yet still within your home state? It really depends on your comfort level and the degree of travel to which you are accustomed. Of course, these days, with air travel being relatively inexpensive, it is quite easy to hop on a plane and be home for the holidays in record time. Nevertheless, many students become homesick. Actually, a student can become homesick even if the campus is close to home. This is a very real possibility, so you will have to gauge how comfortable you are with distance from your home. For other students, the distance between their home and their college or university can represent the final "break away" from the nest. They have finally spread their wings by going off to college. It may also represent a love of travel. The love of travel can be very alluring, and for some students, this may represent the ultimate vacation. Some pundits have even hinted that a university can become almost like a four-year extended vacation for some students. While I neither endorse nor encourage you to consider a university merely a nice getaway, I will recognize the fact that the farther the distance between your university and your home, the greater the likelihood that it will feel, at least initially in your freshman year, like a grand getaway.

Take a Campus Tour

Well before it is recommended that you begin applying to a four-year college or university, I would strongly suggest that you visit your top choices. There is nothing like actually seeing the campus, live and "in the flesh." Most universities offer tours to prospective students and their families. It can be a wonderful adventure to tour these beautiful campuses with your parents or friends. If you have your heart set on a university that is out of state, find out the dates when they arrange for tours, and sign up for one of these tours. Save all the money you can and make it a learning adventure! To make it worthwhile:

- Take a writing pad and a pencil and take notes while the tour is being given.
- Pay close attention to what the tour operator says regarding the vital statistics of the university. You will not want to miss important information regarding the place you might very well be living for the next four years.
- Pay attention for data regarding issues of campus safety, any issues the school may have had with drugs or alcohol, the availability of dorms on campus, and so on.
- Be sure to collect as many fliers and brochures as you can from the school to see what campus and community life is like.
- Additionally, with the widespread availability of the Internet, if you miss out on an important detail, you can always log in to the school website and read up on the data you missed during your initial foray to the campus.

It is good idea to take your parents to these campus tours, for several reasons. First, the journey to college may be something with which they are familiar. They might be college graduates themselves, and therefore, they will be in key positions to help you in answering some of your questions. Who better to help you in this quest than your parents? However, on the chance that they are not college graduates, then this process of learning about the college and university system of the United States can be become a shared family adventure. It can be a wonderful experience for all of you, as a family, to walk the grounds of these campuses and become familiar with some of these marvelous universities. Involving your parents can help them feel like they are a part of the process, that they too have a sense of ownership over your education, and that they have a vested interest in seeing you succeed—as opposed to not being involved in your decision, which could cause them to feel like you are abandoning them. Make sure that you book your tour well ahead of time.

Foreign Universities

The other option open to you is to apply to go to college at a foreign university. Many American students study abroad and find the experience quite rewarding. Even if you have already completed your first two years of community college coursework, go on-line or go to your local library and find books which catalog foreign universities. There can be nothing more thrilling than to know that you will be leaving for Spain, or England, or Switzerland to study at a fine university. You will not only receive a good education, but the mere experience of traveling to a foreign destination and getting to know another culture will be an education itself. These are the experiences that make you grow and expand your horizons, precisely what you are supposed to be doing at this stage, as well as all stages, of your life. Learn Spanish in Madrid, or work out quadratic equations with your classmates in Zurich. Make the most of these years and enjoy the adventure of it all. Do not be discouraged or pessimistic about your chances of being admitted to some of these programs. You will have plenty of time to work off your student loans. But, these opportunities to study abroad might not come back again. Take advantage of them now.

Online Universities

Finally, the last available option for you is to complete your degree online. There is convenience and speed in doing it over the Internet. However, you will miss out on the social aspects of college life. You will gain the textbook knowledge, important to be sure, but you will not gain the opportunity to make lasting friendships with your peers or to bond with your professors. Nevertheless, if you feel that you prefer an online degree, then by all means pursue it. They are real degrees, and some of the online college degree programs are rapidly gaining in popularity and have developed quite a name for themselves. One cautionary note, though: While there are many perfectly legitimate online universities, there are also many non-accredited universities that advertise online. A non-accredited university will not be recognized by other accredited universities or by most employers since it is not regulated nor does it meet the same academic standards that other schools meet. I knew an instructor at my former teaching position who had gotten a PhD from an online non-accredited university. Once this was discovered by the school's administration, he was fired. Most likely, he will have difficulty ever getting a teaching position anywhere. Be sure to investigate any online university that you are interested in thoroughly to ensure that it is, in fact, accredited and reputable so you don't waste time and money only to suffer the same fate. There are many reputable schools online, though, such as the University of Phoenix, so don't rule them out entirely—just be careful.

Whatever option you pursue, take your education seriously, for it is a blessing as well as an investment that will bring you many dividends in the decades to come. *Peterson's Guide* online provides the following summary of six important considerations:

(Association of American Colleges and Universities, January 2001, Greater Expectations National Panel, Briefing Paper #17 Considering College Quality, Ernest L. Boyer, President of the Carnegie Foundation for the Advancement of Teaching and former U.S. Commissioner of Education, Abstract)

Measures of Quality

1. A Clear Mission

Every college should be guided by a clear and vital mission. It should understand its unique role in higher education and present itself honestly to prospective students through its literature and other information outlets. A good measure of the strength of an institution is a well-defined focus and, beyond that, a clear indication that those goals have been turned into a living purpose for the campus.

Of course, you need to determine if a college's stated mission matches your own goals and values. At the very least, you need to know that you will be comfortable at a college and that it will deliver the type of educational experience you're seeking.

2. Attention to Students

The quality of an undergraduate college can also be measured by the extent of its cooperation with high schools and by its willingness to smoothen the transition of students into college. The way you are recruited by a college helps to shape your expectations of that college. A good college conducts its recruitment and selection with the best interests of the students in mind and should, therefore, try to learn more about you than simply your test scores and class rank.

Beyond the admissions process, it is important for a college to continue to demonstrate commitment to you by taking steps to make you feel at home. The first few weeks on campus are a major rite of passage and may have a significant influence on your entire undergraduate experience. In short, you will want to determine whether the freshman year is viewed as something special and whether the college has a well-planned orientation program that addresses the particular concerns of the new student.

Since students need guidance throughout their entire education, a college of quality has a year-round program of academic advising and personal counseling, structured to serve all undergraduates, including part-time and commuting students. You will want to find out if the faculty is available to freshmen to talk about their disciplines and whether they give guidance on career choices. A college worthy of commendation works as hard at holding students as it does at getting them to the campus in the first place. You may wish to investigate a college's retention rate over the past five years and find out whether or not it offers guidance programs for students who are having trouble. These are all measures of a college's dedication to its students.

3. A Planned, Yet Flexible, Curriculum

At a good college, the academic major will broaden rather than restrict the perspective of the student. The major should not only allow you to explore a subject in depth but should also put such study in perspective, presenting, in effect, an enriched major. An enriched major will answer three essential questions: What are the history and traditions of the field to be examined? What are the social and economic implications to be pursued? What are the ethical and moral issues within the specialty that need to be confronted? Rather than dividing the undergraduate experience into separate camps—general versus specialized education—the curriculum at a college of high quality will bring the two together.

Therefore, it is important to determine if the college has a coherent general education sequence—an integrated core—rather than a more loosely connected distribution arrangement. This core academic program should provide not only for an integration of separate academic principles but also for their application and relation to life.

4. The Classroom Climate

The undergraduate experience, at its best, should encourage students to be active rather than passive learners. In measuring the quality of a college, you should ask if the institution has a climate that stimulates independent, self-directed study, where teaching is perceived as more than just lecturing. If a college encourages small discussion sessions in which students work together on group assignments, it may indicate dedication to the undergraduate curriculum. In addition, if undergraduate courses are taught by the most respected and most gifted teachers on campus, it speaks further to this commitment.

Indeed, the strength of the faculty plays a leading role in determining the quality of the undergraduate experience. Students and parents have become increasingly concerned with the balance of time that faculty members spend on research and publishing requirements versus teaching and advising. To uncover how an institution views this balance, you should ask if good teaching is valued equally with research and if it is an important criterion for tenure and promotion. It's important to know if the college recognizes that some faculty members are great teachers, others great researchers, and still others a blend of both. The central qualities that make a successful teacher are simple: command of the material to be taught, a contagious enthusiasm for the play of ideas, optimism about the potential of one's students, and—not least—

sensitivity, integrity, and warmth as a human being. Look for these qualities when you visit colleges.

5. Devoting Resources to Learning

An institution of high quality is one that supports its mission of learning both financially and philosophically. In doing so, a college should allot ample funds to its library and other educational resources. For instance, a good college should devote a minimum of 5 percent of its total operating budget to funding its library, which is often called the "heart" of the college. In terms of its use, you should determine if the library is more than just a study hall and if students are encouraged to spend at least as much time with library resources as they spend in classes. These resources should primarily serve the interests of undergraduate research and not be dominated by narrow scholarly interests of faculty members or graduate students.

Today technology also offers great potential for learning on campus. Some colleges now require that you purchase a computer before coming to campus. Others simply make terminals available to all students in common areas. Particularly if you are looking to advance in computer-related fields, or if you are inclined toward furthering your computer skills, you will want to know if campus terminals are linked to wider networks (including the Internet) and if the college connects labs, dorms, the library, and classrooms.

6. The Campus Culture

A college campus is also a community. A college of high quality will work to make the time spent outside of the classroom as meaningful as the time spent in class. The high-quality college sees academic and nonacademic functions as related and arranges events that support a concern for issues and stimulate productive debate. Campus-wide activities, intended for both faculty and students, should encourage a sense of community, sustain college traditions, and stimulate both social and cultural interaction. Only with such underlying goals can a campus be considered united by more than routine requirements and procedures.

Check also whether faculty members are routinely present at social or extracurricular functions. It is also a good idea to find out if residence halls seem to promote a sense of community through organized activities and informal learning.

A Final Word of Advice

In the end, a high-quality college is concerned about outcomes. It asks questions about student development that go beyond the evaluation of skill. A good college will focus on being sure that their students can think clearly, are well informed, are able to integrate their knowledge, and can apply what they have learned.

Journal Assignment

Looking at the above list from *Peterson's Guide*, make a list that ranks the most important criteria in choosing a university that is right for you. What is the number one most important thing to consider? What's the least important, etc.? Then, look at the website (or take a virtual tour) of a campus you are definitely considering and evaluate it according to your established criteria. Based on what you learned from your web search, did what you discovered about the school differ from what you expected? Explain. What does this knowledge prompt you to do? Make a plan for the schools you intend to apply for, revising if necessary based on your investigations. Describe your plan.

Chapter Twenty

Choosing the Appropriate Classes and Professors

Student Learning Outcome:
Students will dramatize their ability to tolerate criticism through a role-playing exercise that reconstructs scenarios involving constructive and destructive criticism.

"We are born weak, we need strength; helpless, we need aid; foolish, we need reason. All that we lack at birth, all that we need when we come to man's estate, is the gift of education."
—Jean-Jacques Rousseau, philosopher

As you begin your college education in earnest, you will find that you must take many courses that may not always relate to your field. Of course, you will have to take your general education classes. These will be in history, political science, math, English, physical education, music appreciation, and biology, and so on. As you begin taking these classes, you will get to know other students who can recommend a particular teacher for a particular subject. At most colleges and universities, there will be an informal rating system among students. They will usually shrug it off as common knowledge, saying things such as, "Everyone knows that Dr. Smith is the professor to take for Political Science!" or "Don't every sign up with Dr. McDougal for music; he's so boring!" But these rating systems have become more than just an informal system of rating professors; they have also become a very popular system now utilized online. A casual search on the Internet can yield these seemingly popular sites:

- www.ratemyprofessors.com
- www.profrater.com
- www.professorperformance.com
- www.rateaprof.com
- www.myprofessorsucks.com
- www.reviewum.com

This book is not intended to be a guide to these websites. If you wish to use those sites in order to find out what other students are saying about a particular professor, then, by all means, log into the websites and investigate the ratings of professors on your campus or the campuses that you are considering applying to.

Meet with Your Counselor

The best primary source for information about which classes to take in any given semester is your counselor. Make it a habit to meet with your counselor before the start of every semester. This will give you the chance to review, together with your counselor, the classes you will need to take before you sign up for them. This way, you avoid any mistakes, such as signing up for a class that your counselor might later tell you was unnecessary for your major. Later, when you pay for your classes, you can rest assured that the ones in which you have enrolled are the very ones you need for your goal, be it a two-year degree, a career certificate, or to transfer to a four-year college or university.

Manage Your Time

As you prepare for each semester, be sure to pick up a copy of the current *Schedule of Classes* at your college's bookstore or view it online on the college's website. Look through it and be sure that all of the classes you will take that semester are being offered. Knowing which classes to take will depend on several factors. As stated above, your major and educational goal will dictate largely which classes you decide to take. Next, your General Education requirements need to be considered. If you are studying for a career certificate, then you may not need to take general education classes at all. Next, your work schedule will most likely force you to take a set number of units every semester. One of the worst things that you can do to your college education is to make yourself take too many units in one term and experience burnout. I have met many students who told me that they were working thirty to forty hours a week and were also taking eighteen units at the same time! This can make for a very harried and head cold-prone semester. You will run yourself down if you do this, and in the end, you will not really learn anything or retain much information. There is only so much energy that you can expend on any given day and night. Your body requires rest and sleep. It also requires good nutrition and exercise. If you run yourself down by taking eighteen units, which, you will recall, is about six classes, you will be doing yourself a great disservice. Eighteen units require roughly eighteen hours of lecture time per week. That is the equivalent of being in class for six hours straight, three days a week. In the end, you will earn lower grades, and your body will be in a state of

> *One of the worst things that you can do to your college education is to make yourself take too many units in one term and experience burnout.*

269

perpetual exhaustion. If you were to follow this type of regimen, you will run the risk of becoming another countless community college dropout. There is a sizeable population of young people who drop out of community college. They end up working more and more hours which crowds school out. It would hardly be a surprise to learn that they were also taking upwards of sixteen or eighteen units every term. It is no wonder that they do drop out. The body and mind can only take so much pressure and demands.

Prioritize Your Education

In its heart and soul, a college education is meant to be savored. The experiences you will have in college are those which you will carry for the rest of your life. They will also, by the way, shape the views and opinions of college, which you will eventually hand down to your children. If you want your children to have a positive and healthy view of the college experience, then you must allow yourself the opportunity to enjoy your college education experience as much as possible. Imagine two contrasting scenarios. In the first, you are sitting under a tree on campus, leisurely reading your textbook, calmly noting the passages that are important, and perhaps, taking notes every now and then. Two hours later, you get up, stretch a little, and saunter into your next class. In the second scenario, you are rushing across campus, desperately late for class. You nose is running from the latest head cold you have caught. Your immune system is shot, and you also feel tired and achy. You stumble into class, and before long find yourself, alone in the back row of the classroom, falling asleep, as last night you had to study well into the early morning hours for the quiz you are due to take today. Later, you take the quiz, scarcely able to remember what you studied last night, as it was the first time that you had actually

> *In its heart and soul, a college education is mean to be savored. The experiences you will have in college are those which you will carry for the rest of your life. They will also, by the way, shape the views and opinions of college which you will eventually hand down to your children. If you want your children have a positive and healthy view of the college experience, then you must allow yourself the opportunity to enjoy your college education experience as much as possible.*

read the material. Honestly, which of the two scenarios seems more attractive? This is why it is important that you pace yourself. Don't be impatient with the process of getting your college education. Your commencement will come.

Consider Your Preferred Learning Style

Yet another factor which will affect your choice of classes and professors is the fact that we all have different learning styles. Some people are auditory learners, and enjoy hearing a good lecture. Others are more visual and need PowerPoint presentations or overhead projector slides. Yet others may be more kinesthetic and require movement of some sort as they learn. These are the students for whom the physical education component is probably the most enjoyable. Perhaps if you are a more auditory learner, you may want to record the lectures you attend on a voice recorder, either a digital, microcassette, or standard cassette recorder. This way, you can later listen to the recordings at home and take notes from them. If you are more inclined to be a visual learner, you may want to buy multi-colored markers and make different color codes for the information in the text and in your notes. Or, you may want to buy index cards that are colored and sort them by types of information. This way, even if your professors do not accommodate you with the learning style you need, you can at least compensate slightly for that by using the techniques you prefer.

Other Factors

Of course, things are never that simple either. There have been countless other factors that will impinge upon a student's decision whether or not to take a certain professor in college. For instance, do you prefer male or female teachers? Be it nature or nurture, most of us grew up with the image of teachers as being female. This may have been truer for our earlier years of school. Perhaps you had female teachers in pre-school and kindergarten. In elementary school is when one begins to see males here and there teaching classes, but it is still overwhelmingly female. At the high school level, there is a real male presence among the faculty. At the university level, we see large numbers of males on the payroll as faculty members. When you go to college, you may still have the imprinting to prefer female to male teachers. It is purely a matter of subjectivity and personal preference. Perhaps you might feel intimidated by a male professor and would prefer a female professor. Or, if you are a female student, you may want to have a female professor whom you feel is more sympathetic to the feminist cause. Of course, you may be in for a rather rude awakening in taking a female professor precisely for that reason and find out well into the course that she is unsympathetic with feminist ideology! Or, perhaps you may want to have to have male professors. It can be supposed that a male student may have a wish to have male professors in college to serve as role models or mentors. This may be more the case in graduate school, where you will be working closely with a member of the faculty on your thesis. You will be working long hours on your thesis, and your thesis advisor will become like a friend to you. That is what happened to me. When I was at the University of La Verne, I worked closely under the chair of the graduate program. A *chair* is the head of a department or team, especially at a university. He and I had developed a good rapport, and I enjoyed working closely with him. It is important that you have at least a marginal liking for the person with whom you will be devoting long and difficult hours on a paper or project. You will be receiving constructive criticism from him or her. This is someone who will judge your work. Think of the person as you would a mentor, and keep in mind that all business associates, professors, and co-workers do become a part of your social network, so it's a good idea to distinguish yourself, receive constructive criticism as it was intended, and build a good working relationship with that person.

Learning to Handle Criticism

In order to be an effective student, you will have to be prepared for this type of academic criticism. Faculty members can be brutal. If there has been nothing in your past to give you a thick skin, then the competition and constructive criticism that you may receive from your college professors will give you that callous layer. College and university professors can be brutally honest about what they think about your work. Nevertheless, if you have a good and strong connection, even if it is only intellectual, with your faculty advisor, then your work will be more rewarding in college or graduate school.

Remember, if someone really didn't care about you or your success, they would not say anything useful to you—they would just overlook areas where you have room for improvement, or let mediocrity pass by without any comment.

Many students don't take criticism well, and it can be very discouraging to work very hard on a project or paper only to hear that it has flaws and what those flaws are. Keep in mind that the professors you are working with or your bosses at work generally have the best interests of the project or essay or task in mind when they offer suggestions or point out errors or flaws in your work. Their goal, in most cases, is to guide you to getting the best end result you can achieve, so that the relationship is productive. The criticism should be taken as constructive criticism—not a personal attack or form of discouragement. Remember, if someone really didn't care about you or your success, they would not say anything useful to you—they would just overlook areas where you have room for improvement, or let mediocrity pass by without any comment. The intention of feedback on your work is one of concern for you and the project you are working on. Use it to your advantage.

Selecting a Wide Range of Instructors

There will also other, perhaps more personal, reasons for choosing certain faculty members over others. Perhaps you are of a certain political or religious orientation. You can take either of two roads: you can take professors that are sympathetic to your views, which, in a sense, is the safe and easy path. Or, you can take a professor whose views are the opposite of yours. This can have either of two effects. You can either learn to become more open-minded to other people's view of life, politics and religion, or, you can develop the capacity to make truly great debate-style rebuttals. As stated earlier in this book, one of the main aims of getting a good college education is learning the fine art of debate, logic, and rhetoric. If you are not developing these capacities, some of which are hopefully *already* in place by the time you enter college, then you are not getting the education you are paying for. You must be able to sit in front of any professor, be he liberal, conservative, an Evangelical, or a hard-nosed atheist, and be able to listen calmly to his views. If his views are, in your estimation, flawed, then you need to be able state why. This is an important point.

Being Open-Minded to Diverse Points of View

In order to become truly educated, you must do more than simply charge somebody else with being "wrong." Why, in your view, are their views "wrong," at least in *your* mind? We all construct our own realities as we grow up. These views of life are called our *schemas*. They are glasses through which we view the world. Schemata are very necessary for our very survival. Imagine that you are an alien creature from another planet and arrive in the middle of Rockefeller Plaza in New York. You would be inundated with sounds, lights, colors, people, cars, horns blaring, tires screeching, people yelling, running, talking, laughing, even crying. Your mind would be scarcely able to make sense of what was happening. Yet, as we grow up, we are similarly inundated with information and sensory

> *As stated earlier in this book, one of the main aims of getting a good college education is learning the fine art of debate, logic, and rhetoric. If you are not developing these capacities, some of which are hopefully already in place by the time you enter college, then you are not getting the education you are paying for.*

273

input. When we were all babies and infants, our five senses were given information and stimulation. As our brains grew larger and more sophisticated, we began to learn about our world and to discover more about the objects, sights, and sounds in our world. As we grew older, our parents began to explain to us the way the world works. As we became preadolescents, our parents, in their own loving, kind and innocent ways, began to inform us more about the world and our relationship to it. They explained relationships between friends, spouses, and family. This is also when our core beliefs, those which we hold most dear, were handed down to us. You might have already been attending a religious private school since kindergarten, or perhaps you were educated entirely through the public school system. Whatever school system you were put through, your parents also may have sent you to Sunday school in order to develop your faith. You may have attended weekly services at a Synagogue or perhaps a Catholic Mass. Perhaps you were raised as a Muslim and went to the Mosque every week. No matter what system of faith or beliefs you inherited, at a certain point in time, right around the time you enter college, these beliefs become your own. The inheritance becomes full and complete. You are now a full owner of these views and beliefs. By the time you enter college or a university, you will enter an arena where you will be confronted by a plethora of belief systems. There will be times when you might feel that there is little campus support for your views. Perhaps you were raised in a staunchly Republican family and firmly believe in state's rights, low taxes, and private property. Yet, upon arrival at a large public university, you may feel that the atmosphere is more liberal than you prefer. This can be a very jostling experience.

Choose Diverse Learning Environments

As mentioned earlier, you will be faced with certain decisions in regards to choosing the right classes and professors. The first option is to choose classes where your belief systems will be supported and defended. The second option involves choosing classes and professors who will have different views of government, religion, and other controversial subjects. If you choose that path, you will be faced with the choice of opening yourself up to these views, staying silent, or opposing the views of your classmates and professors in a well-conceived manner. Remember, you are there to get an education in thinking, not to tell people in a belligerent manner that they are "wrong."

Practice the Art of Critical Thinking

I have personally always felt that the college or university experience is incomplete without the experience of a debate. A well-regulated debate can expose you to the art of critical reasoning. Once you start enrolling in classes, ask your peers if they know of professors in certain classes who hold these old-fashioned debates. It will be a great experience for you. Once you have been exposed to this style of argumentation, and your skills in it become strong, your mind and intellectual powers will have grown exponentially.

Scheduling Work around School

Another very pragmatic set of conditions that will determine your school schedule is your work schedule. More and more students are working while going to school. If you must work, arrange to have perhaps only two (but no more than three) days devoted to schoolwork. Thus, you should to arrange to have your classes back-to-back, on Tuesdays and Thursdays, or even Mondays, Wednesdays, and Fridays. I found that this was tremendously efficient for me. It saved me effort, gasoline, and stress. This is why it is so important that you read the *Schedule of Classes* well before the start of the semester. Additionally, since classes tend to fill up quickly, you will be ahead of the game by having your classes chosen, and you stand to have a much better chance of getting yourself into those classes. Another good thing to remember as you start generating your schedule for the semester is to have a backup schedule, on the off-chance that you may end signing up for classes that fill up too rapidly, or that perhaps are cancelled, due to low enrollment. There are always going to be little glitches as you progress through the semesters in college. You can count on these surprise occurrences regularly. Colleges and universities are big, cumbersome, and at times, poorly-run institutions. They may have excellent leadership at the top echelons of the hierarchy and a great faculty, but down in the "trenches" at the administrative level, it may be a wholly different situation. However, as the saying goes: "The squeaky wheel gets the grease"; therefore, make it a habit to show up to class, the Admissions Office, or to your counseling appointment and ask about any loose ends that you may have in person in regards to the schedule. At times, this face-to-face inquiry may serve you better, as the administrative staff is right there in front of you, and it saves you the agony on being put on hold for what seems like an eternity over the telephone.

Therefore, enjoy the process of selecting your classes and professors. Most importantly, do not get too stressed over the selection. Think it through as best as you can. You may also want to visit some of the websites mentioned at the beginning of the chapter. Strategize to get the most efficiency out of your time. This is very important if you are commuting to campus and wish to save money on gasoline. In the end, however, the most crucial part is that you make the most out of every single class. Let your mind be filled with all the wisdom your professors can provide.

Journal Assignments

1. Look up one of your current professors on one of the professor evaluation sites mentioned in the chapter. After reading the descriptions of your instructor, compose a brief paragraph that assesses the site's evaluation. Do you agree? Is it accurate? Are there any factual errors, incorrect statements, or unfair attacks against the instructor that you notice? Is the site's evaluation too positive? What else should be indicated to give a complete composite picture of the instructor's ability?

2. With a friend, role-play a situation in which one of you is a boss or instructor and the other is a worker or student. In the role-play exercise, pretend that you are working together on a project, but that the boss / instructor is basically supervising the worker / student's work. Have a conversation that includes constructive criticism of the project so far. Keep the responses professional, despite how you may feel inside. Then, reverse roles and repeat the simulation. In your journal, briefly write what your feelings were during the role-play. What did you react to emotionally? Where did the reactions come from? With which character did you identify most? Why? What did you learn about yourself from the exercise? What do you need to be more aware of when you find yourself in a situation like this, struggling to accept criticism, in real life?

Student Success Profile:

Matthew Plinck

Describe yourself briefly in a short biography (hometown, birthplace, high school experience, family, education).

I grew up in various areas in the Los Angeles area. I was born in Torrance, California, and lived there the majority of my preteen years. Throughout my life I moved sporadically, spending brief periods of time in Texas, Nevada, and North Carolina but I always ended up in the L.A. area. When I became a teenager, my father and mother wanted to get me out of the crime and poverty-stricken streets of Los Angeles; they got blessed with an opportunity to manage some apartments in the wealthy area of Palos Verdes. My parent's efforts backfired. I felt out of place and began to wonder why everyone I went to school with had so many things that my family and I did not. We were only able to afford rent where we lived because as a perk of apartment management, our rent was drastically discounted. I started acting out and became a thief in an effort to make money for clothes and other items we could not afford. During the time I was acting out, my parents' marriage suffered, which eventually lead to their messy divorce. The divorce added to my feelings of being an outcast, and I plummeted into the depths of darkness. My anger grew daily, and I began to graduate from petty theft, to violence and stealing cars. I continually got into fights, and had temper fueled outbursts in class on a regular basis. My mom was at my school talking to the principle continuously. I was getting suspended from school all the time. During middle school, I had beat a boy on the bus ride to school; the MTA police got involved and after a brief meeting with my principal, my chances had run out and I was expelled. I moved in with my dad in Nevada. I went to school in Nevada for a couple months and networked with a group of lost individuals that mirrored my pain. I dropped out of school in the ninth grade. My dad was not opposed to my decision because he was more of a friend than a father at the time. My father was beaten and mistreated by his father, so he did not know how to be a father. His troubled childhood coupled with his broken heart allowed him no energy for caring for an out of control child. I was doing crime and partying on a daily basis; this carried on for some time until my dad could no longer handle me and sent me back to L.A. When I got back to my mother's, I was already well versed in the criminal and gangbanging lifestyle due to a lack of adult supervision in Nevada, where I ran free and wild. I decided that I wanted a place where I belonged and where my skills in violence and crime would be warranted. I joined a gang shortly after I arrived back in L.A. Briefly after I returned to L.A., I started to do juvenile jail time. I was in and out of juvenile facilities until my mom deemed me incorrigible and I became a ward to the state. I spent most of the rest of my teens in placements, which are similar to a group home. While I was in placement, my mom grew close with a new man who had to move to N.C. for a job. By the time my mom was going to move, I was seventeen; my mom proposed to the state of California that if she was to take me out of the state of California, I would be able to get an early release. I was awarded an early release with the stipulation that I left California. My mom and I went to the local high school in N.C. to get me enrolled. My past followed me, and I was not allowed to go to the general population high school; instead, the school officials told me that I would be on a probation period. They allowed me to go to the school, but I attended at a trailer off to the side of the main campus. The trailer was a disciplinary place for troublesome students. I felt they highlighted my foolishness and embarrassed me. I started school without a fresh start and began to act upon my self-fulfilling prophecy. I was expelled from the school in N.C. shortly after I started, and because of this I was kicked out of the house by my mother's new husband. I found a job and slept in my car and the bath tubs of unfinished homes for a few months until my mother and her husband helped me get a place. I worked a couple dead end jobs and moonlighted as a thief at night for extra money. I started selling weed and cocaine and realized I would make far more money selling drugs then working a regular job, so I quit my job. My mom and her husband had to move once again, my sister followed, and they all moved to Virginia. I stayed in N.C for a while and continued my spree of selling drugs, partying, and crime. I eventually left N.C. and went back to L.A. where I fell very fluidly back into my neighborhood and the gangbanging lifestyle. It took no time for me to begin doing prison time. I went in and out of prison from 18 until I was 26. I was a two striker and I had dropped out of school completely in the ninth grade. I got my G.E.D during my last term in prison.

What was your background before coming to community college?
Prior to going to community college, I was released from prison for the third time and I was living in a homeless shelter. While in the homeless shelter, I was attempting to get a job and I was on general relief or state aid. During a meeting at the general relief office, I listened to speakers from a vocational school promoting a medical assisting program. I decided to go to the vocational school and see what it would take to get enrolled. I got enrolled with low expectations of my performance. I did not have any confidence and believed that I was stupid. While in school for medical assisting, I was at the top of my class and began to receive awards for my academic performance. I graduated medical assisting at the top of my class and decided to couple my medical assisting certificate with another certificate that the vocational school offered. I furthered my schooling and got another certificate for phlebotomy. At the time of my graduation, I had moved out of the homeless shelter and into a parolee transitional housing in South Central Los Angeles. I found a clinic in South Central where I did my internship. After my internship, I was offered part time employment at the clinic but I did not feel that the part time work would offer me the financial stability I wanted. I also found that taking blood from children was not something that I enjoyed. Filled with hope and a bit more confidence then I previously had, I decided to further my education at the local community college, which happened to be LASC.

What, if anything, prompted your decision to attend community college? What were your goals upon entering community college (why did you go)? Did they change after you started college? If so, how?
The hopes of financial stability and a better life prompted my deaccessioning to attend community college. My initial community college goals were to gain a degree in business. I had no idea what I was doing I just figured that businessmen make money and I wanted to be a young business man. As my community college experience progressed and I progressed as a man, I found that I wanted to give back and money took a second to my interest and want to help others. I got inspired by a professor and decided to major in psychology in hopes to help others and grow and understand my cognitions as a man.

Describe your experience as a community college student. What were the highlights? Were there any special programs or extracurricular experiences that were memorable or inspiring?

My initial experience as a community college student was intimidating. I had no idea what I was doing; I just jumped in with an open mind. When I first entered community college, I did not believe that I had the capability to be a good student. I had concerns about whether I was smart enough or driven enough to make a degree a possibility for me. As I began to get involved with my community college, I realized that there were plenty of people that did not know me but were concerned about my success. The hearts of the staff at my community college made my experience great. When I started to realize that I could achieve good grades, it sparked a fire in me and gave me excitement to learn. While I was going to community college, I drew upon a variety of programs that the school offered, all of which inspired me in some way. I was involved in EOPS, which is a program that helped to pay for my books. I remember at one time I got my backpack stolen and it had all my books in it. I expressed what happened to the EOPS office and they bought me new books. I was shocked at the kindness that EOPS offered. I was also involved in the TRIO Scholars program. In the TRIO program, I was inspired by the love, concern, and guidance of the counselors. I also took a course that got me involved in the Puente program. The Puente program gave me one of the most inspiring and memorable experiences that I had at community college. While in the Puente program, I was able to go on a college tour. We went to three of the premier universities in California. Being able to see the colleges where I could potentially be one day brought tears to my eyes and gave me extreme motivation to push toward my academic goals. Student services, financial aid, international student services, and the student government office all gave me hope, not just in achieving my goals, but hope that there is good and good people in this world that will work for you if you are willing to work for yourself.

How much time went by between high school and community college for you? What were the biggest challenges that you faced when you began attending community college?
I never really went to high school, but from the time I dropped out of school until the time I went to community college was about 10 years. The biggest challenges that I faced when I began community college were financial, supposed rudimentary and internal challenges. When starting community college, I had no idea how I would pay for my education, and it was initially tough to figure out how to work with the financial aid office to ensure my needs were meet. The supposed rudimentary challenges that I speak of are labeled as such because I believe there to be a faulty generalized thought process that certain things are basically common knowledge: such things as using a computer, checking/sending emails, using Word, and other computer-based knowledge. I was oblivious to basic computer functions and that made it difficult for me to keep up in classes at times. Another problematic base for me in community college was attempting to figure out who I was as a man. I spent so long being someone I could not stand that even to this day I try to figure out who I am and who I want to be as a person. It was a struggle at times to adapt to people and behaviors and to be social with a cohort that was strikingly different, in a good way, than what I had been used to.

Still one of my biggest challenges to this day that rang true in community college was my lack of confidence that causes me to feel that I do not deserve success and also tells me that I do not fit in.

Did you work while attending community college? If so, how did you balance your time between work and school? Do you have any kids or other family responsibilities? If so, how did you balance your time between home and school? Did you have all three? How did you handle that?
I did do a work study in community college. I worked for the International Student Services Office. I was blessed with the work position I had being a work study which ensured that my boss knew the importance of my grades and allocated me flexibility, which offered me the time I needed to study. I do not have any children and my family lives on the east coast, so family responsibility was slim; however, I did live in a half-way house that had some similar challenges. Much like I would assume a house with children would be, I lived in a double room with another guy and a house full of other men. The house was often loud and it offered me no place to study until late at night. I would stay up until everyone went to sleep in order to study. I do not know the struggles that are faced when having children and wanting to gain an education. I do, however, know that one thing is constant regardless of subjective circumstance; if you want something bad enough, you will adapt and make it happen.

Community colleges generally have a high attrition rate, meaning a large percentage of students drop out. Why do you think this happens? What motivated you to persevere through college and transfer to a university?
There are a plethora of subjective contextual circumstances that could be attributed to the reasons for dropping out of school. I don't have time because I need to work and take care of my kids, my family member is sick, I don't have transportation, I need money now, I don't have a place to live, I am arguing with my partner too much or I don't have time to allocate to my significant other, I am not getting the grades I thought I was going to get; these are just a small fraction of assumed reasons that people might have for leaving college. An individual could spend a life time attempting to figure out all of the subjective circumstances or rationalizations one might have for dropping out. I believe that personal circumstances aside, at a simple foundational basis individuals lose motivation and drive via varying life circumstances. Easily put, I believe it important to be honest with oneself and be accountable for whatever reasons that are keeping someone from achieving one's goals. We should all recognize that our rationales are not subjective but holistic, and everyone, although maybe contextually different, has problems when trying to achieve academic success. We should realize that if an education is what is wanted then we have to take the good with the bad and not create reasons to allow ourselves to fail. I cannot specify a single thing that motivated me to persevere, but instead a variety of things that kept me going. My motivators were initially when I started to get good grades. Getting good grades gave me confidence which helped me to push forward, but eventually

281

that was not enough. I then drew on the love I had for my family to push me forward, with the thought that doing this will offer my family a better life. I also was captivated by the fact that the best thing that I was gaining and working toward was not academic success or degrees but instead, daily through my education I was learning about myself and becoming a better human being. When my motivation got low or began to be tested, I also looked to the staff at my community college, friends, and family to help me through my low energetic moments. I also thought in longevity about what my success could bring me, things such as financial freedom, a degree, and a spot at a university of my choice, these things also lifted me up in times of need. I am still continually finding things to motivate my success and I think it is important to grasp for an immense amount of motivators because if someone is trying to push through a gamut of struggle, drawing upon one motivational tool is not enough, at least for me.

Of all the reading assignments you completed in college, which one had the greatest impact on you? What's your favorite book and why?
When I read *Always Running* by Luis J. Rodriguez, I was heavily impacted because through the book I realized that regardless of where you come from, with hard work success is evident. The book also kept me grounded and harbored the perfect median of success and struggle allowing me to realize that even when you are in a place of success, life and struggle still occurs. Even though struggle still happens, it is possible to push through to gain a positive outcome and maintain the success you have earned. One of my favorite books is actually a text book called *Culture Counts* by Nanda Warms. I really enjoyed the book because it offered me a tremendous amount of insight into the ways of other people. It helped me to be more open minded about people in general and allowed me to see that just because people are different and don't go through life according to your own values, does not make them wrong or bad.

Of all the writing assignments you had in college, which are you most proud of and why?
The writing assignment I am most proud of is a writing assignment I did in community college about the California prison system. I am extremely proud of this paper because while doing the paper I did research on the California Department of Corrections and rehabilitation. The knowledge I gained from the research allowed me factual and tangible evidence to convey to my old friends, who were still locked into a negative lifestyle, evidence that showed them the trap they were falling into. I am very proud of the paper because through the process of writing I was able to offer my friends a potential way out of the street life via the truth behind the CDCR's motives.

Attending a college or university can be extremely stressful for many students. Does any particular thing stand out as being the most stressful aspect of going to school? What was it and why was it stressful? What coping skills did you use to overcome stress in order to succeed?

The most stressful thing for me was feelings of inadequacy which led to me feeling like I did not fit in. My feelings of not fitting in caused me to be withdrawn and lowered me into a depressive state. When I got to the university, I felt very out of place and felt like I was continuously being scrutinized and judged by my peers. I fell into a depressive state and my grades fell which worsened my state of mind. I almost dropped out of the university after my first semester. I decided that I worked extremely hard to get here and I needed to stick it out. The following semester, I enrolled in a leadership and personal development class in an effort to be more assertive and gain confidence. I also fought with myself to be more social. I slowly learned that my negative concerns were aggregated internally and did not reflect the beliefs of my peers.

Many community college students give up when faced with adversity or challenges or barriers. You, however, didn't. What was the biggest challenge you faced and how did you overcome it? What advice would you give to a student who feels like he or she just can't do it, has too much going on in his or her life, or is just struggling academically and feels like maybe college isn't the right place?

One of the biggest challenges I faced was love. I told myself when I began to gain an education that I was not going to indulge myself in a relationship because I knew that it could be distracting, but things happen organically and I meet a great girl at school. After the honeymoon phase of the relationship was over, things began to turn and arguments became commonplace. The only thing that I believe in more than gaining my education and could take precedence over my academic concerns is love. I believe if true love is found, it is more valuable than owning a house made of gold. Because of my strong belief in love, I began to allow myself to be drained by supposedly fixing my relationship or attempting to fix it. I was irresponsible and my views were irrational. I fell hard and almost lost my acceptance to my dream UC. I had to reevaluate where my life was going and I had to step back and understand what was happening for my future. I realized that education is my passion, and if I am being drawn away from my passion, I would never truly be happy, and if I am not happy my confidence will wane, and if my confidence is gone then I will continuously be miserable and therefore not be a good man to my woman or my family. I realized that we must be somewhat selfish at times in order to not be selfish, although seemingly paradoxical very true. I meditated, journaled and self-evaluated as much as possible, and I eventually came to a place of understanding with my partner. She was very supportive and we decided to take a break from our relationship for the betterment of us both. If she would not have been understanding, I would have ended the relationship regardless because if anyone is disjointed or incongruent with your passion, the relationship will never work. The strain of pulling in opposite directions will ultimately lead to the demise of a person. The best advice I could give to a student who believes he or she just can't do it is self-evaluate continuously and ensure that you are not making excuses for yourself. I believe that we tend to talk ourselves out of success because of varying circumstances.

Self-evaluation is very important; as humans we tend to take the path of least resistance. An example of this would be that if there is a chair in front of you, you are likely to walk around the chair to get to a destination on the side of the chair as opposed to climbing over the chair to get to that destination. Climbing over the chair would be a bit more difficult, but you would get to your destination quicker. I believe that our minds follow the same logic: it is easier to tell ourselves that life is hard right now and that's why I can't do it, or I am not smart enough so that's why I can't do it; instead of taking the more difficult but more rewarding path of saying to ourselves: Is life really that hard or am I just not ready to allocate the time necessary for school, am I really not smart enough or have I just not been studying enough or not doing my homework or reading assignments on time? It is hard to come to terms with negatively stigmatized words when attributed to the self, such as I am being lazy or I am just not trying hard enough. When we self-evaluate and question our cunning thought process, we can reach the root of our issues and tackle them at the base, it just takes a lot of mental work and accountability. I always attempt to do everything in my power to ensure that I have no regrets on a later date by making a hasty potential cognitive mirage of a decision, really question why your success is not occurring.

Were there any memorable faculty, counselors, other students, administrators or staff (at your community college or university) with whom you established a rapport and who made a difference? Is establishing relationships with people on campus important? Tell a brief story about someone with whom you became close and who was supportive.
I cannot responsibly specify one relationship that I had with a faculty member, student or counselor that had an impact on me because my success and the differences that people at my community college made in my life are holistic. I met so many of the above listed groups of people that made a difference in my life and academic career there; with that being said, I believe it not only important but essential to gain positive relationships with people on campus. Without the support and love of faculty members, students, and counselors at my community college, I would not be where I am today. Gaining an education is by no means a solo journey but a holistic journey of human resources brought about by a common goal and care for one's future and impact on society.

Courage to Learn **discusses building social capital, meaning developing relationships and skills that are like an investment in your own future. What social capital have you gained since entering community college?**
I have gained an extreme amount of social capital since entering community college. I have learned the value of networking. I have met people that are in positions of certain power and that have honed skills that I draw upon to succeed academically. I have met people who are well versed in math, science, and writing, that helped me to push forward when I needed advice in their particular mastery. I have meet professors that have written the books that are studied in their field which helps me to gain insight from a professional standpoint. Through

education, you are put in a circle of the equivalent of movie stars in their field of study and it is invaluable toward one's success.

What was your social life like in college? How important was it to you personally and educationally?
My social life in college is at an adolescent state, and I am continually growing socially in hopes to reach respective social maturity at some point soon. Having a social life is very important to me, and it is something that social people take for granted, but being social is definitely a skill. It is important to me personally because I want to know that I can be valued as a friend, intellectual, and confidant among people that harbor my new life values. It is important to feel a part of humanity in college because it offers a feeling of being one with my success and education. It is important educationally to be social because like I stated earlier being successful is the effort of not just myself but of a collective group of individuals that guide and support each other through the struggles faced in academia.

Deciding what university to transfer to is difficult. What factors did you consider when deciding where to apply and where to attend?
The factors that I considered when deciding what universities I wanted to apply to are factors revolving around social, environmental, and major concerns. I am a psychology major, so I chose to apply to schools that were known for their undergraduate experiences and validity in the psychological field of study. I also chose schools to apply to that harbored the aesthetic that suited my personality. I was also concerned with the namesake and stigma associated with the colleges I applied to. In my particular situation, it was important for me to choose a school that was away from where I had distractions, in my case where I grew up. I wanted to be in a place where I could start fresh and be in a place of peace. I also looked at the social reputation of the school. I am 30 years old and my partying has been done, so I wanted a school where academics were number one and partying was not the focus of social life.

Universities are expensive. Many magazine and newspaper articles highlight the fact that attending a university is an investment that frequently doesn't pay off or isn't worth it. Perhaps you've seen stories about students graduating from various universities under mountains of debt and unable to find jobs. How did you handle the financial burden of attending college and a university? Is it worth it? Are you buried under mountains of debt?
I am a financial aid student so that is how I have contended with the cost of college. I also am going to start a work study which will offer me a way to pay off some of my debt. Once I have a work study where I am working at least 20 hours a week, I will also be eligible for state help which will give me food stamps and cash aid. Prior to entering college, I had never had a bank account or had a credit card; I had no idea how to manage money or was concerned with loans. I am still learning how to be responsible with finance, and because of my lack of knowledge

when it comes to money, I have acquired quite a bit of debt. The debt, however, does not bother me for two reasons: one, I believe through creativity and drive, success is inevitable; secondly, regardless of how much I owe, there is no amount of money that could equate to what I have gained during my college experience. We live in a complex competitive world, and gaining employment that will be financially rewarding can be tough, but my logic is if money is not at the forefront of your thought process and instead a person is consumed with passion, creativity, and drive, it does not matter if you major in the art of paper airplane making, you will achieve financial success with the above listed values at the forefront of your thinking. As far as if I believe my education is worth my debt, I can answer that question without ever gaining a dime off of my degree. YES, my education is worth more than my debt could ever be. The life lessons that I have learned and gained that have made me a better person are absolutely priceless.

If you are working (while still a student or after having graduated), what is that experience like?
I have only done a work study which is working for the school and it is tough. While working, I gained a great understanding of the amount of time in a day; it is extremely important to manage your time well and create a schedule for yourself. If you are aware of your schedule and are responsible enough to abide by the time frames that you have set for yourself for multiple day-to-day items, it is very feasible to be successful in college while working.

How did you manage the transition from a community college to a university? Did you feel prepared or underprepared? What were the biggest challenges that you faced during the transition?
I did not initially handle the transition to the university well; again I struggled to feel a part of the university and to fit in. I did feel somewhat unprepared because going into a research university, I believe that it is important to be aware of how to do research and figure out what you want to research or at least have given it some thought at the community college level. My biggest challenges were attempting to be social and trying to understand the research process.

What plans for the future do you have (educationally, socially, and professionally)? When and how did those goals emerge?
My educational goals for the future are to get a doctorate in psychology and get an MBA in business. I always wanted to get my doctorate in psychology ever since the community college level. I enjoy psychology for multiple reasons; for one I would like to utilize the knowledge that I have gained to help others including my family. I also use psychology as a tool to help me understand myself which is a major goal for me. I decided recently that I would like a degree in business because as I have been learning about myself, I have found that I am completely interested in entrepreneurship. My father was interested in business and was very creative. I have those qualities that my father shared with me as a child, and I realized that I would enjoy creating businesses that contribute to the betterment of society. My social goals are to be more assertive and take chances on social

relationships. I would like to be in a place of confidence where I can easily dismiss the thoughts of how I think others perceive me so that I can gain rewarding lifelong friendships that can grow my social capital. Professionally, I would like to potentially be a professor at a premier university, and I would also like to dive into research. The reason the goal came about of me wanting to teach is because I believe that to teach is the best way to learn and to solidify knowledge. I want to be able to harbor the foundations of psychology so that I can build off of that knowledge and create schools of thought on my own. I want to get involved in research because going to a research university has shown me the importance of research. All of the knowledge base of the world is based on research, and I would like to continue to contribute to that growing body of knowledge.

Looking back, what advice would you give to first year community college students today (i.e. if you could go back in time and talk to yourself on your first day of college, what would you say)?
I would say find your passion: be compassionate of your mistakes gain empathy and understanding of everything and everyone you encounter in the world; stay focused on your goals and never give up.

Chapter Twenty-One

Writing the UC Personal Insight Statement

Student Learning Outcome:
Students will write and refine a draft of their UC personal statement, using the techniques for academic writing and the strategies for developing appealing subject matter discussed in this chapter and chapter 13.

"Life is the most exciting opportunity we have. But we have one shot. You graduate from college once, and that's it. You're going out of that nest. And you have to find that courage that's deep, deep, deep in there. Every step of the way."

—Andrew Shue, actor

The four personal insight questions on your college or transfer application are probably the most important writing you will ever do. Not only are they a required part of your admission application, they are also your opportunity to explain to the application readers why you are an excellent candidate for the college you are applying to. Both the content and the writing quality are crucial elements because the responses are a writing sample *and* an opportunity to distinguish yourself as an individual, share your personal details, your goals and aspirations, your experiences, the obstacles you have overcome, and most importantly *your passion*. Do not put this off until the night before the application is due. Start early, get feedback, and revise until it's the best writing you can produce.

These responses are one part of your overall transfer application, so be aware that all the sections of the application are considered; you won't be accepted or rejected for admission based solely on your personal insight responses alone--but it can be a deciding factor if you apply and are equally qualified with competing candidates in other areas. Therefore, you want to plan out which questions to answer so that each one adds something unique about you to your application. Each of your four responses should show your passion and dedication, each in a different way or about a different subject than the others.

As you begin to plan what you will write, remember to use the personal insight responses to add value to your application: this means, write about topics that are not already covered in your application, address any unusual circumstances or situations that the rest of the application doesn't address, and *show your passion* and drive. It should serve to enhance your application and show you to be a desirable candidate who will succeed at the university to which you are applying.

Getting Started

First, read over your application. Look for patterns in your academic record and your extracurricular activities. Anticipate any questions or assumptions that a reader of your application might have. For instance, was there a gap in your education when you took a few years off for military service, to start a family, to travel, or to get a full time job to support your family? Did you switch majors halfway through your education? How did you get to where you are now? Does the rest of the application really reflect who you are, not only as a student but also as a person? Why or why not? This requires some critical thinking on your part, but anticipate what your readers might think--and don't limit yourself exclusively to the questions above. Those are merely examples that application readers might wonder about (or be impressed by) and which would be helpful to explain in the personal insight responses. Connecting your personal responses to the application, as opposed to writing stand-alone pieces, will strengthen your application.

The UC personal insight questions section of the application consists of eight questions. Transfer applicants respond to a required prompt and choose 3 additional questions to answer from a list of 7 questions; freshman applicants respond to 4 of 8 choices. The only differences between the two lists are that freshman applicants don't have a required question, and they have one question that is different: What's your favorite academic subject? Transfer applicants don't have that question, but they do have a required question which asks about the major prep they have done in community college. Each of your responses should not total more than 350 words.

Generally, the questions allow you to explore different areas of your life: your environment and upbringing, the journey from your family, school, and/or community, and how that made you who you are today; and the characteristics that make you unique, such as special talents, leadership skills, personal qualities and characteristics, and/or special contributions you have made to your family, school, or community.

Look up other examples of personal statements also. You want to find examples of model responses that really jump out at you and attract your attention. Your counselor can help you find good examples of successful personal insight responses as well as assist you with brainstorming for ideas.

Lastly, as you begin to brainstorm ideas to use in your essays, remember that the same people will be reading all of the responses, so you want to write separate responses on each topic. In other words, it wouldn't enhance your application to write about volunteering in the community for two different prompts; write about that for one response, and then write about something completely different for the remaining responses. Think of it as an opportunity to share more about yourself: where you came from and what you are made of.

The University of California Essay Prompts

Freshman Application Questions

You must answer 4 of the following 8 questions.

1. Describe an example of your leadership experience in which you have positively influenced others, helped resolve disputes, or contributed to group efforts over time.

Things to consider: A leadership role can mean more than just a title. It can mean being a mentor to others, acting as the person in charge of a specific task, or taking lead role in organizing an event or project. Think about your accomplishments and what you learned from the experience. What were your responsibilities?

Did you lead a team? How did your experience change your perspective on leading others? Did you help to resolve an important dispute at your school, church in your community or an organization? And your leadership role doesn't necessarily have to be limited to school activities. For example, do you help out or take care of your family?

2. Every person has a creative side, and it can be expressed in many ways: problem solving, original and innovative thinking, and artistically, to name a few. Describe how you express your creative side.

Things to consider: What does creativity mean to you? Do you have a creative skill that is important to you? What have you been able to do with that skill? If you used creativity to solve a problem, what was your solution? What are the steps you took to solve the problem?

How does your creativity influence your decisions inside or outside the classroom? Does your creativity relate to your major or a future career?

3. What would you say is your greatest talent or skill? How have you developed and demonstrated that talent over time?

Things to consider: If there's a talent or skill that you're proud of, this is the time to share it. You don't necessarily have to be recognized or have received awards for your talent (although if you did and you want to talk about, feel free to do so). Why is this talent or skill meaningful to you?

Does the talent come naturally or have you worked hard to develop this skill or talent? Does your talent or skill allow you opportunities in or outside the classroom? If so, what are they and how do they fit into your schedule?

4. Describe how you have taken advantage of a significant educational opportunity or worked to overcome an educational barrier you have faced.

Things to consider: An educational opportunity can be anything that has added value to your educational experience and better prepared you for college. For example, participation in an honors or academic enrichment program, or enrollment in an academy that's geared toward an occupation or a major, or taking advanced courses that interest you — just to name a few.

If you choose to write about educational barriers you've faced, how did you overcome or strive to overcome them? What personal characteristics or skills did you call on to overcome this challenge? How did overcoming this barrier help shape who are you today?

5. Describe the most significant challenge you have faced and the steps you have taken to overcome this challenge. How has this challenge affected your academic achievement?

Things to consider: A challenge could be personal, or something you have faced in your community or school. Why was the challenge significant to you? This is a good opportunity to talk about any obstacles you've faced and what you've learned from the experience. Did you have support from someone else or did you handle it alone?

If you're currently working your way through a challenge, what are you doing now, and does that affect different aspects of your life? For example, ask yourself, "How has my life changed at home, at my school, with my friends, or with my family?"

6. Describe your favorite academic subject and explain how it has influenced you.

Things to consider: Discuss how your interest in the subject developed and describe any experience you have had inside and outside the classroom — such as volunteer work, summer programs, participation in student organizations and/or activities — and what you have gained from your involvement.

Has your interest in the subject influenced you in choosing a major and/or career? Have you been able to pursue coursework at a higher level in this subject (honors, AP, IB, college or university work)?

7. What have you done to make your school or your community a better place?

Things to consider: Think of community as a term that can encompass a group, team or a place – like your high school, hometown, or home. You can define community as you see fit, just make sure you talk about your role in that community. Was there a problem that you wanted to fix in your community?

Why were you inspired to act? What did you learn from your effort? How did your actions benefit others, the wider community or both? Did you work alone or with others to initiate change in your community?

8. What is the one thing that you think sets you apart from other candidates applying to the University of California?

Things to consider: Don't be afraid to brag a little. Even if you don't think you're unique, you are — remember, there's only one of you in the world. From your point of view, what do you feel makes you belong on one of UC's campuses? When looking at your life, what does a stranger need to understand in order to know you?

What have you not shared with us that will highlight a skill, talent, challenge, or opportunity that you think will help us know you better? We're not necessarily looking for what makes you unique compared to others, but what makes you, YOU.

Transfer Application Questions
You must answer the required question and 3 additional questions that you choose from the remaining 7 questions.

Required question

Please describe how you have prepared for your intended major, including your readiness to succeed in your upper-division courses once you enroll at the university.

Things to consider: How did your interest in your major develop? Do you have any experience related to your major outside the classroom — such as volunteer work, internships and employment, or participation in student organizations and activities? If you haven't had experience in the field, consider including experience in the classroom. This may include working with faculty or doing research projects.

If you're applying to multiple campuses with a different major at each campus, think about approaching the topic from a broader perspective, or find a common thread among the majors you've chosen.

Choose to answer any three of the following seven questions:

1. Describe an example of your leadership experience in which you have positively influenced others, helped resolve disputes, or contributed to group efforts over time.

Things to consider: A leadership role can mean more than just a title. It can mean being a mentor to others, acting as the person in charge of a specific task, or taking lead role in organizing an event or project. Think about your accomplishments and what you learned from the experience. What were your responsibilities?

Did you lead a team? How did your experience change your perspective on leading others? Did you help to resolve an important dispute at your school, church in your community or an organization? And your leadership role doesn't necessarily have to be limited to school activities. For example, do you help out or take care of your family?

2. Every person has a creative side, and it can be expressed in many ways: problem solving, original and innovative thinking, and artistically, to name a few. Describe how you express your creative side.

Things to consider: What does creativity mean to you? Do you have a creative skill that is important to you? What have you been able to do with that skill? If you used creativity to solve a problem, what was your solution? What are the steps you took to solve the problem?

How does your creativity influence your decisions inside or outside the classroom? Does your creativity relate to your major or a future career?

3. What would you say is your greatest talent or skill? How have you developed and demonstrated that talent over time?

Things to consider: If there's a talent or skill that you're proud of, this is the time to share it. You don't necessarily have to be recognized or have received awards for your talent (although if you did and you want to talk about, feel free to do so). Why is this talent or skill meaningful to you?

Does the talent come naturally or have you worked hard to develop this skill or talent? Does your talent or skill allow you opportunities in or outside the classroom? If so, what are they and how do they fit into your schedule?

4. Describe how you have taken advantage of a significant educational opportunity or worked to overcome an educational barrier you have faced.

Things to consider: An educational opportunity can be anything that has added value to your educational experience and better prepared you for college. For example, participation in an honors or academic enrichment program, or enrollment in an academy that's geared toward an occupation or a major, or taking advanced courses that interest you — just to name a few.

If you choose to write about educational barriers you've faced, how did you overcome or strived to overcome them? What personal characteristics or skills did you call on to overcome this challenge? How did overcoming this barrier help shape who are you today?

5. Describe the most significant challenge you have faced and the steps you have taken to overcome this challenge. How has this challenge affected your academic achievement?

Things to consider: A challenge could be personal, or something you have faced in your community or school. Why was the challenge significant to you? This is a good opportunity to talk about any obstacles you've faced and what you've learned from the experience. Did you have support from someone else or did you handle it alone?

If you're currently working your way through a challenge, what are you doing now, and does that affect different aspects of your life? For example, ask yourself, "How has my life changed at home, at my school, with my friends, or with my family?"

6. What have you done to make your school or your community a better place?

Things to consider: Think of community as a term that can encompass a group, team or a place – like your high school, hometown, or home. You can define community as you see fit, just make sure you talk about your role in that community. Was there a problem that you wanted to fix in your community?

Why were you inspired to act? What did you learn from your effort? How did your actions benefit others, the wider community or both? Did you work alone or with others to initiate change in your community?

7. What is the one thing that you think sets you apart from other candidates applying to the University of California?

Things to consider: Don't be afraid to brag a little. Even if you don't think you're unique, you are — remember, there's only one of you in the world. From your point of view, what do you feel makes you belong on one of UC's campuses? When looking at your life, what does a stranger need to understand in order to know you?

What have you not shared with us that will highlight a skill, talent, challenge, or opportunity that you think will help us know you better? We're not necessarily looking for what makes you unique compared to others, but what makes you, YOU.

Private Colleges

Private colleges, such as USC, Whittier, Loyola Marymount, Occidental and Pitzer, use the Common Application, which is different from the UC personal insight questions. The personal statement prompt sometimes differs by individual college, so if you plan to attend a private university, research the application prompt so that you can prepare early to write the essay. This personal essay helps the colleges you are applying to become acquainted with you as a person and student, apart from courses, grades, test scores, and other objective data. It will demonstrate your ability to organize your thoughts and express yourself. Often it is a question such as:

Please write an essay (250-500 words) that addresses your reasons for transferring and the objectives you hope to achieve.

Note: Your Common Application essay should be same for all colleges. Do not customize it in any way for individual colleges. Colleges that want customized essay responses will ask for them with supplemental questions.

Beginning to Write

Remember that brainstorming can help you collect the details, insights, and information that you can use in your writing. You want to collect ideas that you can use at three different levels: descriptive, illustrative details to support your bigger points; broader subtopics that contain insights, like ideas that would make good topic sentences in a larger essay; and broad, overarching ideas that link all of your subtopics and ideas together, like those you might use in a thesis statement. It is better to brainstorm and come up with more ideas than you will use so that you can select the best ones to include and discard those that are less insightful or revealing. Start by asking yourself a few questions:

- What is my most important personal quality? What sets me apart from other people and makes me the unique person I am? Why?
- What personal experiences have I had that would show others my true qualities?
- Where do I excel? Where do I feel most comfortable? What makes me feel passionate and excited?
- What activities, adventures, experiences, or achievements really show what I care most deeply about?
- What special talent, skill, life experience, or accomplishment do I have that makes me special?
- What experience(s) led you to choose your major?
- Why do you feel passionate about your major?

Avoid writing about topics that readers might come across frequently; you want to distinguish yourself as unique, so typical or common experiences generally don't work as well. Describing your high school graduation or the experience of becoming a parent are, unfortunately, all too common among university applicants.

As you consider your responses to the questions above, think about which ones led you to reveal or think about something interesting or unique. Then, continue asking questions that probe a bit deeper. Locate yourself as an individual within a larger system (your family, school, or community).

- Are you the first person in your family to attend college?
- Did you or your family struggle to get to where you are?
- Have any obstacles been especially difficult for you to overcome?
- Have you ever volunteered or served the community in some way that was rewarding?
- Have you ever participated in any sort of political activity or been an activist?

These questions are starting points; begin with them, but then progress forward and probe more deeply. For example, to progress from a superficial observation to a deeper level insight, you might frame your questions to yourself as the example below illustrates:

In what courses do I get my highest grades? What activities do I love? What are the reasons I am interested in English literature and writing? Why do I love to go to poetry slams?

How can I share my love of literacy and writing with others in my community which has low levels of literacy and a lack of interest in the literary arts?

Finally, reread the prompts above and decide which ideas will best work to respond to each prompt. Remember, you want to convey different ideas and a different, appealing view of yourself in response to each one.

Organizing Your Ideas

Next, sort out the ideas you came up with while brainstorming. Look over your notes in response to the questions above and seek patterns or "constellations" of ideas that fit together, and decide which groups of ideas fit together best. Then, decide which prompt they work for most effectively. Finally, look for ways to organize your ideas.

The progression of family-school-community works well as an organizing principle, but it's not the only one. However, remember that you are looking to make an argument and write persuasively that you are the ideal candidate for admission to the university. Being able to show that you "live your major" can be very persuasive. Show your reader that your whole life has led up to this moment--and that you will take what you learn to heart, back to your home, and out into the community. Universities like to think that by giving successful candidates the opportunity that they will benefit others as well as you, others such as those people in the community and in your home.

Using the above example for an English major, you might consider how literacy can impact all of those locations.

4. Home: What can I do to increase the level of literacy in my family, for my parents and siblings, by serving as a role model?
5. School: How did my participation in a campus-wide reading event or open mic poetry slam inspire others to want to read and use language to take political action?
6. Community: How has my involvement in a local book fair or how has my volunteer work at the local library inspired others to love to read?

Once you have organized your thoughts and ideas into clusters, consider which cluster of ideas, or topic, would best respond to the prompts. How will you answer each of the prompts? Consider the following:

- Topic: What topic will each response focus on? This is a short essay or story, so one topic per prompt is better than an overview. You can't tell your life story, but you can provide one illustration that shows the impact or significance of your life.
- Persuasiveness: Will that topic that you've chosen make a strong argument on your behalf for admission to the university? Does it answer any concerns that the rest of your application raises? Does it showcase you in your best light?
- Storytelling: Whether you ultimately choose to write persuasively in the form of a story or an argumentative essay, each should contain vivid and specific details. You will need to illustrate and support assertions you make in your writing or you will need to tell an engaging story. Choose a topic that lends itself well to illustration because it is dramatic or shocking or unique, or because it showcases you as a remarkable candidate.

Finally, decide, based on the criteria above, what topics you will focus on. Generally, the stories about community involvement work best because you can also include their relevance to you personally or to your family or school by referencing those precedents as influences or as inspiration.

Writing Strategies

In addition to those writing strategies discussed in the chapter on writing effective essays, keep in mind the strategies and tips below. Remember that the UC responses are short (350 words maximum)--shorter than most essay assignments for class--so you really want to make every word count and avoid unnecessary details. The following tips apply to both the UC responses and the Common Application Essay.

- Get to the point: Don't wander in writing. Get right to the point. Be assertive and abrupt if necessary. Make a point and support it. Tell a story and be direct.
- Begin with a strong opening: Use a quote, tell an anecdote, begin with an analogy or simile, use a description, make a bold statement. Get your readers' attention!

- Use specific, concrete, vivid details: Avoid general statements like "I love reading and writing." State specifically why you love reading and writing and immediately provide an example of a book you read or some writing you did that shows this. Don't repeat ideas. You may have tons of examples of books you read and loved, but just choose the best one, the one that enlightened you, the first one that opened your eyes to the world of reading, or the one that had the strongest impact on you personally. Additional examples should serve only to expand on what you've already said, or add another dimension.

- End strongly: Leave your readers with a memorable point. Consider ending your essay as you began it, i.e. with a quote, anecdote, analogy, etc.

- Stick to the word count: If you end up over, go back through and remove unnecessary words. If the word doesn't add something to the meaning of the sentence, then delete it.

- Make sure that the personal insight responses complete your application effectively: These responses are an extension of your application, so they are your opportunity to respond to any anticipated questions that may arise from your application. Did you explain any gaps in your education? Did you explain any semesters where you performed poorly for just that one semester because of a personal or family tragedy? Do they repeat too much of what was already covered? The responses should provide new information and showcase you as you.

Read and Revise

The personal statement and personal insight responses are an opportunity for you to reveal your passion for learning and for your major, for you to argue persuasively for why you deserve admission to the university over other candidates (who may be equally or more qualified than you), and it is also a writing sample. No matter what your intended major is, universities want to know that you can write and think critically. That's why those topics were covered in this book! The readers of your personal statement are looking for a response that clarifies, contextualizes, or expands on information provided in your application as well as the following: organization and clarity; an persuasive thesis statement, analytical topic sentences, and illustrative examples.

Your thesis statement, here as always, is especially important. Thesis statements generally contain the following:

- A Concession (optional): "Although..." or "Despite the fact that...", an acknowledgment that there may be conditions under which your thesis is not true or does not apply. This is your opportunity to complicate or sophisticate your ideas, establish premises that your argument is predicated upon, or acknowledge an opposing argument--an opinion that differs from yours.

- An Assertion: This is your argument, your main point.

- Reasons: This is a synthesis of your supporting reasons, a list of subtopics that you will address in the essay which support, expand on, or illustrate your main point.
- Significance: This part highlights the importance, significance, results, or implications of your main point.

Finally, proofread. I can't stress this enough. Your personal statement is a writing sample and you need to show its readers that you can write at a university level, without grammatical or other types of errors. Seek help from a trusted instructor, your counselor, and a tutor. It should be perfect! Ideally, get as much feedback from as many people as you can. Almost every college and high school has workshops on writing college application responses. Go to one! Your personal statement is yours, but the more feedback you get, the closer to perfect it will be!

Journal Assignment

Following the tips and suggestions in this chapter, begin to write drafts of your personal insight statements earlier in the chapter. If you will be applying as a freshman, respond to the freshman applicant prompts; if you will be applying as a transfer student, respond to the required prompt and the additional optional ones.